THE GIFT OF
THE HOLY SPIRIT
TODAY

D1159121

THE GIFT OF
THE HOLY SPIRIT
TODAY

by

J. Rodman Williams

Logos International
Plainfield, New Jersey

BT
121.2
.W56
c.2

Unless otherwise indicated, all scriptural quotations are from the Revised Standard Version of the Bible.

THE GIFT OF THE HOLY SPIRIT TODAY
Copyright © 1980 by Logos International
All rights reserved
Printed in the United States of America
Library of Congress Catalog Card Number: 80-82142
International Standard Book Number: 0-88270-413-3
Logos International, Plainfield, New Jersey 07060

to

the Spirit of Glory

Other books by the same author:

Contemporary Existentialism and Christian Faith
Ten Teachings
The Era of the Spirit
The Pentecostal Reality

CONTENTS

PREFACE

One of the most extraordinary Christian facts of our time is the claim of many people to be freshly experiencing "the gift of the Holy Spirit." They speak of "receiving the gift of the Holy Spirit" or simply "receiving the Holy Spirit,"[1] and declare variously that this has been a unique experience of the presence and power of God in their lives.

Because I believe this claim is valid, and also that it represents a rediscovery of a basic dimension of Christian faith, I have written this book. A number of years ago I ran across a statement in *The Beginnings of Christianity* by Jackson and Lake, to the effect that in "the study of the beginnings of Christian thought. . . the starting-point for investigation is the experience called 'the gift of the Holy Spirit'; for this is the most important constant factor throughout the first Christian generation."[2] If this statement is true—and I believe it essentially is—there could scarcely be a better or more important time in the history of the Church to make such an investigation. Also if the contemporary claim to the experience of "the gift of the Spirit" is valid—and I believe it largely is—then what is happening among many people in this late Christian generation is extremely significant: it is verily the renewal of a most important aspect of first-generation Christianity.

What this book accordingly intends to do is to investigate the significance of the gift of the Holy Spirit in its earliest Christian form and to pursue this investigation in the context of contemporary Christian experience.[3] Thus what is written in the pages to follow will by no means be simply a dispassionate academic

---

[1] Some use terminology such as experiencing the "release of the Spirit," "renewal of the Spirit" or the "renewal of the gift of the Spirit."

[2] *Op. Cit.*, Part I, *The Acts of the Apostles*, ed. by F.J. Foakes-Jackson and Kirsopp Lake (London: Macmillan and Co., Ltd., 1920), p. 322.

[3] The contemporary Christian experience referred to is that represented in the present day "charismatic renewal." This renewal, an outgrowth of "classical Pentecostalism" (a term frequently used to refer to the Pentecostal movement beginning in the early

exercise in "Christian origins," but a deeply concerned exploration of a vital aspect of original Christianity reappearing in our time.

It is just possible that fresh study and experience in the area of the gift of the Holy Spirit can make for profound renewal of Christian faith in the late twentieth century.

---

twentieth century), began to occur in mainline churches in the 1960s and is now found among Protestants of many denominations, Roman Catholics and Greek Orthodox. Earlier, it was known as Neo-Pentecostalism, but within recent years has come increasingly to be called the "charismatic renewal," or even "the renewal." The main point for those participating is that it is a renewal in the Holy Spirit.

INTRODUCTION

An exploration of "the gift of the Holy Spirit" in first-generation Christianity means turning basically to the New Testament record. Non-canonical writings, such as those of the Apostolic Fathers, are of some help, but we are on sure ground only when we listen to the New Testament witness. For it is here that primitive experience of this gift is set forth with authority and challenge.

If it is true that the experience of the gift of the Holy Spirit belonged to the first Christian generation, then whatever the exact nature of that gift, it will directly or indirectly inform the New Testament throughout. However, our focus will be largely on the portion of the New Testament, namely the book of Acts, that specifically records the giving and receiving of the Holy Spirit. Other New Testament materials of course have relevance—the Gospels pointing forward to the gift and the Epistles representing persons and communities who have already received the gift—but it is only the book of Acts that records the actual experience.

In turning most often to Acts we shall find ourselves considering several accounts of the giving and receiving of the Holy Spirit. These will include accounts of the disciples in Jerusalem (Acts 2:1-21), the people in Samaria (8:5-24), Saul in Damascus (9:1-19), the Gentiles in Caesarea (10:1-48) and the disciples in Ephesus (19:1-6).[1] There will be reference also to other incidents that may less directly refer to the gift of the Holy Spirit.

As was suggested in the preface, we shall be dealing with

---

[1]In two of these accounts the language employed does not include "the gift of the Holy Spirit," "receiving the Holy Spirit," etc. However, it is obvious that the whole story of Acts 2:1-21 is that of the gift of the Spirit being received. This is presupposed later in Acts 2 when Peter speaks of the gift of the Spirit also being promised to his audience (vv. 38-39), and is specifically referred to in Acts 10 when Peter speaks of the Gentiles at Caesarea as "people who have received the Holy Spirit just as we have" (v. 47). In the case of Saul of Tarsus, though gift language is not employed, he is said to experience being "filled with the Holy Spirit" (9:17). We shall later note how this is one of the general expressions that relate to the gift of the Holy Spirit.

first-generation Christianity and the gift of the Holy Spirit from a perspective of vital existential concern. It will be our purpose to learn all we can about the New Testament witness as it relates to contemporary experience.

THE GIFT OF
THE HOLY SPIRIT
TODAY

CHAPTER ONE

BACKGROUND

It is important at the outset to reflect upon the background for the gift of the Holy Spirit. For what took place in first-generation Christianity, as recorded in the book of Acts, happened against the background of certain objective factors preparing the way for the giving of the Holy Spirit.

A. *The Divine Promise*

Most immediately apparent is the fact that the gift of the Holy Spirit is a direct fulfillment of the promise of God. It is grounded in God's intention and purpose and therefore has behind it the divine integrity. As a promise of God, like all divine promises, it is dependable and sure.

We may begin by noting on the Day of Pentecost that Peter, speaking for the disciples in Jerusalem who have just received the gift of the Holy Spirit, says: "This is what was spoken by the prophet Joel: 'And in the last days it shall be, God declares, that I will pour out my Spirit upon all flesh. . .' " (Acts 2:16-17). In other words, the gift of the Spirit that has been received is in fulfillment of God's promise through the Old Testament prophet. Similar Old Testament promises are found elsewhere: "Thus says the Lord . . . I will pour my Spirit upon your descendants and my blessing on your offspring" (Isa. 44:2-3); "I will not hide my face any more from them, when I pour out my Spirit upon the house of Israel, says the Lord God" (Ezek. 39:29). Though Isaiah and Ezekiel speak specifically of Israel, and Joel universally ("all flesh"), the divine promise contained in all three books may be viewed as being initially fulfilled in Acts, since the Spirit was first poured out upon Israel (Acts 2), and thereafter upon the Gentiles (Acts 10 and elsewhere), thus "all flesh."

Next, moving closer to the actual giving of the Spirit as recorded in Acts, we find more immediate references to the divine promise as "the promise of the Father." First, there are the final words of Jesus: "And behold, I send the promise of my

Father upon you" (Luke 24:49). Next we read: "And while staying with them he charged them not to depart from Jerusalem, but to wait for the promise of the Father, which, he said, 'you heard from me' " (Acts 1:4). Then we have the words of Peter: "And having received from the Father the promise of the Holy Spirit, he [Jesus] has poured out this which you see and hear" (Acts 2:33). Thus it is the promise of God the Father which stands as immediate background for the gift of the Holy Spirit on the Day of Pentecost.

Thereafter, on the same day the promise is likewise extended to Peter's audience and to their children, and to those of other times and places. So says Peter: "You shall receive the gift of the Holy Spirit. For the promise is to you and to your children and to all that are far off, every one whom the Lord our God calls to him" (Acts 2:38-39).

Finally, turning to the Epistles we find two references to the promise of the Holy Spirit. First, Paul writes in Galatians about receiving the Spirit (3:2) and then adds, a few verses later, words about receiving "the promise of the Spirit through faith" (3:14). Second, Paul writes to the Ephesians that they were "sealed with the promised Holy Spirit" (literally, "the Holy Spirit of promise"—Eph. 1:13). So in these two letters, written to communities of Christians who have received the gift of the Holy Spirit, the Spirit is described as the "Spirit of promise." Hence, once again it is the divine promise, the promise of God, that stands behind the gift of the Holy Spirit.

What is exciting about this promise is that it was by no means limited to the New Testament period. As we have noted, Peter declares it is "unto you and to your children and to all that are far off," hence people of all places and generations. The promise of the gift of the Holy Spirit therefore belongs to us also in our time.

This last statement brings us to the opening words in this book, namely, that many people in our day are claiming a like experience of the gift of the Holy Spirit. If this is the case, there surely stands behind them the divine promise. Their experience of the Holy Spirit therefore is grounded firmly in the never failing promise of God.[1]

B. *The Exaltation of Jesus*

Next, the gift of the Holy Spirit comes from the exalted Jesus. This is the Jesus who has been exalted to the right hand of the Father; it is He who sends (or pours) forth the Holy Spirit. The centrality of the exalted Lord Jesus is accordingly critical to a proper understanding of the gift of the Holy Spirit.

Here we must take our direction from the New Testament, for the Old Testament prophecies do not include reference to a Messianic figure who will be communicator of the Spirit of God. The most direct New Testament statement concerning the role of the exalted Jesus is that found in Acts 2:33 (quoted in part above): "Being therefore exalted at the right hand of God, and having received from the Father the promise of the Holy Spirit, he has poured out this. . . ." Jesus, the risen Lord, had said just before His ascension: "Behold, I send [or "send forth"][2] the promise of my Father upon you. . ." (Luke 24:49). Thereafter he "parted from them" and they, awaiting the fulfillment of the promise, were "continually in the temple blessing God" (Luke 24:53). Thereafter Jesus, risen from the dead and exalted at the Father's right hand, sends forth the Holy Spirit.

We turn next to the Fourth Gospel and note the statement that it is the glorification of Jesus that is essential background for the gift of the Holy Spirit. For we read that "as yet the Spirit had not been given,[3] because Jesus was not yet glorified" (John 7:39). Since the word "glorified" in the Fourth Gospel signifies "exalted,"[4] it follows again that the exaltation of Jesus must precede the giving of the Holy Spirit.

---

[1]As a vivid illustration, see "The Promise of the Father" in *Set My Spirit Free* (Plainfield, NJ: Logos, 1973) by Robert C. Frost. Dr. Frost testifies: "He knew my need and desire and had faithfully promised He would endue my life with the power of His Spirit. And it happened—just like He promised. For me it was a mighty Baptism of love that flooded my life inside and out. . . . My Heavenly Father had kept His word and performed His promise—and He will do the same for you" (p. 12). Dr. Frost is a biologist and popular lecturer in the contemporary spiritual renewal.

[2]The Greek word is *exapõstello*—to "send out" or "send forth." It is a parallel to the term in Acts 2:33, *execheen*, meaning "poured out" or "poured forth."

[3]The preponderance of Greek manuscripts omit the word "given," so that the text could be read simply, "the Spirit was not yet." However, English translations usually provide the word "given." This appears to be the intended meaning.

[4]See also John 12:23, 26, 28; 17:5. Cf. Acts 3:13—"The God of Abraham and of Isaac and of Jacob . . . glorified his servant Jesus."

Later in the Gospel of John there are several references by Jesus to the future sending, or giving, of the Holy Spirit. Particularly relevant to our concern are the words of Jesus: "I tell you the truth: it is to your advantage that I go away, for if I do not go away, the Counselor [the Paraclete][5] will not come to you; but if I go, I will send him to you" (John 16:7). The "going away" of Jesus is, of course, a reference to His return to the Father; from there He will send the Holy Spirit. Similar to this is the statement of Jesus: "But when the Counselor comes, whom I shall send to you from the Father, even the Spirit of truth, who proceeds from the Father, he will bear witness to me" (John 15:26). It is to be noted here that Jesus says He will send the Holy Spirit, and since the Spirit comes "from the Father," the implication is that this will happen when Jesus has returned to the presence of the Father. Thus both of these Johannine passages specify—as do the ones quoted from Luke and Acts— that the sending forth of the Holy Spirit is from the exalted Lord Jesus.

In two other Paraclete passages of the Fourth Gospel the Holy Spirit is said to be sent or given by the Father: "The Counselor, the Holy Spirit, whom the Father will send in my name, he will teach you all things. . ." (John 14:26); and "I will pray the Father, and he will give you another Counselor, to be with you for ever, even the Spirit of truth. . ." (John 14:16-17). One cannot stop with the exalted Jesus but must again go back to the Father.

Who then sends the Holy Spirit? If one reads these four passages in the actual order of their being set down, beginning with John 14:16-17 and concluding with John 16:7, the picture is this: (1) The Father will give the Spirit at the request of Jesus; (2) The Father will send the Spirit in Jesus' name; (3) The Son will send the Spirit from the Father; and (4) The Son will send the Spirit.

Thus, as Jesus unfolds the mystery of the sending of the Holy Spirit there is a progression from the Father to the Son. The Father is primary in all activity, and therefore ultimately He

---

[5]*Paraclētos*—the Paraclete: word used in the Fourth Gospel for the coming of the Holy Spirit. It conveys the idea of one who appears in another's behalf: advocate, helper, intercessor, advisor, counselor.

gives or sends the Holy Spirit,[6] as the first two Johannine passages disclose; however, even in these two passages the Son is intimately involved, for it is at His request that the Father sends the Spirit, and He does so in the Son's name. But once it has been clarified that the Father is the primary actor, Jesus moves on to state that it is through himself that the Spirit comes. Then follows the beautiful transition in the third passage where Jesus says that He (not the Father this time) will send the Spirit but that the Spirit is "from the Father." Here the extraordinary balance is shown: for while it is Jesus finally who sends the Spirit, nonetheless the Spirit is from God, the Father. Having stated in the three passages these relationships between the Spirit and the Father, and only against that background, does Jesus finally say—with no reference to the Father—that the Son will send the Holy Spirit.

One additional point before reflecting further on the sending, or giving, of the Holy Spirit, is that Jesus, in one of the Fourth Gospel passages, speaks of the Spirit as proceeding from the Father: "the Spirit of truth who proceeds from the Father" (John 15:26). Thus not only is the Father the primary agent in the sending of the Spirit, but He is also the source of the Holy Spirit: the Holy Spirit "proceeds" from Him. This procession of the Spirit from the Father is important to recognize; for it emphasizes that when the Holy Spirit is given, it is a continuation of the eternal procession[7] of the Spirit from the Father. Thus the Holy Spirit goes back to the eternal source of all things. The Holy Spirit is from God, the Father, and is therefore himself also God. Therefore, when the Holy Spirit is sent to the world, nothing less than the eternal God himself comes.

To return now to the sending of the Holy Spirit: we may say that both the Father and Son send the Holy Spirit[8] in the sense that the Father sends the Spirit *through* the Son. There is no sending of the Holy Spirit by the Father except through the

---

[6]Even as he gives or sends the Son. "God so loved the world that he gave his only Son . . . For God sent the Son into the world. . ." (John 3:16-17).

[7]Since the Holy Spirit did not come into existence (He always has been), the procession is an eternal one. He eternally proceeds from the Father within the mystery of the triune godhead. It would seem improper, therefore, to speak of the Holy Spirit as "proceeding from the Father and Son" (as, for example, in the Western *filioque* [and the Son] addition to the Constantinopolitan Creed).

[8]Though the procession of the Holy Spirit is from the Father alone (as we have observed).

Son, and therefore the Holy Spirit who is sent by the Father is received only through the mediation of Jesus Christ. Thus, in the ultimate sense, the Holy Spirit is sent from the Father, but in a proximate sense He comes from the Son.

This brings us back in our reflection to the exalted Jesus. For the Son through whom the Holy Spirit comes is the One at the Father's right hand. He who has been exalted by the Father to the place of honor and majesty sends forth the Holy Spirit. The Holy Spirit thus comes from heaven to earth: even from the Lord Jesus.

The coming of the Holy Spirit accordingly is not a divine event to which Jesus may be only peripherally related, but a coming in which He is the essential channel. The Holy Spirit, though distinct from Jesus, is the Spirit issuing from Jesus. He is sent by Jesus. Thus it is not as if the exalted Jesus were one force among many from whom the Spirit might come. "All authority in heaven and on earth" (Matt. 28:18) has been given the exalted Lord, and from Him alone does the Holy Spirit go forth.

Now to return to the contemporary scene: the central focus is the exalted Jesus. Wherever people today speak of the gift of the Holy Spirit it is invariably against the background of Jesus as the channel or medium. The focus is not on the Holy Spirit, but on Him through whom the Holy Spirit comes.[9] There is, to be sure, the recognition that ultimately the Spirit comes from God, the Father, but in no way so that the exalted Jesus is secondary or unessential. The contemporary spiritual renewal is Jesus-centered (or Christocentric) through and through.[10]

---

[9]". . . our testimony was not about tongues; not even primarily about the Spirit. But wherever we went, our talk was about Jesus Christ. . . ." Kevin and Dorothy Ranaghan, *Catholic Pentecostals* (New York: Paulist Press, 1969), p. 42. The words quoted refer to the first small group of Roman Catholics in the contemporary spiritual renewal.

[10]It is also obviously Trinitarian. From what has been said in the above paragraphs, Father, Son, and Holy Spirit are equally involved. This needs emphasis especially in light of the importance of Christian experience attesting to the fullness of the divine reality. On the matter of the focus being on Jesus Christ—which is universally true in the renewal of our time—there is some misunderstanding by critics who view the renewal as a shifting away from Christ to the Holy Spirit. (For example, see F.D. Bruner, *A Theology of the Holy Spirit* [Grand Rapids: Eerdmans, 1970], who speaks of how in Pentecostalism faith is "directed primarily to the Holy Spirit," p. 115. Though Bruner is dealing in his book mainly with classical Pentecostalism, his viewpoint also includes Neo-Pentecostalism, or the charismatic movement.) Actually, the focus

C. *The Work of Redemption*

Finally, the background for the gift of the Holy Spirit is the work of redemption. What God has wrought in Jesus Christ for the salvation of the world is essential preparation. The gift of the Holy Spirit follows upon the completion of God's gracious, redeeming work in the life, death and resurrection of Jesus, the Son of God.

We have been observing that the Holy Spirit is sent forth from the exalted Jesus at the Father's right hand. Now we move on to the recognition that this exaltation is of the *risen* Lord. The statement, earlier quoted, "Being therefore exalted at the right hand of God . . . he has poured out this . . ." (Acts 2:33) is preceded by "This Jesus God raised up. . ." (Acts 2:32). Hence, it is to be emphasized that the Holy Spirit does not come from the eternally glorious Son of God[11] but from the One who has been raised from the dead and exalted to the Father's presence. It is *this* exalted Jesus who sends forth the Holy Spirit.

Now we need to look back past the Resurrection to the whole cycle of Jesus' birth, life and death. For the exaltation of Jesus is of One who was willing to forgo His heavenly glory, be born in human flesh, suffer at the hands of ruthless men, die on the accursed cross, and experience the agonies of hell itself. Such was His incomparable act of self-humbling from the heights of heaven to the depths of hell. It is this Jesus, who knew humiliation vaster than the mind can begin to comprehend, who was raised from the dead and exalted to the right hand of the Father. This exalted Jesus pours forth the Holy Spirit.

The event of the life, death and resurrection of Jesus is clearly proclaimed in Acts 2:22-32 as background for the sending forth of the Holy Spirit. Peter speaks first, briefly, of the life of Jesus: "a man attested to you by God with mighty works and wonders and signs . . ."; next of the Crucifixion and death of Jesus: "you crucified and killed by the hands of lawless men"; and then, at much greater length, of the Resurrection: "But God raised him up, having loosed the pangs of death. . ." etc. It is only after all

remains throughout on Christ within the context of a Trinitarian frame of reference.
[11]That is, the pre-incarnate Son who is eternally with the Father. Jesus speaks in John 17:5 of the "glory" He had with the Father "before the world was made." Surely the Son was, is and will be forever glorious; but His exaltation follows upon His resurrection from the dead.

7

this that Peter comes to the outpouring of the Holy Spirit.

Years later, Peter is again preaching, this time to the Gentiles at Caesarea, and, as at Pentecost, he rehearses the events of Jesus' life, death and resurrection (Acts 10:34-43). Shortly thereafter "the Holy Spirit fell on all who heard the word" (Acts 10:44). It is again apparent that the whole cycle of Jesus' life, death and resurrection is background for the giving of the Holy Spirit.

But what is more deeply involved in this recounting of the story of Jesus is the declaration of God's work of redemption. This is far more than the narrative of an extraordinary life, of a person willingly dying a horrible death and of God miraculously raising someone from the grave. That in itself would be a vivid and memorable story, and might afford an example of heroic living and God's blessing on it. However, it is much more: it is God's plan of salvation—"Jesus, delivered up according to the definite plan and foreknowledge of God" (Acts 2:23)—being worked out in the life, death and resurrection of Jesus. It is victory over sin and death; the Resurrection is raising up of life; and the exaltation is the triumph of Jesus over all dominions and powers.

It is the life, death and resurrection of Jesus, wherein God's plan of redemption is fulfilled, that precedes the giving of the Holy Spirit. Without such redemption being wrought, the way would not be prepared. But with the victory won through Jesus Christ, the Holy Spirit may now be sent.

We have mentioned earlier the error of those who would view the gift of the Holy Spirit as only peripherally related to the person of Jesus Christ. Now, we must emphasize, it is also a very serious mistake to think at all of the gift of the Holy Spirit except against the background of the work of Christ. It is because of what God has done in and through the life, death and resurrection of Jesus that the Holy Spirit is sent forth. The gift of the Holy Spirit follows only upon the work of redemption.

In the contemporary renewal there is strong emphasis on the work of redemption in connection with the gift of the Holy Spirit. People everywhere who claim to have received the gift testify that because of what God has done in Christ in their lives they have come to experience the gift of the Holy Spirit. It was only as they came to know Jesus as the mediator of redemption that they experienced Him as the mediator of the Spirit.[12] As those who have become participants in the wonder of salvation through Jesus Christ they have likewise become recipients of the blessed Holy Spirit. Jesus has become both Savior and Lord.[13]

---

[12]Accordingly, this movement of renewal is not simply a form of "Christ mysticism" in which there is personal identification with Jesus Christ—a being caught up in His mystical presence. To be sure, there is the sense of Christ-relatedness, even Christ-identification, but this is consequent to the experience of redemption through Him.

[13]On the matter of the work of redemption in connection with the gift of the Holy Spirit, the reader is invited to see my book, *The Era of the Spirit* (Plainfield, NJ: Logos, 1971), especially pp. 51-53. Herein I emphasize that whereas the Holy Spirit is active in the work of redemption "applying the work of God in Christ and making new life an actuality," there is also "a movement of the Spirit *beyond* redemption. . . ." *The Era of the Spirit* was my first attempt to express in writing what had been recently happening to many people, and to follow this up with some theological reflection.

DIMENSIONS

We come now to a consideration of the actual giving of the Holy Spirit. The Holy Spirit promised by the Father, sent by the Son, becomes an event in time and history. God gives His Spirit to human beings. It is therefore our concern to reflect upon some of the dimensions of this event that include both God and man. We shall mainly note the biblical text and thereafter make some reference to the contemporary scene.

The first thing we may observe in the Scripture is that God gives His Spirit in *abundance.* In the words of the Fourth Gospel, "It is not by measure that he gives the Spirit" (John 3:34).[1] The gift of the Holy Spirit is one of plenitude and boundlessness. The Spirit is lavished upon men, and those who receive this gift participate in the divine, abundant self-giving.

It is the word "outpouring"—the outpouring of the Spirit— that in the Scriptures particularly expresses this theme of abundance. We have already given several quotations from both Old and New Testaments where the word "outpouring" or "pouring out" occurs. Let us review the New Testament passages already mentioned. First, Peter on the Day of Pentecost identifies what has just happened with the prophecy of Joel concerning "the last days" when God would "pour out" his Spirit "on all flesh." Second, thereafter, as Peter proclaims the gospel, he states it was the exalted Jesus who "poured out" the Holy Spirit.

Now we may turn to another account of the gift of the Holy Spirit—to the Gentiles at Caesarea. Again, we find the expression, "outpouring." The relevant text reads that "the gift of the Holy Spirit had been poured out [also][2] on the Gentiles" (Acts

---

[1]It is unclear in this text whether the subject of the giving is the Father or the Son. In either case it is a divine giving. Incidentally, the King James Version adds "unto him" (in italics, signifying that the words are not found in the Greek) which, I believe, misses the important note that to *whomever* God gives the Spirit it is without measure.

[2]Rather than "even" which appears in the Revised Standard Version. The Greek word

10:45). Thus the Gentile gathering at the house of Cornelius was blessed in the same manner as the disciples at Jerusalem. They likewise experienced the abundance of God's gift of the Holy Spirit.

One other passage, outside Acts, in the epistles should also be noted. It is found in Titus 3:5-6 where Paul speaks of "the washing of regeneration and renewal in the Holy Spirit, [whom][3] he poured out upon us richly through Jesus Christ our Savior." This is a beautiful statement that connects very closely the idea of outpouring and abundance: the Holy Spirit "poured out . . . richly"—and it happens through Jesus Christ.[4]

To summarize: what we have observed in these passages concerning the gift of the Holy Spirit is the lavishness of God's action. He does not stint, He does not mete out something of himself, something of His Spirit, but He gives in totality. God gives His Spirit in abundance.

As we turn briefly from the biblical record to the contemporary spiritual renewal, it is apparent that many people testify to the abundance of what they have received. There is often the sense of the lavishness of God in holding back nothing of His Spirit. There may have been a growing hunger and thirst for the deep things of God, then a critical spiritual breakthrough came and God poured out His Spirit. For some there was such a plenitude of the divine presence and power, such a copiousness of God's blessing, such totality of the Spirit's bestowal that it seemed almost more than human existence could bear. It was all of God that man could receive of the eternal glory.[5]

---

kai may in this context be translated as "also" or "even." I would judge that "also" (the translation given in King James and several modern versions) is preferable. It is true that Peter and those with him were surprised when the gift was poured out on the Gentiles; thus it could be: "even on the Gentiles." However, I believe the more significant matter here is that the Gentiles were *also* receiving the gift of the Spirit.

[3]Rather than "which" in King James (KJV) and Revised Standard Version (RSV). See New American Standard (NAS) and New International Version (NIV) for translation as "whom." The Greek word is *ou*, which is either masculine or neuter; however, the masculine translation as "whom" seems more fitting in light of the personal reality of the Holy Spirit.

[4]Another passage that might be noted about the Holy Spirit and outpouring is Romans 5:5 where Paul writes of how "God's love has been poured into our hearts through the Holy Spirit . . . given to us." However, Paul is speaking here of a *result* of the Spirit being given, namely, God's love "poured out."

[5]"I felt the breath of God and tasted of His glory. I knew God was revealing only a minute portion of Himself, had it been anything greater I would not have been able to survive. I

We turn, in the second place, to a number of related themes that suggest the way God gives the Holy Spirit. Here we shall note such matters as the *divine sovereignty*, the *suddenness* and *forcefulness* of the gift. All of these, I believe, are contained in the idea of the Holy Spirit "falling upon" persons.

Two of the incidents in the book of Acts relating to the gift of the Holy Spirit make use of the language of "falling." First, the account of the Holy Spirit being given to the Gentiles at Caesarea: "While Peter was still saying this [his message to the Gentiles], the Holy Spirit fell on all who heard the word" (10:44). Later Peter, rehearsing the event, says: "As I began to speak, the Holy Spirit fell on them just as on us at the beginning." Thus not only what happened to the Gentiles at Caesarea but also earlier to the disciples at Jerusalem on the Day of Pentecost was a "falling" of the Holy Spirit.

The other incident in which the language of "falling" is used is that concerning the gift of the Holy Spirit to the Samaritans. Before they received the gift, the Holy Spirit "had not yet fallen on any of them" (8:16). Hence, when the Samaritans received the gift later, by implication, the Holy Spirit then fell upon them.

The aspect of God's sovereign action is unmistakably present in the gift of the Holy Spirit. The word "falling" connotes an action "from above," from heaven to earth and therefore totally initiated by God. God may give the Holy Spirit according to some specified pattern,[6] or He may transcend all usual modes and freely send down the Holy Spirit. The sovereign "falling" of the Holy Spirit occurred in both Jerusalem and Caesarea, and therefore may happen again and again.

Related to this is the note of *suddenness*. It is apparent that in Jerusalem the Holy Spirit suddenly came. On the Day of Pentecost the disciples were all gathered together when "sud-

---

would have died. . . . I felt the Spirit of God surging in as the waters of the Red Sea must have rushed together after the children of Israel had marched through to freedom." So writes Arthur Katz in his autobiography, *Ben Israel: Odyssey of a Modern Jew* (Plainfield, NJ: Logos, 1970), pp. 204-5. This is the climactic moment in the pilgrimage of a "son of Israel" wherein, after a "new-found relationship with the Messiah" (p. 171), he experienced the outpouring (the "surging") of God's Spirit and the presence of eternal glory. Arthur Katz is a leading spokesman in the contemporary spiritual renewal.
[6]This will be discussed later.

denly a sound came from heaven like the rush of a mighty wind . . ." (Acts 2:2). This was unmistakably the coming of the Holy Spirit—sent from heaven—and happened with no advance notice. It is equally apparent that the outpouring of the Spirit upon the Caesareans was sudden. For Peter's sermon was interrupted by the falling of the Holy Spirit, obviously to the surprise of everyone gathered, Jew and Gentile alike.

When God acts, He acts quickly. There may be many factors preparing the way, but when He sends His Spirit, there is a sudden movement from "on high," and the Spirit falls. There may be a period of time leading up to it (as the days of waiting prior to Pentecost),[7] but when the time comes, God moves rapidly. Suddenly—the Spirit comes.

The third aspect mentioned is that of *forcefulness*. We have already observed the statement in Acts about the sound "from heaven like the rush of a mighty wind." The coming of the Holy Spirit at Pentecost was forcible,[8] strong, driving. There was nothing quiet or hidden about it: and it made an impact on all. The expression "fall upon" suggests the same note of forcefulness; for when something—or someone—falls upon a person or a group, the effects will doubtless be felt! Of course, we are here dealing with the Holy Spirit, not a thing or force; nonetheless, His coming is with memorable impact.

This leads us again to the contemporary scene where testimonies abound to the "falling" of the Holy Spirit.[9] Sometimes

[7]See Acts 1:4ff. The period of waiting was about ten days.

[8]The word translated above as "mighty" in the Greek is *biaias*, meaning "violent" or "forcible."

[9]"There came a day and hour when the Spirit of God invaded our small Saturday evening prayer group, where we met to pray for the Sunday worship service. Literally, the Spirit fell! He electrified everyone in the room! . . . Immediately the gifts of the Spirit began to be distributed among us and we began to see signs, wonders, and miracles that have never ceased to this day!" Words of Rev. James H. Brown, Presbyterian minister, in an article entitled "Signs, Wonders and Miracles" in *Presbyterians and the Baptism of the Holy Spirit* (Los Angeles: Full Gospel Business Men's Fellowship International, 1963), pp. 6-7. Such a testimony about the Spirit's "falling" is frequently found in the renewal of our time. It is interesting to observe that the language of "falling" was earlier used by Agnes Ozman, whose experience is usually viewed as the beginning of twentieth-century Pentecostalism: ". . . the Holy Spirit fell upon me and I began to speak in tongues, glorifying God. . . . I had the added joy and glory my heart longed for and a depth of the presence of the Lord within me that I had never known before. It was as if rivers of water were proceeding from my innermost being." See Klaude Kendrick, *The Promise Fulfilled* (Springfield, MO: Gospel Pub-

reference is made to what has been experienced in a gathering of people when, perhaps after witness has been borne about God's readiness to pour out His Spirit, suddenly the Spirit falls. This frequently occurs unexpectedly—even to the shock and surprise of those to whom it happens. Here, seemingly, was a sovereign act of God occurring in the midst of his gathered people. And—it is to be added—often this takes place with such forcefulness that the recipients have literally reeled under the impact. This "falling" of the Spirit, so people attest, may occur privately as well—and there is no limit to time or place: at any hour in church, in one's prayer closet, driving a car, on the job, indeed anywhere. It is God's action, and of such a character that one can never thereafter forget.

We move on to recognize, in the third place, that the Holy Spirit comes to *take possession*. The Holy Spirit lays claim upon a person, or community, so as to be the controlling and guiding reality. Henceforward one is to move under the direction of the Holy Spirit.

The expression "come upon" is the primary one in the book of Acts that conveys this meaning. It is the language used by Jesus prior to Pentecost in telling His disciples they are to be His witnesses: "But you shall receive power when the Holy Spirit has come upon you; and you shall be my witnesses . . ."(1:8). Jesus had been giving them "commandment through the Holy Spirit" (1:2), so the Holy Spirit was already at work in their midst. But this was not yet the "coming upon" whereby the Holy Spirit would become the controlling factor in their lives.

The language of "coming upon" is also used in the later account of Paul ministering to the Ephesians. The climactic moment is stated: "And when Paul laid his hands upon them, the Holy Spirit came on them . . ." (Acts 19:6). Thus the Ephesians experience essentially the same possession by the Spirit as did the disciples at Pentecost.

Here a point needs to be emphasized, namely, the possession referred to in Acts intends to be a continuing matter. When the Holy Spirit comes upon the disciples at Pentecost, this is

lishing House, 1961), pp. 52-53. We shall speak of tongues in the next chapter; the point here to note is that the imagery of falling is used in this early Pentecostal testimony.

an endowment for their continuing life and ministry. From then on they are to be persons moving under the guidance and authority of the Holy Spirit.

There are also a number of references in the Old Testament to the Spirit coming upon various persons. It is said of several of the judges that the Spirit of the Lord "came upon" them, "took possession of" them or "came mightily upon" [10] them. The same is said of Saul and David.[11] Also, it was earlier said of one incident concerning Moses' elders,[12] also of the prophesying of Balaam.[13] However, all of this is largely a temporary matter to enable a person for a time to fulfill a certain role or function: judging, ruling, prophesying.[14] Further, the Spirit only came upon a few now and then. With the outpouring of the Spirit beginning at Pentecost the situation is quite different: the coming of the Spirit is both abiding and universal ("all flesh").

Here we might also quote the words of Jesus: "stay in the city, until you are clothed with power from on high" (Luke 24:49). The picture of being clothed, or endued, with the Holy Spirit likewise contains the note of a continuing endowment. When the Holy Spirit comes and endues, not only will there be a total possession but also movement thereafter will be vested with His presence and power.

It is to be noted that the described "coming upon" and "clothing with" are two aspects of the same operation of the Holy Spirit. The former terminology, in the active voice, expresses the divine side, namely, that the Holy Spirit thereby lays claim to or possesses a person. The latter terminology, in the passive voice, expresses the human aspect, namely, that a person is thereby invested with the Holy Spirit. One does not himself put

---

[10]For example, concerning Othniel: "The Spirit of the Lord came upon him, and he judged Israel" (Judg. 3:10); Gideon: "The Spirit of the Lord took possession of Gideon, and he sounded the trumpet . . ." (Judg. 6:34); Samson: "The Spirit of the Lord came mightily upon him . . ." (Judg. 14:6, 19; 15:14).

[11]"The Spirit of God came mightily upon Saul . . ." (1 Sam. 11:6); "The Spirit of the Lord came mightily upon David from that day forward" (1 Sam. 16:13).

[12]"Then the Lord . . . took some of the spirit that was upon him [Moses] and put it upon the seventy elders; and when the spirit rested upon them, they prophesied" (Num. 11:25).

[13]Balaam: "And the Spirit of God came upon him, and he took up his discourse . . ." (Num. 24:2).

[14]David is the Old Testament exception. As a prior footnote shows, David's endowment of the Spirit was "from that day forward."

on the Holy Spirit; rather does the Spirit clothe the person. Possession *by* the Spirit and investment *with* the Spirit: these are two aspects of God's gracious action.

In the contemporary situation, we now observe, there is a striking sense of the Holy Spirit's possession and investment. Whatever may have been the relation to God before, this represents a fresh and total claim upon one's life. "I may have had the Spirit before, but now the Spirit has me"—such is a typical expression of persons in the spiritual renewal. Nor is there any thought of lack of freedom in such possession; quite the contrary, there is a tremendous sense of moving and acting freely under the Spirit's direction. Moreover, the experience of the Spirit's abiding endowment, so that one is vested henceforward with His presence and power, makes for an extraordinary new level of Christian commitment and activity.[15]

Before going further it is important to stress that all the terminology thus far used in this chapter about the "outpouring," the "falling upon," and the "coming upon" of the Holy Spirit points definitely to the gift of the Holy Spirit as a gift from without or beyond. The experience of the gift therefore is not some kind of mystical participation in the immanent presence of God. Rather, it is a profound experience of the transcendent God coming powerfully to His creature. In some ways it is a kind of spiritual invasion: from the heights to the depths. But the coming from without is by no means to break down or destroy; it is a gracious act whereby human beings may better become participants in the purpose and activity of God.

In the fourth place, those to whom God gives His Spirit are *enveloped* with His presence and power. The Spirit promised by the Father, sent forth by the Son, surrounds, encloses, immerses

---

[15]Leon Joseph Cardinal Suenens, contemporary Roman Catholic leader in the spiritual renewal, writes in his book, *A New Pentecost?* (New York: Seabury Press, 1974): "We are not alone any more, we know we are guided by the Holy Spirit; our life unfolds in response to him. As we dispossess ourselves, our being is possessed by God. The void is filled. . . . Those who allow themselves to be possessed by God, resemble the log that little by little becomes white-hot. Their life, nourished by the fire of the Holy Spirit, becomes fire in its turn. Is not this the fire of which Jesus spoke when he said: 'I have come to bring fire to the earth . . .' (Luke 12:49)? This is what it means to experience the Holy Spirit who alone can renew the face of the earth!" (p. 70).

those to whom He comes. Nothing is left untouched or unaffected. It is as if one were bathed in the reality of God.

The biblical term that expresses most vividly this aspect of envelopment is *"being baptized."* This reference is made not to water but to the Spirit, to being baptized with, or in,[16] the Holy Spirit. By such a baptism, one is totally enveloped within the reality of the divine presence.

In the book of Acts this expression is found twice. It is used in connection with the gift of the Holy Spirit to the disciples at Jerusalem and to the Gentiles in Caesarea. Prior to the Jerusalem Pentecost, the words of Jesus are recorded: "John baptized [in][17] water, but before many days you shall be baptized [in][17] the Holy Spirit" (Acts 1:5). Following the Gentile Pentecost, Peter, in his words to the apostles and brethren in Judea, refers to what had happened to the Gentiles as also a being baptized in the Holy Spirit: "As I began to speak, the Holy Spirit fell on them just as on us at the beginning. And I remembered the word of the Lord, how he said, 'John baptized [in] water, but you shall be baptized [in] the Holy Spirit' " (Acts 11:15-16). Thus although the expression, "baptized in the Spirit," is not used on the occasions of the gift of the Spirit to Jew and Gentile (Acts 2 and Acts 10), it is apparent that both occasions are baptisms in the Holy Spirit.[18] By extension, since we have noted the use of other terms such as "outpouring," "falling" and "coming on," for these and other events recording the gift of the Holy Spirit, we may properly speak of all these incidents as occasions of being baptized in the Holy Spirit.

---

[16]The Greek preposition regularly found is *en* which may be translated "with" or "in." "With" expresses the idea of the Holy Spirit coming to encompass or surround; "in" conveys the note of the Holy Spirit as the element within which one is submerged. "In" is preferred by many for two reasons: it avoids any idea that the Holy Spirit is the baptizer ("with" often means "by"); second, "in" follows quite naturally upon the word "baptize" (*baptizō*) which means to "immerse," "plunge under," "submerge within," etc. However, the fact of envelopment may well include both ideas: to be surrounded with as well as to be plunged within.

[17]In accordance with our previous footnote we shall henceforward render *en* as "in," thus not following the RSV. Most modern translations use "with"; however, a marginal note usually accompanies the translation giving the other possibility of "in."

[18]The noun "baptism" is not used in these passages (nor in others which we shall notice shortly). The gift of the Spirit in each case is an event, a dynamic occurrence, a "being baptized." However, I do not think it improper to use the substantive form (similarly with "outpouring," which as such does not occur either; the text each time is "poured out") if one bears in mind its eventful quality.

The importance of this expression is further enhanced by the fact that all four Gospels likewise contain references to a spiritual baptism. At the beginning of the ministry of Jesus, John the Baptist points to it as a future event: "I have baptized you [in] water; but he [Jesus] will baptize you [in] the Holy Spirit [and fire]."[19] There is no suggestion in the Gospels that this promised baptism in the Spirit is fulfilled during the period of the life, death and resurrection of Jesus.[20] It is only with the completion of the work of Christ in redemption that the Holy Spirit is given—and people thereafter are baptized in the Holy Spirit.

In the Gospels it is evident that Jesus will be the baptizer: "He [Jesus] will baptize you." By implication the same is true in the book of Acts where, as noted, the text reads: "You shall be baptized in the Holy Spirit." The Holy Spirit is not depicted as the baptizer, as if one were being baptized by[21] the Holy Spirit. Rather, Jesus is the baptizer and the Holy Spirit is the element wherein the baptism occurs. Even as water is not the agent in water baptism, neither is the Spirit the agent in Spirit baptism. Water and Spirit are the elements in which baptism takes place. This is an important fact to keep in mind, for it leads one properly to understand baptism in the Spirit as not an action by the Spirit but by the exalted Lord who immerses people in his Spirit.

We have briefly discussed the four Gospel instances and the two in Acts that specifically refer to baptism in the Holy Spirit. There is one other possible instance in the New Testament: "For by one Spirit we were all baptized into one body—Jews or Greeks, slaves or free—and all were made to drink of one Spirit" (1 Cor. 12:13). It could be argued that Paul is dealing with a different matter here, namely, a baptism by the Spirit, so that

---

[19]Mark 1:8. In Matthew 3:11 and Luke 3:16 the words "and fire" are added. In John 1:33 the wording is: "I myself did not know him; but he who sent me to baptize [in] water said to me, 'He on whom you see the Spirit descend and remain, this is he who baptizes [in] the Holy Spirit.' "

[20]This is true even with the interpretation that John's Gospel refers to it in 20:22 where Jesus says, "Receive the Holy Spirit." This "Johannine Pentecost" (as it is sometimes called) still *follows* the events of Christ's life, death and resurrection.

[21]Though the Greek word *en* can be translated "by," it is more often "with" or "in" (see earlier footnote). "By" would clearly be a mistake here, since the Holy Spirit is not the agent in Spirit baptism.

the Spirit (unlike the cases in the Gospels and Acts) is the agent. However, since the Greek word translated "by" is the same as the word translated "in"[22] in the prior six cases, it would seem preferable to translate it thus: *"In* one Spirit we were all baptized.. . ." Accordingly, the Holy Spirit is again depicted as element and not as agent, and Christ (though not mentioned directly) is implied to be the agent. [23] That this seems to be the more likely interpretation follows also from the second half of the verse which again does not show the Holy Spirit as agent: "all were made to drink of one Spirit." Incidentally, this latter statement may also be translated: "all were imbued [or saturated] with one Spirit."[24] This translation sounds much like our previous description of baptism in the Spirit as immersion in or saturation with the Holy Spirit. However, whichever translation is followed, the Holy Spirit is not said to be the agent in 1 Corinthians any more than in the Gospels and Acts.

To summarize: the importance of the expression "being baptized in the Holy Spirit" cannot be denied. It depicts vividly the idea of being totally enveloped in the reality of the Holy Spirit. Even though this baptism in the Holy Spirit is set in contrast with John's baptism in water (in the Gospels and Acts), the same term is used for both; so drawing upon the picture of water baptism one sees more clearly the operation of Spirit baptism. Since to be baptized in water means literally to be immersed in, plunged in, even saturated with the surrounding element,[25] then to be baptized in the Holy Spirit can mean no

---

[22]*en.*

[23]John R. W. Stott writes: "If 1 Corinthians 12:13 were different [from the Gospels and Acts passages] and in this verse the Holy Spirit were himself the baptizer, what would be the 'element' with which he baptizes? That there is no answer to this question is enough to overthrow this interpretation, since the baptism metaphor absolutely requires an element, or the baptism is no baptism. Therefore, the 'element' in the baptism of 1 Corinthians 12:13 must be the Holy Spirit, and (consistently with the other verses) we must supply Jesus Christ as the baptizer." *The Baptism and Fullness of the Holy Spirit* (Downer's Grove: Inter-Varsity Press, 1964), p. 27.

[24]Thayer's *Greek-English Lexicon of the New Testament* (New York and London: Harper and Brothers, 1899) article on *potizō* suggests "imbued" as translation for *epotisthēmen* in this verse.

[25]Practices of water baptism of course vary. Our concern here, however, is to note the literal meaning of the word "baptize," the Greek *baptizo*, which signifies to "dip" or "immerse"—also "plunge, sink, drench, overwhelm " (see Arndt and Gingrich, *A Greek-English Lexicon of the New Testament and Other Early Christian Literature* [University of Chicago Press, 1957]).

less. No part of the body is left untouched by water baptism; everything goes under. So with Spirit baptism the whole being of man—body, soul and spirit—is enveloped in the reality of God. Likewise, the community of those who are enveloped in the divine reality is affected in its total life. Both individual and community are touched in every area by the presence and power of the Holy Spirit.

Through being baptized in the Holy Spirit, life takes on a fresh quality of divine nearness and intimacy. Moreover, the origin of this baptism is from beyond, from Jesus Christ. It is not a kind of mystical immanence without transcendent source, but a being plunged into the sphere of the divine totality by the activity of the exalted Lord. Such is the marvelous sense of immediacy that is known by those who are thus enveloped in the reality of the divine presence.

Now to return specifically to the spiritual renewal in our day: there is no expression more commonly used than that of being "baptized in [or with] the Holy Spirit." For what has been said in the preceding paragraphs about the entire being of man enveloped—immersed, saturated, imbued—in the reality of God is the testimony of countless thousands of people.[26] This may have happened to a community of people or to an individual, but the situation is extraordinarily the same. If to a community, its whole existence is thereby enveloped anew in the divine glory: every aspect of its life touched by the divine presence. If to an individual, one has then been submerged in the presence and power of God—to use a common expression—"from the top of the head to the soles of the feet."

In passing, it is significant to observe that the biblical expression of "baptized in [or with] the Spirit" has had little use in the long history of the church. Much of course has been said about baptism in (or with) water[27] but little about baptism in the Holy Spirit.[28] It may well be that the revival of this biblical

---

[26]"Talk about a baptism, it was just like I was being plunged down into a great sea of water, only the water was God, the water was the Holy Spirit. . . ." Testimony of one of the first Roman Catholics in the contemporary renewal of his "baptism in the Holy Spirit" (*Catholic Pentecostals*, p. 16).

[27]See hereafter (Chapter 6) for discussion of water baptism in relation to Spirit baptism.

[28]It might be mentioned that Charles G. Finney, nineteenth-century evangelist, and later founder of Oberlin College, did use this expression about his early experience. A

expression is one of the key signs of the renewal of New Testament vitality in our times.

Fifth, and finally, the recipients of God's gift are *inwardly pervaded* by His Holy Spirit. Man in the totality of his being is claimed by the Spirit of God. There is penetration through the level of consciousness to the subconscious depths. The Holy Spirit probes the inward regions of soul and spirit, and possesses human existence in its entirety.

The word used in the scriptural record to express this inward possession is "filled"—to be "filled with the Holy Spirit." Let us note its usage first in the account of the disciples at Jerusalem.

It is interesting to observe that the first thing said about what happened to the disciples at Pentecost is that "They were all filled with [29] the Holy Spirit" (Acts 2:4). Peter later speaks of this as the "outpouring of the Holy Spirit" (as we have noted before), but the primary description is their being "filled."[30] They were pervaded by God's presence and power.

Looking in more detail at the Pentecostal picture, we find that before the disciples were filled, the house was filled. The sound from heaven came "like the rush of a mighty wind" (as we have earlier noted), and "it filled all the house where they were sitting" (Acts 2:2).[31] The house being filled suggests the presence

---

few hours after what Finney described as a face to face encounter with Christ, he says: "I received a mighty baptism of the Holy Ghost . . . without any recollection that I had ever heard the thing mentioned by any person in the world, the Holy Spirit descended upon me in a manner that seemed to go through me, body and soul. . . . Indeed it seemed to come in waves and waves of liquid love. . . . It seemed like the very breath of God . . . it seemed to fan me, like immense wings. . . . I wept aloud with joy and love; and I do not know but I should say, I literally bellowed out the unutterable gushings of my heart. These waves came over me, and over me, and over me, one after the other, until I recollect I cried out, 'I shall die if these waves continue to pass over me'. . . yet I had no fear of death." See *Charles G. Finney: An Autobiography* (Old Tappan, NJ: Revell, 1876), pp. 20-21. Finney's experience of "a mighty baptism" of the Spirit is recurring variously around the world in the late twentieth century.

[29]Or, more literally, "filled of the Holy Spirit"—*eplēsthēsan pneumatos hagiou*. Similarly in other passages we shall note.

[30]Thus being "filled with the Holy Spirit" is one of the expressions—along with "outpouring," "falling," "coming upon" and "baptized in"—used in Acts to describe what occurs when the Holy Spirit is given.

[31]The Old Testament parallel to the filling of the house at Pentecost is that of the filling of the Tabernacle and Temple with the divine glory—"the glory of the Lord filled the tabernacle [or temple]" (see Exod. 40:34-35 and 2 Chron. 7:1-2). Of course, the far greater thing at Pentecost was that *people*—not just a tabernacle, temple or house— were filled with the Holy Spirit.

of God in an intensive manner throughout the place of assembly. Those gathered know themselves to be surrounded by and enveloped in the presence of the Holy Spirit. Then what is felt outwardly in fullness becomes an inner total experience. They are all—as community and as persons—filled with the Spirit of God.

Also, just before the disciples are filled, the Scripture reads that "There appeared to them tongues as of fire, distributed and resting on each one of them" (Acts 2:3). Two comments: first, this calls to mind the words that Jesus will baptize with "the Holy Spirit *and fire*"; second, the tongues "resting on each" contains the imagery of the Holy Spirit descending upon—as in the language of "pouring out on," "falling on" and "coming on" —so that the movement is from heaven to earth. Hence, the disciples are filled from beyond themselves. It is not simply an intensification of an inward spiritual presence: it is a divine visitation in fullness.

Next, we turn to the account of Saul of Tarsus, and note how he was filled with the Spirit. Three days after Saul's encounter with the glorified Jesus a disciple named Ananias goes to the blinded Saul: "So Ananias departed and entered the house. And laying his hands on him he said, 'Brother Saul, the Lord Jesus who appeared to you . . . has sent me that you may regain your sight and be filled with the Holy Spirit' " (Acts 9:17). So does Saul, later to become Paul, receive the gift of the Holy Spirit.

Thus the experience of Saul of Tarsus was like that of the disciples at Jerusalem who were also filled with the Spirit. It came from the exalted Lord Jesus in each case, and prepared both the disciples and Saul for the work that lay ahead. Indeed, it was the gift of the Holy Spirit promised by God to all He calls to himself. Accordingly, being "filled with the Holy Spirit" in these two cases is clearly identical with the experience of the Samaritans, the people at Caesarea, and the disciples at Ephesus. It was the initial experience of receiving the gift of the Holy Spirit.

There is one other report in Acts of a being "filled with the Holy Spirit" that might likewise relate to such an initial experience: "The disciples were filled with joy and with the

Holy Spirit" (Acts 13:52).[32] This text refers to those in Antioch of Pisidia who had been disciples for some time.

Outside of this, other references in Acts to "filled with the Spirit" concern persons who have earlier been filled. It is said of Peter, when he later addressed the high council of Jews, that he, "filled with the Holy Spirit," spoke to them (4:8), and that afterward when Peter and the company of disciples prayed for boldness to speak the word "they were all filled with the Holy Spirit . . ." (4:31). Saul of Tarsus, now called Paul, is described as "filled with the Holy Spirit" as he discerns the evil intentions of Elymas the magician and speaks against him (13:9). It would seem from these passages that in addition to the initial experience of being filled there may be subsequent fresh fillings with the Holy Spirit.[33]

There is also reference to a condition of fullness: some persons are said to be "full of the Holy Spirit." Stephen and Barnabas were described as men "full of the Holy Spirit and faith,"[34] and the requirement for those elected to serve tables (including Stephen) is that they be men "full of the Spirit and of wisdom."[35] Indeed, it is also important to note that Jesus himself, just

---

[32]The Greek word for "filled" here is *eplērounto*, the imperfect tense, and may be translated as "were continually filled" (NAS) or "continued to be full" (Phillips). However, the imperfect can also mean that they were being filled one after another— thus an initial experience. (I am inclined to agree with Howard M. Ervin, *These Are Not Drunken As Ye Suppose*, [Plainfield, NJ: Logos, 1968], p. 72, on this point.) A similar imperfect is found in Acts 8:17: "And they received [*elambanon*] the Holy Spirit"—which might be more accurately translated: "they were receiving," that is, one by one.

[33]Mention should also be made that prior to Pentecost there are a few references to "filled with the [Holy] Spirit." In the Old Testament Bezalel, craftsman for the tabernacle, was "filled . . . with the Spirit of God . . . to devise artistic designs . . ." (Exod. 31:3); and Micah the prophet declares, "I am filled with power, with the Spirit of the Lord . . . to declare to Jacob his transgression and to Israel his sin" (Mic. 3:8). In the New Testament, Elizabeth was "filled with the Holy Spirit and . . . exclaimed with a loud cry [to Mary], 'Blessed are you among women, and blessed is the fruit of your womb' " (Luke 1:41-42); and Zechariah was "filled with the Holy Spirit and prophesied . . ." (Luke 1:67). In all these cases the filling with the Spirit was for a limited function (tabernacle designing, prophesying, word of supernatural knowledge), and therefore a temporary manifestation of the Holy Spirit. Such instances prepare the way for the filling at Pentecost that is identical with the outpouring of, or baptism in, the Holy Spirit. One other pre-Pentecost instance of Spirit filling is that of John the Baptist, of whom the angel said, "He will be filled with the Holy Spirit, even from his mother's womb" (Luke 1:15). Here, it would seem, is the one instance of a lifetime of spiritual fullness, thereby marking John as the greatest of the prophets, the forerunner of Jesus' spiritual baptism, and preview of Pentecost.

[34]Acts 6:5; 7:55; 11:24.

[35]Acts 6:3.

following his baptism by John, is described as "full of the Holy Spirit": "And Jesus, full of the Holy Spirit, returned from the Jordan . . ." (Luke 4:1). The language of spiritual fullness bespeaks God's abundant gift of the Holy Spirit.

Thus along with the initial reception of the gift of the Holy Spirit which is described as "filling" in the case of the first disciples and Saul of Tarsus,[36] there are later repetitions of being filled as well as emphasis on continuing fullness. Hence, the concept of filling is quite complex in richness and meaning.

What then is the overall significance of being "filled" or "full"? It would seem to point to that dimension of the Spirit's bestowal that relates to interiority, that is to say, the whole community and/or person is inwardly pervaded by the Holy Spirit. Even as the sound of something like a mighty wind filled all the house—which signifies every room, nook and corner—so for all persons who are filled, this means every aspect of individual and communal life. The human situation is claimed in a total way by the Spirit of the living God.

In the spiritual renewal of our time there are countless numbers of persons who testify to the reality of being filled with the Holy Spirit. There may have been a sense of emptiness for some time, but now God has come in His fullness; there may have been an increasing yearning to glorify God in all that one is and does, and now God had flooded one's being with His ineffable presence; there may have been a deep desire to be used more effectively in sharing the Good News of the grace received in Jesus Christ, and now God has filled one's life and speech with fresh power. Such testimony to being filled with the Holy Spirit points to a profoundly internal experience of the Spirit of God moving throughout like wind, or fire, until all barriers are breached and the Holy Spirit pervades everything.[37]

---

[36] And perhaps the believers in Antioch (as noted).

[37] "How could a man think he was passing out the bread of life every Sunday and still remain so utterly hungry himself? I was empty, and I knew it. This was the end of the line." So writes Erwin Prange about his situation as a Lutheran pastor in his first parish. Then, "all at once a voice seemed to come from nowhere and everywhere. . . . 'The gift is already yours. Reach out and take it.' " As Prange then stretched out his hands toward the altar, palms up, jaws tightening and mouth open: "In an instant, there was a sudden shift of dimensions, and God became real. A spirit of pure love pervaded the church and drenched me like rain. He was beating in my heart, flowing through my blood, breathing in my lungs, and thinking in my brain. Every cell in my body, every

25

This is totality of penetration with the Holy Spirit whereby, in a new way, all areas of one's being—body, soul and spirit (the conscious and subconscious depths)—become sensitized to the divine presence and activity. Likewise, a community of people filled with the Holy Spirit find that not only their relationship to God but also to one another becomes suffused with a profound sense of God moving in and through whatever takes place. Further, the experience of being filled may occur afresh—by God's sovereign action and in response to new situations. However, any renewed filling is against the background of the original breakthrough of God's Spirit when the Spirit moved throughout and all barriers were broken down. For the Holy Spirit is free to move again and again—as all of life becomes redolent with the presence and wonder of Almighty God.

Finally, let us hear the exhortation which remains to all generations: "Be filled with the Spirit. . ." (Eph. 5:18). For it is the divine intention that God's people should know the life of continuing spiritual fullness[38] and thereby ever live to the praise and glory of God.

---

nerve end, tingled with the fire of His presence." See Prange's autobiographical account, *The Gift is Already Yours* (Plainfield, NJ: Logos, 1973), pp. 52-53. Though the language is not precisely that of being "filled with the Holy Spirit," the whole experience was one of moving from emptiness to fullness, and such a fullness as Prange vividly describes.

[38]The Greek verb for "be filled" is *plērousthe* which is present imperative signifying continuity: "Be continuously filled with the Holy Spirit."

CHAPTER THREE

RESPONSE

The human response to the giving of the Holy Spirit is essentially the *praise of God*. When human existence—individually and in community—is bathed with the divine presence, there is only one truly significant response, namely, the glorifying of God. God has acted through Jesus Christ to pour out His Spirit, and so marvelous is its occurrence that nothing else can capture it but the high praise of God. So does the praise of God ring forth—praise for His mighty deeds in creation, redemption and sending His Holy Spirit. It is the extolling of God that springs from the lips and hearts of those who are acclaiming Jesus as Lord.

This praise that is rendered is not to an absentee God but to one who is present in the midst of His people. The fullness of His grace in Jesus Christ has been experienced, and now His glory is being shed abroad in the Holy Spirit. There is a deep sense of the goodness of the Father, the Lordship of Jesus Christ and the dynamism of the Holy Spirit.

The whole focus of this praise is God. It is not a glorying in the self—as if perchance one had suddenly become an extraordinary person by virtue of the gift of the Holy Spirit. It is not a glorying by people who look at themselves as spiritually superior to others because of what they have received. Far from it: the direction is totally away from human existence as all things are lifted up to the praise and blessing of God.

Something like what we have been describing took place originally in Jerusalem at Pentecost. For when the disciples were filled with the Holy Spirit they all began to praise God. This is apparent from the words of Acts 2:11 which record the multitude saying: "We hear them telling in our own tongues the mighty [wonderful, magnificent][1] works of God." We are not

---

[1]The Greek word is *megaleia*.

told for what "mighty works" they praised God; but it is not hard to imagine that, having so recently lived through the events of Jesus' life, death and resurrection, they were praising Him, among other things, for having performed the mighty work of redemption. Also He had just now fulfilled the promise to pour forth the Holy Spirit. How much they had to praise God for!

Again, something of the same thing happened years later in Caesarea: another occasion of the glorifying of God. This time it was the Gentiles upon whom the Holy Spirit came, and others (Peter and his fellow Jews) "heard them speaking in tongues and extolling [magnifying][2] God" (Acts 10:46).

We should also note the connection between being filled with the Spirit and praise in Paul's letter to the Ephesians. Paul writes: "Be filled with the Spirit, addressing one another in psalms and hymns and spiritual songs, singing and making melody to the Lord with all your heart" (Eph. 5:18-19). As a result of being filled with God's Spirit, psalms, hymns, spiritual songs break forth—the heart is filled with melody, rejoicing in the Lord. Thus is praise offered up in manifold ways to Him who has given His blessed Spirit.

Let us reflect for a moment upon the praise of God in the worship of the church. In all true worship there is a desire to offer up worthy praise and adoration to Almighty God. And according to the intensity of the sense of the Lord's presence, there is yearning to find further ways of showing forth this praise. Ordinary language may seem to be inadequate, and perhaps some language of the past (Greek or Latin, for example) will be used in the desire for more worthy expression. There may be the use of praise language such as "Hallelujah!" or "Hosanna!" often repeated to voice an intensity of adoration. Or in the sensing of the wonder of God's grace, there may even be yearning for multiple tongues[3] as a means of declaring what is being deeply experienced. Such ways are examples that bespeak a growing concern to get beyond ordinary speech into another,

---

[2] *Megalunontōn.* It may be noted that the same Greek root is found in Acts 2:11 and 10:46—*megal*—which connotes mightiness, magnification. Thus in both Jerusalem and Caesarea they "magnify" the "magnificent" works of God.

[3] For example, the hymn of Charles Wesley beginning, "O for a thousand tongues to sing My great Redeemer's praise" exhibits this intense yearning.

or higher, mode of worshiping God.

Here, of course, is where music occupies an important role. By moving into lyrical modes of expression, by adding melody to words, there may well be more satisfying worship of heart and soul. Thus human utterance is caught up to higher levels by the singing forth of God's praises. Yet music, even as ordinary speech, is ever seeking among ardent worshipers of God to find ways to reach still more sublime heights.

Now we come to the recognition in the book of Acts of the close connection between praise and *tongues*. As we have noted, the Gentiles at Caesarea were heard to be "speaking in tongues and extolling God." In Jerusalem the Jews on the day of Pentecost were heard to be speaking in other tongues than their own, and the speech served one purpose: the praise of God. From the Pentecostal narrative it is apparent that tongues are not ordinary speech, but represent the worship of God in a speech that is other than one's own native language. Hence, speaking in tongues might be called *transcendent praise*: praise that goes beyond ordinary capacity and experience.

We may better understand this by focusing upon the situation of high spiritual intensity resulting from the outpouring of God's Holy Spirit. The sense of God's abundant presence evokes a breaking forth in praise expressive of the occasion. Ordinary language, even music, may be inadequate to declare the wonder of God's gift. This is not to deny or discount the various modes of human expression with all their possibilities to rise to greater heights. However, there may be a speech or language more suitable to the experience of the richness of God's spiritual gift. Humanly speaking, this is impossible, but—and herein is marvel—God through His Spirit may go beyond what has been uttered or sung before and bring forth a new language![4]

---

[4]Many of the things said in the paragraph above are reflected in the contemporary spiritual renewal. Two illustrations may suffice, the first from a young Roman Catholic layman, Larry Tomczak: "As thanksgiving and praise erupted from within, a profound sense of God's presence began to well up in me. I felt the rapturous and exultant joy of the Lord surging through me, and the more profuse my praise, the more intense became my desire to magnify the name of my Savior. I grew impatient with the inadequacy of the English language to fully express all that I was feeling, how much I loved God. Then, just at the right moment, new words began to flow from my heart. . . . I could not restrain my tongue, and my lips began to stammer, as a new language hopped, skipped

All of this is possible because of the new situation created by the gift of the Holy Spirit. God, while remaining transcendent, scales the heights and plumbs the depths of creaturely existence, thereby effectuating a fresh situation of divine-human immediacy. In this very moment human existence is so penetrated by the Holy Spirit that response may come forth in a new spiritual key. A transposition thereby occurs wherein human language—as representative of the divine-human immediacy—can become, in an extraordinary way, the vehicle of the Holy Spirit for the praise of Almighty God.[5]

This brings us again to the picture of what happened on the Day of Pentecost: "They were all filled with the Holy Spirit and began to speak in other tongues, as the Spirit gave them utterance" (Acts 2:4). The Spirit of God filling all present pervades the speech of each one and brings forth "other tongues." The disciples speak—not the Holy Spirit—but it is the Spirit who gives them the utterance.[6] And the speech is speech

---

and somersaulted from my mouth. The language was foreign to my ears, a heavenly language only God could understand. It was praise that had surged through my whole being to seek expression through the Holy Spirit in a new transcendence" *Clap Your Hands!* (Plainfield, NJ: Logos, 1973), pp. 112-113. More briefly, words from a Reformed pastor, Harald Bredesen: "I tried to say, 'Thank You, Jesus, thank You, Jesus,' but I couldn't express the inexpressible. Then, to my great relief, the Holy Spirit did it for me. It was just as if a bottle was uncorked, and out of me poured a torrent of words in a language I had never studied before. Now everything I had ever wanted to say to God, I could say." *Yes, Lord* (Plainfield, NJ: Logos, 1972), p. 59.

[5]C.S. Lewis in his address entitled "Transposition" (in *Transposition and Other Addresses* [London: Geoffrey Bles, 1949]) describes how a transposition occurs whenever a higher medium reproduces itself in a lower. If viewed merely from the perspective of the lower, the higher may be completely missed. Concerning glossolalia (speaking in tongues) "all non-Christian opinion would regard it as a kind of hysteria, an involuntary discharge of nervous excitement" (p. 9). However, ". . . the very same phenomenon which is sometimes not only natural but even pathological is at other times . . . the organ of the Holy Ghost" (p. 10). "Those who spoke with tongues, as St. Paul did, can well understand how that holy phenomenon differed from the hysterical phenomenon—although . . . they were in a sense exactly the same phenomenon . . ." (p. 17). Lewis later speaks about "the inevitableness of the error made about every transposition by one who approaches it from the lower medium only" (p. 19). "Transposition" accordingly is an excellent term to express what happens when the Holy Spirit, the higher medium, is expressed in the lower, the human spirit. For the vehicle of expression, human language, becomes transposed into a new dimension of utterance.

[6]The word translated "utterance" is *apophthengesthai*, literally "to speak out." *Apophthengesthai* is a term used of "the speech of the wise man [in Greek literature] . . . but also of the oracle-giver, diviner, prophet, exorcist, and other 'inspired' persons. . ." (Arndt and Gingrich, *A Greek-English Lexicon of the New Testament and Other Early Christian Literature*, article on *apophthengomai.)* This "inspired" speech is given by the Holy Spirit through the lips of men.

of transcendent praise, for what they are declaring are "the mighty works of God" (Acts 2:11).

Before proceeding further it is to be recognized that many persons hold the view that speaking in "other tongues" signifies a miraculous speaking in a language of mankind one has not learned. This is claimed, first, on the basis of the narrative in Acts 2 that, since in the assembled crowd "each one heard them speaking in his own language," the disciples must have been speaking the various languages of the listeners. However, what may have been happening was not the hearing *of* one's own language but hearing *in* one's own language. What the Apostle Paul speaks of in 1 Corinthians as the Holy Spirit's work of interpretation following upon a tongue (1 Cor. 12:10; 14:5 and 13) may have been occurring at Pentecost, so that those who heard "other tongues" had this immediately translated—by the Holy Spirit's activity—into their own native speech. Actually not everyone on the Day of Pentecost seems to have understood: "All were amazed and perplexed, saying to one another, 'What does this mean?' But others mocking said, 'They are filled with new wine' " (Acts 2:12-13). Those mocking seemed to hear and understand nothing; the speech of the disciples did not impress them as being their own speech—or any speech for that matter. Hence, it would scarcely seem that the disciples were speaking the various languages of the multitude. For those who had ears to hear, the Spirit gave them understanding; for others, the disciples' speech was but the babble of drunken persons.[7]

A second claim that "other tongues" refers to speaking in other languages of mankind is drawn from some contemporary experience. Many testimonies in the spiritual renewal of our time are heard of people speaking foreign languages they did not learn. The evidence for this invariably given is the witness of others that they actually heard their own languages being

---

[7]I do not mean to say in the paragraph above that only a miracle of understanding is involved; there is also clearly a miracle of speech. It is by no means enough to say that whereas the disciples may have spoken their own language (Aramaic), each in the crowd—miraculously—heard his own tongue being spoken. There is *both* a miracle of speech—other, different, spiritual tongues—*and* a miracle of understanding: each made possible by the Holy Spirit.

spoken by someone who had no knowledge of that language.[8] However, there are no assured proofs that the language spoken was actually a foreign language. Tongues spoken on various occasions have been recorded and checked thereafter as to language content, but the evidence for their being a language of man is lacking. This, of course, does not rule out the possibility— even likelihood—that through the Holy Spirit's interpretation a person might understand what is being said. It would seem more probable that speaking in "other tongues" refers—as was earlier mentioned—to the utterance of transcendent praise. "Other" would mean different—different, that is, in quality[9]— from what had been spoken before. Thus rather than the speaking of an additional human language, it would be transcendent speech, and in that sense an unknown tongue. It would be language addressed to God and known by Him alone.[10]

Let us reflect upon a number of significant matters about this utterance. First, the extraordinary and unique fact is that while people do the speaking, it is *the Holy Spirit who provides the language.* It is spiritual, not natural, utterance. The human apparatus—mouth, tongue, vocal cords—is in full operation, but the words are not from the speaker: they are from and by the Holy Spirit. One speaks *as* the Holy Spirit gives to speak out.

---

[8]See, for example, *Spoken by the Spirit: Documented Accounts of "Other Tongues" from Arabic to Zulu,* by Ralph W. Harris (Springfield, MO: Gospel Publishing House, 1973).
[9]Thayer in his *Greek-English Lexicon of the New Testament* has two headings under *heteros* ("other") referring to (1) Number (2) Quality. "Number" would point to other tongues as additional; thus in the case of Acts 2:4, the speaking of additional languages (such as Arabic, Greek and Chaldean); "quality" would signify difference in kind—"not of the same nature, form, class, kind" (Thayer).
[10]So does Paul write the Corinthians: "For one who speaks in a tongue speaks not to men but to God; for no one understands him, but he utters mysteries in the Spirit" (1 Cor. 14:2). Here clearly "a tongue" is not a human language—"no one understands him." Incidentally, the KJV reads, "For he that speaketh in an *unknown* tongue. . . ," while adding a word "unknown" not in the Greek original, conveys a proper understanding of what "a tongue" is. It is not a foreign language, but an "other" language, known to God alone, and only by interpretation to men (see 1 Cor. 14:5, 13, 27-28). Thus, there is no basic difference between tongues, or glossolalia, at Pentecost, in Caesarea, Ephesus and Corinth. So writes Philip Schaff: "The glossolalia [on the Day of Pentecost] was, as in all cases where it is mentioned, an act of worship and adoration. . . . The Pentecostal glossolalia was the same as that in the household of Cornelius in Caesarea after his conversion, which may be called a Gentile Pentecost, as that of the twelve disciples of John the Baptist at Ephesus, where it appears in connection with prophesying, and as that in the Christian congregation at Corinth" *(History of the Christian Church* [New York: Charles Scribner's Sons, 1910], Vol. I, pp. 230-231).

Thus there is no sense of compulsion or coercion. The Holy Spirit does not assume control, thereby forcing this speech to occur. There is no divine seizure. Rather, the person freely does the speaking, and the Holy Spirit generously provides the language. Human integrity is fully maintained—even as individuals are given to speak forth praise in a way transcending anything they have before experienced.

It may also be observed that the uniqueness of this speech is also related to the fact that the Holy Spirit is speaking through the human spirit. For the Spirit of God pervades the depths of the human spirit and speech flows therefrom. The level is deeper than—or higher than—the level of mind where speech is that of human conceptualization and articulation. The level is also more profound than that of human feelings where speech has a large emotional content. It is that level of human spirit where the Spirit of God, speaking in and through the spirit of man, communicates with the transcendent God.[11] To speak in other tongues is to go beyond one's native speech into the realm of spiritual utterance. Thereby the praise of God may sound forth in a new and glorious way.

The utterance, secondly, has *intelligible content*. It is address to God, and not babbling nonsense[12] or irrational expression. It

---

[11]"The language was being given me from the central place in me where God was, far beyond the realm of my emotions. Speaking on and on, I became more and more aware of God *in* me. . . God living in me was creating the language. I was speaking it—giving it voice, by my volition, and I was speaking it to God Who was above and beyond me. God the Holy Spirit was giving me the words to talk to God the Father, and it was all happening because of God the Son, Jesus Christ." So writes Dennis Bennett in *Nine O'clock in the Morning* (Plainfield, NJ: Logos, 1970), p. 23. Father Bennett, Episcopal priest, is often described as "spiritual father" of the neo-Pentecostal or charismatic renewal. His experience of "baptism in the Spirit" and speaking in tongues occurred in 1960 while he was rector of St. Mark's Church in Van Nuys, California.

[12]". . . this speech of tongues is not the babbling of babes, but it is a mode in which the inexpressible *verbal* form of the heavenly world (1 Cor. 12:3; 1 Cor. 13:1) breaks into this human world of ours." So Peter Brunner writes in his book, *Worship in the Name of Jesus* (St. Louis: Concordia, 1968), p. 270. Brunner describes tongues, however, not as speech but as a disintegration or rupture of speech in which the mode mentioned breaks in, all of which is due to the impact of the approaching kingdom of God. "The New Testament shows us that the verbal vessel of our language may disintegrate under the impact of the onrushing new eon. This takes place in the language of tongues, which is no longer speech, but which appears as babbling and outside the bonds of molded words." Then comes the statement: ". . . this speech of tongues, etc." Another beautiful passage follows: ". . . this rupture of intelligible speech in the speech of tongues shows us that the word will not remain unaffected by the approaching might of the kingdom of God.

is speech, language; hence, there is intelligibility, even if this utterance is other than one's own ordinary language.

Again, let us return to the Day of Pentecost. They speak on that day in "other tongues" or "languages."[13] Hence, there is intelligible content even though the disciples themselves do not provide it. This intelligibility is demonstrated in the fact that the assembled crowd understands the disciples to be declaring "the mighty works of God" (Acts 2:11). The same thing is implied later at Caesarea where the people are heard to be "speaking in tongues and extolling God" (10:46). There is intelligible content in both cases: the magnifying of God.

It is important to stress that the intelligible content of speaking in (other) tongues is that provided by the Holy Spirit. It is the Spirit of God flowing through the human vessel—most profoundly the human spirit—communicating with God. It is the worship of God *"in* spirit and truth" (John 4:23).

Thirdly, speaking in tongues is the language of *exalted utterance.* We have spoken of its intelligible content; now it is to be observed that the language is that of exaltation, of rapture, of transport.[14] As we have noted, some mockingly said, "They are full of new wine," which suggests (despite the lack of spiritual sensitivity of some in the audience) that the manner and speech of the disciples were not unlike inebriation. Here, though, was

It, too, will be drawn symbolically into the future eschatalogical transformation of all things" (page 270). Brunner here employs language about the inbreak of "the heavenly world," "the onrushing new eon," "the approaching might of the kingdom of God" which, while different from terminology we have used, expresses the wonder of the coming of the Holy Spirit. What is important is his strong emphasis on "tongues" as resulting from the impact of the inbreaking spiritual reality, and that tongues are not babbling nonsense but a form of expression beyond all human capacity.

[13]The Greek word is *glōssais.* It may mean either tongues or languages.

[14]I hesitate to use the word "ecstasy" because of the possible connotation of frenzy, uncontrolled behavior: speech that is irrational, emotional utterance without intellectual content. For example, in the statement of Mark 3:21: "He is beside himself" the Greek word is *exestē*, a form of the verb *existēmi*, the noun *ekstasis.* Thus, though "ecstasy" may be used of transport, joy, etc., it also tends to suggest unbalance, lack of control, even madness. *Ekstasis* can also mean "amazement," or "astonishment," in a situation of confusion and bafflement. For example, the multitude hearing each in his own language ". . . were amazed [*existanto*]. . . and wondered [or 'marveled'] saying, 'Are not all these who are speaking Galileans?' " (Acts 2:7). Accordingly, it was the crowd hearing the tongues who were "ecstatic," not the disciples speaking them! On this point also see Larry Christenson, *Speaking in Tongues* (Minneapolis: Dimension Books, 1968), P. 24. Christenson is a Lutheran pastor and leader in the contemporary renewal.

not wine of the grape, but wine of the Spirit, and an exuberance transcending anything earth could produce.[15] When the Holy Spirit is poured out and men experience this abundance of God's grace, it can but follow that there will be great joy and exaltation.

Here also is the place to comment that this language of exalted utterance may be that of song. Earlier, mention was made of how, through music, the ardent worshiper may seek to go beyond speech into lyrical expression, thereby conveying his worship and adoration of Almighty God. Now we take a step further by making reference to "singing in the Spirit."[16] Such singing may not be in conjunction with the outpouring of the Spirit; indeed, it often takes place later. However, it is an aspect of "tongues," a singing in tongues—but with the added factor of the melody also being provided by the Holy Spirit. This often happens in a group at worship, and may be a climactic moment in the total worship experience.[17]

Before proceeding let us stress again that the basic human

[15]Recall Paul's words: "Do not get drunk with wine, for that is debauchery; but be filled with the Spirit . . . singing and making melody to the Lord with all your heart. . ." (Eph. 5:18-19). The true wine of the Spirit makes not for dissipation but for the praise of God with all one's being.

[16]The words of Paul in Ephesians 5:18-19 were partially quoted in the preceding footnote. The fuller quotation, which seems particularly relevant here, is: "Be filled with the Spirit, addressing one another in psalms and hymns and spiritual songs, singing and making melody to the Lord with all your heart." The "spiritual songs" are ōdais pneumatikais, songs given by the Spirit, probably representing the exalted utterance of singing in the Spirit. (Incidentally, in a footnote to Colossians 3:16, where "spiritual songs" are also mentioned, the Jerusalem Bible says that these songs "could be charismatic improvisations suggested by the Spirit during liturgical assembly.") For a reference to "singing with the spirit"—which seems likewise to refer to spiritual singing—see 1 Corinthians 14:15. Note also that Paul differentiates such singing from "singing with the mind."

[17]"We were lifted out of ourselves in the worship of the Lord. There was a period of singing in tongues, and the variety in the sound was matched only by its harmony and the unanimity with which it began and ended, almost as if at the signal of a conductor; but there was no conductor—at least, not a human one." So writes Michael Green, Anglican rector, about his visit to a church "full of the Holy Spirit" (I Believe in the Holy Spirit [Grand Rapids: Eerdmans, 1975], pp. 158-59). In an earlier book I described the experience of "singing in the Spirit" thus: ". . . there may be long periods of joyful, lilting music, quite unplanned, moving back and forth through psalms, hymns, choruses, and the like—as the Spirit guides the meeting. But the climax is the moment when not only is the melody given by the Spirit but also the language, as words and music sung by the assembled worshipers blend into an unimaginable, humanly impossible, chorus of praise. Here is 'singing in the Spirit' at its zenith—the sublime utterance of the Holy Spirit through the human spirit to the glory of Almighty God" (The Era of the Spirit, p. 33).

response to the gift of the Holy Spirit is the praise of God. The focus is not on tongues but on praise. Where, however, praise under the impact of the outpouring of God's Spirit seeks to express itself, it may become transcendent. The breakthrough into the heights of praise is made possible by the Holy Spirit taking human speech and carrying it beyond itself into spiritual utterance. *There may be praise without tongues, but where tongues are spoken there is always praise.* The essential matter is, and continues to be, praise.

This leads, fourthly, to the recognition of tongues as a *peculiar sign* of the gift of the Holy Spirit. Those who have experienced the outpouring of God's Spirit and spoken in tongues bear in their own speech evidence of a miracle. They never had spoken so before—though there may have been many other spiritual experiences. This was a sign of something new and different in their lives. Furthermore, they know they did not manufacture this speech,[18] that in all of its strangeness (never becoming really comprehensible) such speaking remains testimony to a special visitation of God. The particular joy and elation of the original moment of the divine gift may come and go, even fade somewhat, but not the memory of this strange utterance. And this is all the more enhanced by the fact that, insofar as such speaking continues in the personal life and community life,[19] there is a visible, audible reminder of the extraordinary fact of the outpouring of God's Holy Spirit.

In this matter of tongues as a peculiar sign, it is apparent in the biblical witness that there is no record of speaking in tongues before the first outpouring of the Holy Spirit. Many other phenomena such as prophecy, healings, exorcism, etc. had

---

[18]Samarin, in *Tongues of Men and Angels* (New York: Macmillan, 1972), says that "anybody can produce glossolalia if he is uninhibited and if he discovers what the 'trick' is . . ." (pp. 227-8), namely, the uninhibited expression of nonsense syllables. To reply: anyone who has truly spoken in tongues knows that there is no possible comparison of it with human gibberish. As Simon Tugwell, Dominican priest, succinctly says: "You cannot engineer tongues. . ." *(Did You Receive the Holy Spirit?* [London: Darton, Longman, & Todd, 1972], p. 63).

[19]Most persons continue speaking in tongues in their prayer life. No reference to a continuation of tongues beyond the initial gift of the Spirit is found in Acts. However, Mark 16:17, many verses in 1 Corinthians 12-14, Ephesians 5:19, Colossians 3:16, and possibly Ephesians 6:18 and Jude 20 suggest continuation. (On Ephesians 6:18 and Jude 20 see later discussion.)

occurred previously—but not tongues. Thus it is the particular sign of the gift of the Holy Spirit. Also, in at least one case where speaking in tongues occurs in Acts, it is designated as peculiar, undeniable evidence that the Holy Spirit has been given. I make reference to the Caesarean account where the text reads: "The gift of the Holy Spirit had been poured out even on the Gentiles. For they [those accompanying Peter] heard them speaking in tongues and extolling God" (Acts 10:45-46). Speaking in tongues was the sure evidence—the unmistakable sign—that the Holy Spirit had also been given to the Gentiles.

Indeed, in the book of Acts wherever speaking in tongues is mentioned, it is immediately after the gift of the Spirit. The disciples at Jerusalem: "were all filled with the Holy Spirit and began to speak in other tongues" (Acts 2:4). The Gentiles at Caesarea: the Holy Spirit falls on them and at once they are "speaking in tongues and extolling God" (Acts 10:46). Likewise the Ephesians: "The Holy Spirit came on them; and they spoke with tongues and prophesied" (Acts 19:6). It would seem unquestionable that Acts points to speaking in tongues as an immediate and unmistakable sign of the gift of the Holy Spirit.[20]

A sign, however, is not identical with the reality to which it points. The gift of the Holy Spirit is the primary reality, and speaking in tongues is the sign that the gift has been received. It demonstrates further that the human response of transcendent praise has occurred. So tongues are not constitutive of the gift of the Spirit (as if it were not possible to have one without the other), but are declarative, namely, that the gift has been received. Tongues are—and remain—a peculiar sign.[21]

---

[20]This is true even though Acts does not mention tongues in the two other primary cases of the gift of the Spirit (the Samaritans, Acts 8, and Saul of Tarsus, Acts 9). But where they are specifically mentioned, in each instance, it is immediately after the gift, and thus tongues have a peculiar significance. Alan Richardson in his *An Introduction to the Theology of the New Testament* (New York: Harper & Brothers, 1958) says that "St. Luke regards 'speaking in tongues' (glossolalia) as an unmistakable sign of the gift of the Spirit" (p. 119).

[21]A helpful discussion of this matter is to be found in the chapter, "Speaking in Tongues as 'Sign,'" by Larry Christenson in his book, *Speaking in Tongues*, pp. 30-70. E.g., "To consummate one's experience of the baptism with the Holy Spirit by speaking in tongues gives it an objectivity . . . regardless of feelings, that sign of the 'new tongue' is there to remind one in a special way that the Holy Spirit has taken up His dwelling in one's body," pp. 55-56. Don Basham in his book, *Face Up With a Miracle* (Northridge, CA:

Fifthly, tongues are to be understood as a *universal possibility*. It is the same Holy Spirit, the same reality of the gift of the Spirit, the same called-for response of praise, and the same opportunity to voice this praise in tongues. That it is a possibility for all is surely a matter of God's grace wherein He grants the privilege for persons to enter into His highest praise.

Let us look again at the biblical record. In the book of Acts on every occasion when people speak in tongues *all* are involved. On the Day of Pentecost the waiting disciples were "all filled with the Holy Spirit and began to speak in other tongues" (2:4); at Caesarea "the Holy Spirit fell on all who heard the word" (10:44) and others heard "them [all] speaking in tongues. . ." (10:46); and at Ephesus "the Holy Spirit came on them; and they [all] spoke with tongues" (19:6). Where speaking in tongues is mentioned, all who have received the gift of the Holy Spirit participate. It is not the activity of a few, but that of the whole body of believers.[22] No one is left out.

This universal possibility is also apparent in the words of Mark 16:17: "And these signs will accompany those who believe . . . they [all] will speak in new tongues." The same is suggested in the words of Paul to the Corinthians: "I want you all to speak in tongues" (1 Cor. 14:5). Likewise since "praying with the spirit" refers to praying in tongues (1 Cor. 14:14-15),[23] the admonition to believers generally to "pray in the Holy Spirit"

Voice Christian Publications, 1967), describing his baptism in the Spirit and tongues, says: ". . . this *was* God moving in my life more powerfully than ever before. . . . I had made entry into a new and deeper spiritual dimension, clearly marked by the experience of praying in a language utterly unknown to me" (p. 60). "Clearly marked" points up the significance of tongues as an objective and unforgettable sign.

[22]Sometimes the statement is made that the Apostle Paul, in his first letter to the Corinthians, presents a different picture. In Chapter 12 Paul describes tongues as one of several apportionments of the Holy Spirit—"to another [person] various kinds of tongues" (v. 10), and later asks, "Do all speak with tongues?" (v. 30). The implied answer is "No, not all do." Does this contradict the accounts in Acts? Not at all, when one understands that Paul is dealing in Corinthians with ministry in the church, and how the Holy Spirit uses a diversity of gifts for building up the body. That all at Corinth are capable of speaking in tongues is evident from the words of Paul thereafter: "I want you all to speak in tongues" (1 Cor. 14:5). But when it is a matter of the edification of the body, if all so speak it only causes confusion and disorder. The Holy Spirit therefore manifests himself variously (see 1 Cor. 12:7): prophecy, tongues, healings, etc. Incidentally, prophecy is also listed as one of the several gifts apportioned; yet Paul makes clear that prophecy is not limited to a few: "You can all prophesy, one by one. . ." (1 Cor. 14:31).

[23]"For if I pray in a tongue, my spirit prays but my mind is unfruitful. What am I to do? I will pray with the spirit and I will pray with the mind also. . . ." Praying with (or "in"—the Greek is simply *tō pneumati)* the spirit is unmistakably praying in a tongue.

(Jude 20), or to "pray at all times in the Spirit" (Eph. 6:18) may contain the note of glossolalic utterance—and thus again represent a universal possibility.

The universality of speaking in tongues has been confirmed again and again in the contemporary spiritual renewal. So widespread is the experience that—though the nomenclature is misleading—the renewal is frequently called "the tongues movement."[24] Untold numbers of people have found there is no limitation to a few, but that all may praise God in tongues. Wherever the Spirit is moving in fullness, tongues—the language of the Spirit—are to be found.

Now, returning to the record in Acts, it is to be recognized that though all speak in tongues wherever tongues are mentioned—hence the universal character—not every account that records the giving of the Spirit mentions speaking in tongues. In the five stated instances of receiving the gift of the Spirit, three of them (as previously noted) specify speaking in tongues, the other two do not. However, in the case of the Samaritans, tongues may be implied. For just after the statement that "they received the Holy Spirit" are the words: "Now when Simon [the magician] saw that the Spirit was given through the laying on of the apostles' hands, he offered them [Peter and John] money. . ." (Acts 8:18). The text may be suggesting that what Simon saw was the Samaritans speaking in tongues, something extraordinary beyond his previous manifold occult practices, and that he was willing to pay for the power to lay hands on others for similar miraculous results. I think this interpretation is quite likely, and that the Samaritans did speak in tongues.[25]

---

[24]Usually this expression is used in a critical fashion by those who would like to make of the renewal a kind of sensationalism or exhibitionism, as if the basic emphases were on speaking in tongues and getting others to do the same. The emphasis, of course, is not on tongues but on the outpouring of the Holy Spirit and the response of praise, which in becoming transcendent does move into the language of exalted utterance. The movement accordingly is "a Holy Spirit movement," not a "tongues movement." Incidentally, however, the labeling of the movement as "tongues" does express (what most critics do not like to admit) that tongues are universally present!

[25]A.T. Robertson states that the word structure in Acts 8 "shows plainly that those who received the gift of the Holy Spirit spoke in tongues" (Word Pictures in the New Testament [New York: Harper and Brothers, 1932], III, p. 107). F.F. Bruce affirms that "the context leaves us in no doubt that the reception of the Spirit was attended by external manifestations such as had marked His descent on the earliest disciples at Pentecost" (Commentary on the Book of the Acts, "The New International Commentary on the New Testament" [Grand Rapids: Eerdmans, 1954], p. 181.). Johannes Munck

In the case of Saul of Tarsus and his being filled with the Spirit, nothing is said about his speaking in tongues (see Acts 9:17f.); however, by Paul's own testimony to the Corinthians—"I thank God I speak in tongues more than you all" (1 Cor. 14:18)— we know he did. It is quite possible, though Luke does not so specify,[26] that Paul first spoke in tongues when he was filled with the Holy Spirit. However, it may also be that he began to speak at a later time.

To summarize: in the majority of cases—three out of five— people who had received the gift of the Holy Spirit definitely did speak in tongues; there is strong likelihood of such in four out of five; and a possibility that in all five instances people did speak so. Based on the evidence in Acts we can draw no absolute conclusion that speaking in tongues invariably followed the reception of the Spirit; however, the texts do incline in that direction. This is further suggested by the fact that, as already noted, wherever tongues are explicitly mentioned, all speak; it is not the expression of one or two but of everyone who has received the Holy Spirit. The universality of speaking in tongues would strongly suggest their occurrence, whether or not directly mentioned, in all situations wherein the Spirit was given.

---

writes that "Simon, who by virtue of his earlier life closely observed all wondrous faculties and powers, was struck by the apostles' ability to make the baptized prophesy and to speak in tongues by the laying on of hands" *(The Anchor Bible: The Acts of the Apostles* [Garden City, NY: Doubleday and Co., 1967], p. 75). Foakes-Jackson says that in this passage "the gift [of the Spirit] is manifested openly, possibly (though this is not stated) by *glossolalia" (The Moffatt Commentary: The Acts of the Apostles* [New York: Harper and Brothers, 1931], p. 73).

[26]Since Luke does not actually say that when Ananias laid hands on him Saul was filled with the Holy Spirit—yet the whole context implies that Saul was so filled—it is quite possible that tongues are also implied. We have just observed the clear-cut statement in Acts 8 that the Samaritans did receive the Holy Spirit, and the strong implication that they spoke in tongues. Acts 9 is less direct on the reception of the Spirit by Saul, while strongly implying it, and has nothing as such about tongues—but Luke may be asking the reader to supply both. If both the reception of the Spirit and tongues were common knowledge and experience (as I believe they were) to Luke's readers, he scarcely needs to repeat each time. Incidentally, this same point may be made about belief in Christ and baptism in water. Often Luke specifically mentions water baptism in connection with faith in Jesus Christ (see Acts 2:38, 41; 8:12-13, 35-38; 9:18; 10:48; 16:14-15, 31-33; 18:8; and 19:5); on other occasions he describes people coming to faith without reference to water baptism (see Acts 9:42; 11:21; 13:12, 48; 14:1; 17:12, 34). However, it is very likely that Luke would have the reader assume the occurrence of water baptism when not mentioned. Such baptism was doubtless common experience and practice in the early church.

Again, in the present-day spiritual renewal, the intimate connection between receiving the gift of the Holy Spirit and speaking in tongues is recognized everywhere. It happens again and again that when people are filled with the Holy Spirit they immediately begin to speak in tongues.[27] Indeed, since praise is the initial response to the gift of the Spirit, and tongues represent transcendent praise, one follows readily upon the other. In some instances, speaking in tongues may occur later;[28] but that it *does* occur is the common testimony of the renewal through the world. Tongues are the Spirit-given opportunity for fullness of praise.

Some of the things said in this chapter about transcendent praise through tongues may seem a bit strange since there has been a tendency in the Church to neglect this opportunity and vehicle of praise. However, there have always been those who, flowing in the Spirit, have experienced and maintained this high worship of God. It is quite possible also that out of this praise in tongues has come some of the great music in the Church.[29]

A similar, fascinating, activity in the history of the Church has been that of *jubilation.* To jubilate is to go beyond ordinary

[27]See, for example, John L. Sherrill, *They Speak With Other Tongues: The Story of a Reporter on the Trail of a Miracle* (New York: McGraw-Hill, 1964). The climax of Sherrill's own experience was that of being prayed for to receive "the baptism in the Spirit" (p. 139). Shortly thereafter: "With a sudden burst of will I thrust my hands into the air, turned my face full upward, and at the top of my voice I shouted: 'Praise the Lord!' It was the floodgate opened. From deep inside me, deeper than I knew voice could go, came a torrent of joyful sound. . . . After that one shattering effort of will, my will was released, freed to soar into union with Him. No further conscious effort was required of me at all, not even choosing the syllables with which to express my joy. The syllables were all there, ready-formed for my use, more abundant than my earth-bound lips and tongue could give shape to. . . . And so I prayed on, laughing and free, while the setting sun shone through the window, and the stars came out" (p. 141).
[28]As possibly in the case of Paul. In our present day there may be a delay, often because of fear or uncertainty. Among many people there is prejudice against tongues, and barriers of inner resistance are built up. However in view of the strong desire to respond in praise to God, and the Holy Spirit surging within, the inevitable movement is toward such transcendent speaking.
[29]"The glossolalia of the early Eastern Church, as the original musical event, represents the germ cell or the original form of sung liturgical prayer. . . . In the sublime levitation and interweaving of the old Church tones, and even in Gregorian chant to some extent, we are greeted by an element that has its profound roots in glossolalia." Words of Werner Meyrer in *Der erste Korintherbrief: Prophezei,* 1945, Vol. II, 122 et seq. (tr. by Arnold Bittlinger). See *Sounds of Wonder* (New York: Paulist Press, 1977) by Eddie Ensley, p. 117.

speech into a praise of God that even the most expressive words cannot convey. "Jubilation is an unspeakable joy, which one cannot keep silent; yet neither can it be expressed (in words) . . . it is beyond comprehension."[30] Jubilation represents various wordless outcries of joy and exaltation; hence, though it may not be identified as such with "other tongues" (the emphasis being on wordless praise rather than praise in a new language), the connection is quite close. Each is motivated by the same intense yearning: to express the inexpressible—thus to go beyond ordinary speech into the realm of transcendent praise.[31]

We close this chapter on the theme of the praise of God as the ultimate human response to the gift of the Holy Spirit. Praise be unto God for all His mighty and wonderful works!

---

[30]Words of St. Thomas Aquinas in his Commentary on Psalms, as quoted in *Sounds of Wonder*, p. 53. Ensley, in this important book, gives many instances of jubilation in the history of the Church, and states that "Indications are that jubilation is a continuation of the glossolalia of the New Testament" and that "plainsong and the musical parts of the liturgy emerged from the early practice of glossolalia" (pp. 115 and 117).

[31]Tongues are described as "a special language of jubilation" by Gerhard Delling in his book, *Worship in the New Testament* (Philadelphia: Westminster Press, 1962). "The working of the Spirit brings about . . . an enthusiasm which expresses itself in a special language of jubilation, in a *praising of God which rises above the normal manner of speaking*"(italics: Delling), p. 38. Incidentally, Delling's evaluation of glossolalia is also worth quoting: "It is an intimation (certainly an imperfect and, in Paul's opinion at least, an inadequate one) of the praise and worship of God in the heavenly service; and thus at the same time an *anticipation of the future glory*. Men knew that they stood in the midst of the irruption of the coming age; they knew that in the gift of the Spirit they had received an earnest /ἀρραβὼν/ of the consummation; furthermore the Spirit when bestowed did not remain simply a gift in the hidden chambers of the heart; it pressed for expression in special intimations in Worship" (p. 35).

CHAPTER FOUR

PURPOSE

The central purpose for the gift of the Holy Spirit is *power*. The biblical term is *dunamis*—power, strength, might, force—and as the gift of the Holy Spirit, it represents an endowment of spiritual power.

We have earlier spoken of how the gift of the Holy Spirit signifies the coming of God's Spirit in fullness so that a new divine-human immediacy is thereby established. God is now present in a total kind of way, and man is bathed in the reality of the divine presence. And, as noted, the human response is that of praise to God. Now we proceed to observe that this gift of the Spirit is the gift of spiritual—transcendent, supernatural—power.

Thus we come to the words of the risen Jesus: "You shall receive power when the Holy Spirit has come upon you . . ." (Acts 1:8). That this power is transcendent is emphasized in the similar words of Jesus: "But stay in the city, until you are clothed with power from on high" (Luke 24:49). Hence spiritual—"from on high"—power is the intention of the gift of the Holy Spirit.

The close connection between the gift of the Holy Spirit and power may also be seen in the example of Jesus' own life and ministry. It is recorded in all the Gospels that at the baptism of Jesus the Holy Spirit "descended upon"[1] Him; thereby He received the gift of the Holy Spirit. Afterward, "Jesus, full of the Holy Spirit, returned from the Jordan . . ." (Luke 4:1), and following his wilderness temptation, He "returned in the power of the Spirit into Galilee" (Luke 4:14). Thus, clearly, the endowment of the Holy Spirit was one of power. In a summary of Jesus' ministry by Peter we read "how God anointed Jesus of Nazareth with the Holy Spirit and with power . . ." (Acts 10:38).

---

[1]See Matthew 3:16; Mark 1:10; Luke 3:22; John 1:32. The Greek verb is *katabainō*—"come down." Thus it parallels expressions before noted for the gift of the Spirit such as "coming upon," "falling on," etc.

The close connection between the endowment of the Holy Spirit and power in Jesus' ministry is unmistakable.[2]

It follows that it is the intention of Jesus that the same Spirit of power that rested upon Him should rest upon His disciples— hence, the words already quoted concerning their receiving power when the Holy Spirit would come upon them. Thereby the disciples would likewise be able to move in the power of the Spirit for the ministry that lay ahead.[3]

More, however, needs to be said. It was not that they were simply to receive the Holy Spirit *as* He did, but the Spirit who was to come upon them was to be *through* Him. Ultimately the Spirit was from the Father, but it would be Jesus, the Son, who would mediate the Spirit's coming.[4] Thus by the Spirit's coming the exalted Jesus would actually continue His ministry through them.[5] They would carry on their work not only in the power of the Spirit as He did, but also with the Spirit of Jesus impelling them.[6]

It is apparent that the gift of the Holy Spirit is for that power which enables the ministry of Jesus to be carried forward. It is not power in a general sense—that is, an increment of supernatural strength that could have many uses—but power for ministry that flows from the Father through the Son. As such, what Jesus did—and even more[7]—will be done through His

---

[2]In John 6:27 Jesus says that "on him [Jesus himself] has God the Father set his seal"— literally, "this one God the Father sealed" (*touton ho patēr esphragisen ho theos*). The idea of sealing here would seem clearly to refer to this anointing with power at the Jordan— "to dedicate, to consecrate . . . to endow with heavenly power" (*Theological Dictionary of the New Testament*, Vol. VII, [Grand Rapids: Eerdmans, 1971], p. 949, fn. 83).

[3]Thus when Pentecost occurred, in the words of Lindsay Dewar, "the members of the infant Church were by this momentous event lifted up to a new and supernatural level, the level of the Spirit-filled humanity of the Incarnate Lord" (*The Holy Spirit and Modern Thought* [New York: Harper and Brothers, 1959], p. 43.)

[4]Recall our earlier discussion of this in Chapter 1.

[5]It is significant to note that in the book of Acts, Luke says, "In the first book [the Gospel of Luke] . . . I have dealt with all that Jesus *began* to do and teach. . . ." Thus the book of Acts will deal with what Jesus *continued* to do and teach, but now as the exalted Lord through the power of the Holy Spirit.

[6]Accordingly, even as Jesus was anointed (Acts 10:38) with power and sealed (John 6:27), likewise are His disciples after Him. So does Paul write the Corinthians: "It is God who establishes us with you in Christ, and has commissioned [*chrisas*—"having anointed"] us; he has put his seal upon us . . ." (2 Cor. 1:21-22). To seal, in this context means to " 'endue with power from heaven' " (*A Greek-English Lexicon of the New Testament*, article on "seal," σφραγίζω , 2b).

[7]The extraordinary words of Jesus affirm this: "Truly, truly, I say to you, he who believes in me will also do the works that I do; and greater works than these will he do, because I

disciples upon the earth. What a prospect this opens up!

Hence, though the *response* of man to the gift of the Holy Spirit is the praise of God, and therefore directed upward, the *purpose* of the gift of the Spirit is the service of man, and therefore directed outward. It is the power of God through Jesus Christ enabling His ministry to be carried forward and fulfilled.[8]

This brings us next to the recognition that the power given by the Holy Spirit is first of all power for *being witnesses* of Christ. We have earlier recalled the words of Jesus: "You shall receive power when the Holy Spirit has come upon you. . . ." Hence there is close connection between the Holy Spirit and power. Jesus immediately continues with the words: "and you shall be my witnesses in Jerusalem and in all Judea and Samaria and to the end of the earth" (Acts 1:8). Thus a close connection is affirmed between power and being witnesses.

In the book of Acts with the outpouring of the Holy Spirit at Pentecost, as we have noted, there is the response of praise and Peter's explanation of what has just occurred (2:1-21). This explanation climaxes with the words, "And it shall be that whoever calls on the name of the Lord shall be saved" (v. 21). Thereupon Peter begins to proclaim the gospel, and his whole message is one of testimony to the life, death and resurrection of Jesus. It is throughout a matter of bearing witness, of testimony, with the climax being the resurrection. The words are unmistakable: "This Jesus God raised up, and of that we all are witnesses" (Acts 2:32). The proclamation is witnessing proclamation; it is done in the power of the Holy Spirit—and the results: "there were added [to their number] that day about three thousand souls" (Acts 2:41).

---

go to the Father" (John 14:12). In this astounding declaration Jesus is pointing to the fact that His going to the Father will make possible "greater works" by His disciples. The reason would seem to be that they will receive the *total* impact of the Spirit coming from Father and Son. They will do the works of Jesus—and more.

[8]See Michael Harper, *Power for the Body of Christ* (London: Fountain Trust, 1964) wherein Father Harper stresses that the same power of the Spirit is available in our time: "Our knowledge of Him [the Holy Spirit] may be correct. But what of our experience of His power? The power is still available for the Body of Christ and for each of its members. The Baptizer [Jesus] stands ready on the banks of the Holy Spirit to do again for the Church what He did on the day of Pentecost" (p. 56). Michael Harper, Anglican priest, is an international leader in the contemporary renewal.

The gift of the Holy Spirit, therefore, is power for witness that leads to salvation. It is effectual witness—witness that brings about the knowledge of what God has done in Christ (Acts 2:22-36), the conviction of sin (those who heard Peter's message were "cut to the heart" [Acts 2:37]), repentance and forgiveness ("Repent and be baptized every one of you in the name of Christ for the forgiveness of your sins" [Acts 2:38]), and thereby the receiving of salvation. It is life-giving, life-renewing witness brought about by the power that comes through the gift of the Holy Spirit.

What is being said here is extraordinary indeed. God enables human beings by the power of the Holy Spirit to become channels for *the radical transformation* of human existence! There is no greater miracle on earth than the miracle of regeneration—the "second birth"—brought about through profound conviction of sin, sincere repentance, and God's gracious forgiveness. Herein a person becomes wholly new in Jesus Christ—"the old has passed away, behold, the new has come" (2 Cor. 5:17). This is all of God: for He alone can create and re-create. But the marvel that stands behind this re-creation is that, through the power of His Spirit, God makes the witness of human beings the means through which this transformation takes place.

There is always the danger that proclamation, even well intended, may go forth not in the power of the Holy Spirit. Peter, and the others of his company, knew the message before Pentecost, but they did not yet have the power that could make it bring about salvation. They could have spoken, and perhaps even attracted some to join their fellowship, but there would have been no re-creation of life. Some might have had feelings of remorse about the past, yet not really a conviction that cuts "to the heart"; some might have turned momentarily away from the old life, but not have fully repented (i.e., turned around totally); some might even have been baptized "for forgiveness" but without that genuine faith through which the cleansing of the old and the coming of the new occurs. It is possible for the proclaimer to be "fervent in spirit"[9] but not necessarily in the Holy

---

[9]In this connection the name of Apollos, teacher in Ephesus, comes to mind. Luke describes him as "an eloquent man, well versed [literally: "mighty"—*dunatos*] in the scriptures . . . instructed in the way of the Lord; and being fervent in spirit, he spoke

Spirit—and despite all efforts no power of God unto genuine salvation.

Let us move on to note the record in Acts likewise makes clear that Saul of Tarsus was given the Holy Spirit for the purpose of witness. We have already observed how Ananias lays hands on Saul and prays for him that he might be "filled with the Holy Spirit" (9:17). What we did not note is that the purpose for Ananias coming to Saul had already been spoken by the Lord in a vision: "The Lord said to him [Ananias], 'Go, for he is a chosen instrument of mine to carry my name before the Gentiles and kings and the sons of Israel . . .'" (9:15).[10] Thus the gift of the Holy Spirit will be for the purpose of carrying forward this kind of far-reaching witness.

It is not so clear in the other incidents which specifically relate the giving of the Holy Spirit that the primary purpose is power for witness. Nothing is said directly in the instances of the Samaritans, Caesareans and Ephesians; however, this purpose is doubtless implied.[11]

In the case of the Samaritans, while it is Philip the evangelist who proclaims the gospel so that they come to faith and baptism,

---

and taught accurately [or "carefully"—akribōs] the things concerning Jesus, though he knew only the baptism of John" (Acts 18:24-25). Hence the fervor of Apollos was not the fervor brought about by the Holy Spirit: it could lead none to salvation, no matter how eloquent, how well versed in Scripture he was. So it is that Priscilla and Aquila "took him and expounded to him the way of God more accurately" (v. 26). Nothing is said by Luke directly about their leading Apollos into baptism in the name of Jesus and receiving the Holy Spirit; however, looking ahead to Acts 19 where Paul does exactly these things for the Ephesian disciples (probably earlier instructed by Apollos), who likewise knew only the baptism of John, it is quite conceivable that Priscilla and Aquila's expounding the way "more accurately" included a further experience of the Lord. In any event, it is interesting to note that after Priscilla and Aquila have ministered to Apollos, he goes on from Ephesus to Achaia where "he greatly helped those who through grace had believed, for he powerfully confuted the Jews in public, showing by the scriptures that the Christ was Jesus" (Acts 18:27-28). Greatly helping true Christian believers, powerfully confuting Jews—surely a different Apollos is at work now!

[10]In Acts 26:16, where Paul is recounting this event, the words to Saul from the risen Lord are similar: "I have appeared to you for this purpose, to appoint you to serve and bear witness to the things in which you have seen me and to those in which I will appear to you. . . ." The note of bearing witness is quite pronounced here.

[11]According to R.R. Williams, "throughout Acts, the Holy Spirit is thought of as the means whereby Christians receive power to witness [to] Christ and His resurrection" (The Acts of the Apostles, Torch Bible Commentaries, p. 36). Quotation found in The Holy Spirit in the Acts of the Apostles by J.H.E. Hull (Cleveland and New York: World Publishing Co., 1968), p. 46.

it is Peter and John who come down from Jerusalem to lay hands on them for the Holy Spirit. The reason for this would seem to be that the Samaritans might receive the same empowering for witness that Peter and John had received at Pentecost and thus become also a vital part of the witnessing community. It is not so much that the Samaritans become thereby incorporated into the Jerusalem church[12] as it is that they are invested with power necessary for the ongoing mission of the gospel. Since Jesus had said to His disciples, "You shall be my witnesses in Jerusalem and in all Judea and Samaria and to the end of the earth" (Acts 1:8), reference to Samaria could signify not only a people *to* whom witness is to be made but also *by* whom it is to be continued.

This would seem to follow logically from the principle, which now needs to be enunciated vigorously, that the Holy Spirit is a "missionary spirit";[13] that wherever He comes upon a people they are driven beyond themselves into a witness for Christ; and that they become participants thereby in the continuing outreach of the gospel to the ends of the earth. Even as the Holy Spirit is a "proceeding" Spirit,[14] so those who are anointed by Him cannot possibly remain confined in their faith but must "proceed" forth to tell the Good News everywhere.

Thus in the book of Acts there is an ever-widening missionary circle: Jerusalem, Judea, Samaria, Caesarea, Ephesus—all representing further outreach of the gospel—and additional areas that through the gift of the Holy Spirit become participant in the witness to Christ. Hence, though nothing is said directly in the biblical narratives about the Samaritans, Caesareans and Ephesians bearing witness to the gospel, the fact that they also receive the Holy Spirit—the "missionary Spirit"—would

[12]It is sometimes suggested that the Samaritans needed the ministry of the Jerusalem church (represented by Peter and John), so that long-standing separation and antagonism between Jew and Samaritan might be overcome. While this may have been a valuable byproduct of Peter and John's ministry, it would hardly seem to be the primary purpose.

[13]I know of no more forceful presentation of this theme than that found in Roland Allen's *The Ministry of the Spirit* (Grand Rapids: Eerdmans, 1960). See especially Chapter I, Section II, "The Spirit Revealed as the Inspirer of Missionary Work." Also see Michael Green, *I Believe in the Holy Spirit*, Chapter 5, "The Spirit in Mission."

[14]Recall the earlier discussion of how the Holy Spirit is said to "proceed" from the Father. This eternal procession becomes temporal in the gift of the Holy Spirit, and He continues to proceed from the lives of all those to whom He is given.

suggest that they too become proclaimers of the Good News.

In moving to the contemporary scene one finds a renewed emphasis on the gift of the Spirit and power for witness[15]—and the Spirit as a "missionary Spirit." Persons who have received this gift thereby become Christ's witnesses in a fresh way, often their very being and manner so filled with God's presence and power that others are profoundly affected thereby. The witness is primarily that of *being* rather than word: by the gift of the Spirit they become transparent for the Divine, channels of grace and power. Also words and actions are laden with new potency so that there is both wisdom and incisiveness in testifying to the gospel. In some cases people may have borne witness to Christ for years with varying degrees of success, but now there is a further breakthrough that brings about deep and abiding results.[16] The "missionary Spirit" is present—as many demonstrate in their daily work or in their carrying the Good News both far and wide.

The gift of the Spirit accordingly makes for an "anointed" witness. Even as Jesus was "anointed with the Holy Spirit and

---

[15]See, for example, the chapter entitled "Power to Witness" in *As the Spirit Leads Us* (New York: Paulist Press, 1971) by Kevin and Dorothy Ranaghan. In this chapter two spiritually renewed Roman Catholics, Leon and Virginia Kortenkamp, describe how "it seems to be universally true that those who have come into this experience [i.e. baptism in the Holy Spirit] are taught not so much by one another but by the direct power of God, that every tongue (including theirs) is meant to proclaim that Jesus is Lord" (p. 103). Thus there is power for witness they never knew before.

[16]Dwight L. Moody, nineteenth-century evangelist, after many years of preaching, related how two women would say to him regularly, "*You* need the power of the Holy Spirit." Moody reflected thereafter: "I need the power! Why I thought I had power"—because—"I had the largest congregation in Chicago and there were many conversions. I was in a sense satisfied." Soon though, the two godly women were praying with Moody, and "they poured out their hearts in prayer that I might receive the filling of the Holy Spirit. There came a great hunger into my soul. . . . I began to cry out as I never did before. I really felt that I did not want to live if I could not have this power for service." Some time later Moody related this: "One day, in the city of New York—oh, what a day!— I cannot describe it, I seldom refer to it; it is almost too sacred an experience to name. Paul had an experience of which he never spoke for fourteen years. I can only say that God revealed himself to me, and I had such an experience of His love that I had to ask Him to stay His hand. I went to preaching again. The sermons were not different; I did not present any new truths, and yet hundreds were converted. I would not now be placed back before that blessed experience if you should give me all the world. . . ." (W.R. Moody, *The Life of D.L. Moody* [New York: Fleming H. Revell, 1900], pp. 146-47, 149.) Moody had witnessed to the gospel for many years and with some obvious effectiveness, but after his being filled with the Spirit there was an anointing never before experienced in his life. Moody, while of course not a participant in the current spiritual renewal, is surely a precursor of those who likewise in our time are being filled with the Spirit and thereby finding a fresh power for witness.

power," so are all who receive the gift. There is a certain indefinable, but quite apparent, difference between one who witnesses without such an anointing and one who does. In the former case there may be fervency in spirit, but not in the Holy Spirit; there may be earnestness to bring people to salvation but without convicting power of the Spirit; there may even be the response of many to the message proclaimed but without undergoing a genuine transformation of life. Through the gift of the Spirit persons are anointed for bearing witness to Jesus Christ.[17]

This brings us to the next consideration that the gift of the Holy Spirit makes for the *universalizing of prophetic utterance.* When the Holy Spirit is poured out, and people receive this fullness, they are enabled thereby to prophesy. No longer is this a possibility for the few but becomes the possibility of all.

In an early period of Israel's history, Moses had expressed the wish that the people of God might all be able to prophesy— "Would that all the Lord's people were prophets" (Num. 11:29). This wish becomes a matter of future declaration in the words of Joel: "And it shall come to pass afterward, that I will pour out my spirit on all flesh; your sons and your daughters shall prophesy . . ." (Joel 2:28). Finally, the wish and declaration come to fulfillment in the book of Acts as Peter, explaining to his Jerusalem audience what has just happened, says: "This is what was spoken by the prophet Joel: 'And in the last days it shall be, God declares, that I will pour out my Spirit upon all flesh, and your sons and your daughters shall prophesy . . . yea, and on my menservants and my maidservants in those days I will pour out my Spirit; and they shall prophesy' " (Acts 2:16-18). Peter, while affirming that the words of Joel are now fulfilled, namely, the universalizing of prophecy among all God's people, is yet

---

[17]In accordance with what has been said about the "missionary spirit" and "anointing"— that the Holy Spirit is given for power to witness—it is important not to confuse this gift with becoming a Christian, salvation, regeneration, etc. James Dunn makes this mistake in his book, *Baptism in the Holy Spirit* (Naperville, IL: Allenson, 1970), for example, where he writes: "The gift of the Spirit . . . is the gift of saving grace by which one enters into Christian experience and life, into the new covenant, into the Church. It is, in the last analysis, that which makes a man a Christian . . ." (p. 226). Rather, it is by the gift of the Spirit that *one can help others* enter into Christian life and experience. It is not the gift of saving grace, but, presupposing this, it is the gift of power for witness.

more specific: not only will "sons and daughters" prophesy but also "menservants and maidservants." The universalizing of prophecy is threefold: first, it now goes beyond one race, the Jews, and includes all races and nations; second, there is no sexual exclusiveness, for both male and female will prophesy; and third, class differentiations disappear, for servants themselves are also now able to speak prophetically. All this is possible through the gift of the Holy Spirit.

It would seem apparent that Peter's own words to the gathered multitude in Jerusalem, first, describing what has just happened to him and the other disciples (Acts 2:15-21) and, second, proclaiming the gospel (2:22-36), are prophetic utterances. His message begins thus: "Peter, standing with the eleven, lifted up his voice and addressed ["spoke out to"][18] them, 'Men of Judea and all who dwell in Jerusalem, let this be known to you, and give ear to my words' " (Acts 2:14). Here Peter, an uneducated, common man[19]—a rough fisherman—speaks as he has never spoken before. He addresses the whole nation of Israel, as gathered in Jerusalem, and does so with the authority, forcefulness and wisdom that could only come from the full anointing of the Holy Spirit.

But, in accordance with the words of Joel and the affirmation of Peter, it is not one man only who is now anointed to speak prophetically but all of those who have received the fullness of God's Spirit. The mention of the eleven other apostles standing with Peter signifies that through Peter, as the mouthpiece, all

---

[18]The Greek word is *apephthenxato*, the same verb as in Acts 2:4 in connection with speaking in tongues: "They began to speak in other tongues, as the Spirit gave them utterance" (literally, "to speak out"). See footnote in previous chapter where it was commented that this Greek word is frequently used for "the oracle-giver, diviner, prophet, exorcist, and other 'inspired' persons." Hence, even as they "spoke out" in tongues to God by the inspiration of the Holy Spirit, so now do they (the eleven standing with Peter) "speak out" to people in prophetic utterance under the anointing of the same Holy Spirit. Meyer in his Acts Commentary (*Critical and Exegetical Handbook to the Acts of the Apostles*, by H.A.W. Meyer [New York: Funk and Wagnalls, 1883], p. 57) writes that the *prophēteusousin* (they shall prophesy) of Joel 2 "is by Peter specially recognized as a prediction of *that* apocalyptically inspired speaking, which had just commenced with the *heterais glōssais* [other tongues]." That is to say, the word in Joel concerning universal prophesying is recognized as covering both the speaking in tongues and the "inspired speaking" that follows.

[19]Of Peter and John it is said in Acts 4:13: "they [the Jewish council] . . . perceived that they [Peter and John] were uneducated, common men [or "unlettered laymen"— *agrammatoi idiōtai*]."

51

are speaking. But this is by no means limited to the twelve apostles, for on a later occasion after Peter and John have been released from the Jewish council that had threatened them and they have returned to their own people,[20] the company of those gathered pray for courage "to speak [God's] word with all boldness." As a result, "when they had prayed, the place in which they were gathered together was shaken; and they were all filled with the Holy Spirit and spoke the word of God with boldness" (Acts 4:29-31). Since the company of believers by this time includes many others than the apostles, it is clear that the prophetic word is being voiced by the larger Spirit-filled community.

In this same connection we turn again to the disciples at Ephesus. We have already observed that when they received the gift of the Holy Spirit, all of them spoke in tongues. They all prophesied, for the text reads in full: "And when Paul had laid his hands upon them, the Holy Spirit came on them; and they spoke with tongues and prophesied. There were about twelve of them in all" (Acts 19:6-7). So all prophesied—in accordance with the words of Joel and Peter. What they prophesied is not stated,[21] but that the Ephesians are further evidence of the universalizing of prophetic utterance is apparent.

Mention might be made also of the daughters of Philip who on one occasion were said to prophesy. Luke writes concerning Paul and his visit in Caesarea that "we entered the house of Philip the evangelist . . . and stayed with him. And he had four unmarried daughters, who prophesied"[22] (Acts 21:8-9).

---

[20]Acts 4:23: ". . . they went to their friends. . . ." The term for "friends" is *tous idious*, literally, "their own."

[21]It is probable that the Ephesian prophetic utterance was not proclamation of the gospel as was that of Peter and the others mentioned. As we have noted, Peter and company were bearing witness concerning Christ in order to bring people to faith. The Ephesians may rather have prophesied to one another, since the text does not suggest that other people were present to be addressed. If this is the case, their prophesying was more akin to Paul's description in 1 Corinthians 14 of prophecy as being for believers: "prophecy is not for unbelievers but believers" (v. 22). It should be added that Paul in this context is speaking only of the gathered community, the body of believers, wherein prophecy is addressed to believers for their edification (see discussion hereafter). This community function of prophecy would not preclude the role of prophecy in another situation as bearing witness to the Good News of Jesus Christ. Prophecy is a speaking of God's word to man whether it be in an evangelistic or community context.

[22]Literally, "prophesying" (*prophēteuousai*). Hence, the text does not state that they were "prophetesses" (NAS) or "possessed the gift of prophecy" (NEB), but that on this occasion they "did prophesy" (KJV). "Prophets" are mentioned elsewhere in Acts, viz., 11:27-28;

This incident is directly in line with the words of Joel, repeated by Peter at Pentecost, that "your daughters shall prophesy" (Acts 2:17). Philip himself was a man "full of the Spirit" (Acts 6:3, 5), hence he had experienced the outpouring of the Spirit. Thus, not only was he used by God to bear witness to the gospel (as, for example, to the Samaritans and the Ethiopian eunuch—Acts 8), but also all four of his daughters were overflowing with prophetic utterance.

In the letters of Paul frequent reference is made to prophecy and prophesying. There are places where Paul speaks of prophecy as a particular gift. For example, in Romans 12 he delineates various "gifts" (*charismata*) that "differ according to the grace given to us" and immediately adds: "let us use them: if prophecy, in proportion to our faith" (v. 6). In 1 Corinthians 12 Paul again lists a number of charismata, each being apportioned by the Holy Spirit, including prophecy—"to another prophecy"; and further on in the chapter he rhetorically asks, "Are all prophets?" (v. 29). However, despite these words, Paul later says, "You can all prophesy . . ." (1 Cor. 14:31). A careful study of the Pauline text makes clear that prophesying may: (1) be a particular manifestation of the Holy Spirit when the fellowship gathers for worship and ministry—and thus limited in exercise; (2) be performed by one who holds the office of a prophet, and thus again limited in exercise; and (3) in principle, be done by all—"you can all prophesy."[23] It is this universal note which, without denying certain limitations, informs the New Testament witness.

To summarize: this universalizing of prophetic utterance is a very important aspect of the gift of the Holy Spirit. It signifies that all persons who receive this gift may be spokesmen for God.[24]

13:1; 15:32; and 21:10. It is important to differentiate between the act of prophesying, which Philip's daughters performed, as a universal possibility since Pentecost, and the office of prophet which belongs to certain persons. In 1 Çorinthians, Paul likewise distinguishes between those who are prophets (12:27, 29) and prophesying which may be done by all (14:1, 5, 31). Incidentally, there is no suggestion that the office of prophet is limited by race, sex, or class either. If all may prophesy, it follows that out of that universal possibility, regardless of background, some will be designated especially to the office of prophet.

[23]Thus there is a parallel with tongues. We have earlier spoken of the universal possibility of speaking in tongues along with certain limitations. Tongues and prophecy are basic, dynamic expressions of the Holy Spirit that pervade the Spirit-endowed community.

[24]To "prophesy" means essentially to "for speak" (*pro* plus *phēmi*), hence for God. It may

It is not that they become persons of superior knowledge or virtue; rather, they become channels for God to speak His word. Whether it is to proclaim the way of salvation or to exhort believers,[25] it is wholly a matter of God speaking through them. Hence, traditional distinctions of class, sex, race, or education all fall away—as God has free rein in people's lives.

Prophetic utterance, it should be added, is not the same as teaching. There is no suggestion that the outpouring of the Holy Spirit grants to all the possibility of teaching. For teaching is a function that, while surely needing the guidance of the Holy Spirit, calls for some native capacity plus preparation, study, careful training and experience. It is a task of such fearsome responsibility that James warns: "Let not many of you become teachers, my brethren, for you know that we who teach shall be judged with greater strictness" (James 3:1). Prophesying, on the other hand, and prophetic utterance in general, is the God-given possibility for all who are filled with His Holy Spirit.

It is also to be observed that prophetic utterance may come forth with a "Thus says the Lord" and the message delivered in the first person, for example, "I speak unto you . . . ;" or it may be given as a message about the Lord, His will, intention, etc. But in either case the distinctive feature is that the speech, while uttered in the common language, is God-inspired, that is to say, it is not the result of human reflection but comes directly from God through the Holy Spirit. The Holy Spirit speaks through the human spirit in the known tongue and declares a divine message.[26]

also have the temporal significance of "fore speak," where prophecy contains the element of prediction (e.g. the case of Agabus in Acts 11:28 and 21:11). In any event, prophesying is a "forth speaking," namely, a word, a message, on behalf of God.

[25]In Acts, the emphasis is more on the former; in 1 Corinthians it is on the latter. "Primitive Christian prophecy is the inspired speech of charismatic preachers through whom God's plan of salvation for the world and the community and His will for the life of individual Christians are made known" (*Theological Dictionary of the New Testament*, Vol. VI, p. 848). Both are included—as God's message is one of both salvation of unbelievers and direction (or edification) of believers.

[26]Thus there is a likeness to tongues in that the message originates with the Holy Spirit and is expressed through the human spirit—hence, a direct utterance of God. The difference, of course, is that tongues is an utterance in an "unknown language" whereas prophecy is in the common speech. Tongues is the highest possible utterance on earth—transcendent speech addressed to God; prophecy is next to it, being God-given speech addressed to man. In neither case does the speech result from human meditation or conceptualization but comes immediately from the Holy Spirit.

54

Prophetic utterance occupies the place of highest significance in the life and ministry of the church. While it may be divinely inspired speech proclaiming God's truth to the world (as we have noted)—and therefore quite important—it occupies a critically vital role in the life of the community of faith. Paul writes the Corinthians: "Earnestly desire the spiritual gifts, especially that you may prophesy" (1 Cor. 14:1). And the reason for this is that "he who prophesies speaks to men for their upbuilding and encouragement and consolation" (v. 3).[27] Accordingly, prophecy, which has this distinctive function of edifying the body of believers, is much to be desired.

It is apparent that the universality of prophetic utterance, made possible by the gift of the Holy Spirit, makes both for proclamation of the gospel and the upbuilding of community life. Therefore, the word of God may go forth with increased power and effectiveness.

To return to the contemporary scene: one of the truly significant features is the widespread occurrence of prophetic utterance. First, this is the case in the proclamation of the gospel: there is no limit. Those who are caught up in the high tide of the Spirit—whether young or old, male or female, master or servant (employer or employee!)—are speaking the word with extraordinary effectiveness. The words of Joel 2, affirmed in Acts 2, are again being fulfilled in our time. Youth, full of the Spirit and vision, are testifying on every hand and believing God for the transformation of the world. Older men are dreaming great things for God and regardless of advancing years are stepping out for God. Women (young and old) are not left behind as they find fresh ways and a new freedom to witness to the gospel in

---

[27]Paul adds that, "He who speaks in a tongue edifies himself, but he who prophesies edifies the church. Now I want you all to speak in tongues, but even more to prophesy" (vv. 4-5). In the previous footnote I spoke of the primacy of tongues over prophecy, but does not Paul say otherwise here? No, for two reasons: first, Paul is speaking to the Corinthians about community edification and in that situation prophecy, which is addressed to men, has the primary role, but tongues first of all build up or edify the believer (without which there could be little community edification); second, even in the community, tongues *may* be no less significant than prophecy if interpretation follows, for Paul continues (in v. 5): "He who prophesies is greater than he who speaks in tongues, unless he interprets [*ei mē diermēneuē*], so that the church may be edified." Tongues could then, if interpretation follows, be equally "great" since (as Paul earlier says) "one who speaks in a tongue . . . utters mysteries in the Spirit" (v. 2). Interpretation would then be the declaration of those divine mysteries.

55

the power of the Spirit. Employers and employees with spiritual anointing are equally, and in multiple fashion, bearing witness to Jesus Christ. There is a fresh release of prophetic proclamation around the world among the spiritually renewed people of God.[28]

It is also a fact that prophetic utterance for community edification is freshly occurring wherever the spiritual renewal has spread. Indeed, one of the most distinctive features of the renewal is the way in which, wherever people gather together for worship and ministry, there is the expectation and occurrence of prophetic utterance.[29] There is utterly no distinction between age, sex, socioeconomic levels—or otherwise. In some instances clergy and laity may be present, but prophecy springs from either or both; there may be priests and nuns, and either or both prophesying; there may be highly educated and semi-literate people together but prophecy is limited to neither; there may be professors and students, both prophesying as the Lord leads. As the Apostle Paul said, "You can all prophesy one by one, so that all may learn and all be encouraged" (1 Cor. 14:31)—and this is precisely what is happening in our time.

The universalizing of prophetic utterance is one of the extraor-

---

[28]Many concrete illustrations could be given of the things mentioned in the paragraph above. The author has had opportunity to view this in many parts of the world where people have received the Spirit's anointing, and also at home base: the Melodyland School of Theology in Anaheim, California. As president of the School of Theology—or "School of the Prophets"—it has been for me a particular joy to work with some 500 to 600 students (men and women, young and old, employers and employees) and witness their total dedication to the proclamation of the gospel. It is Joel 2 and Acts 2 all over again!
[29]An extraordinary demonstration of this occurred during the meeting of some ten thousand "charismatics" in Rome—May, 1975. One of the occasions (which the author attended) was the gathering in St. Peter's Church where Cardinal Suenens celebrated the Eucharist and prophecies began to be uttered from within the audience. There was no prior preparation—but the atmosphere was full of expectation. One prophecy declared: "My people, I speak to you of a new day. I speak to you of the dawning of a new age in my church. I speak to you of a day that has not been seen before, of a life on the earth not seen before for my church. Prepare yourselves for me—prepare yourselves for the action I begin now, because the things you see around you will change. The combat you must enter into now is different, it is new. You need wisdom from me you do not have now. You need the power of my Holy Spirit in a way you have not possessed before. You need an understanding of my will and of the way I work that you do not have now. Open your eyes, open your hearts, prepare yourselves for me and for the day I announce now. My church will be different, my people will be different. Difficulty and trial will come upon you—comfort that you know now will be far from you. But the comfort you will have is the comfort of my Holy Spirit. They will seek for you to take your life, but I will support you. Come to me—bind yourselves together around me because I proclaim a new day of victory and triumph for your God. Behold it is begun!"

dinary features of the contemporary renewal in the Spirit. Thereby the people of God in their entirety become spokesmen for God.

Let us now move on to note how the gift of the Holy Spirit enables the *performance of mighty works*. The witness to Christ is not only that of word but also deed. There is, as we have observed, the powerful word of testimony to Christ whereby persons become vehicles for the transformation of human life, and prophetic utterance may go forth with great directness and forcefulness. But the witness is likewise that of deed wherein mighty works in the name of Christ are also performed.

It is apparent that not only did the early disciples speak about Jesus but also they did extraordinary things. The first mention of this follows upon the narration about Pentecost where the text reads: "And fear came upon every soul; and many wonders and signs were done through the apostles" (Acts 2:43). The fact of the multiplicity of extraordinary things—"many"—is first to be noted; second, their description as "wonders" and "signs" suggest their character both as miracles and pointers;[30] and third, these many wonders and signs are done "through" the apostles, the apostles being channels, and not agents, of their occurrence. The whole atmosphere is charged with awe—"fear . . . upon every soul"—as the exalted Lord does His work through them.

It should be quickly added that signs and wonders are done not only through the apostles but also through other disciples. On a later occasion Peter and John, after being threatened to speak no more about Jesus, return to their own people who pray for a common courage: "grant to thy servants to speak thy word with all boldness, while thou stretchest out thy hand to heal, and signs and wonders are performed through the name of thy holy servant Jesus" (Acts 4:29-30). As we have already noted, in reference to boldness, the immediate result following upon the shaking of the place is that "they were all filled with the Holy

---

[30]The combination of "wonders and signs" (*terata* and *sēmeia*) points to deeds that are miraculous (a miracle being a "wonder") and as such are expressive of God's supernatural activity (hence are "signs"). These "wonders and signs," or miracles, are particularly attestations of the gospel.

Spirit and spoke the word of God with boldness." Doubtless, the implication is not only that the prayer of the company for boldness of speech is answered for all, but also that they are all granted the performance of signs and wonders through the name of Jesus.

Further to examine the above matter: though it is said more than once that the apostles did wonders and signs,[31] it is apparent that others such as Stephen the martyr and Philip the evangelist did likewise. "And Stephen, full of grace and power, did great wonders and signs among the people" (Acts 6:8). "And the multitudes with one accord gave heed to what was said by Philip, when they heard him and saw the signs which he did" (8:6). "Even Simon [the magician] himself believed, and after being baptized, he continued with Philip. And seeing signs and great miracles[32] performed, he was amazed" (8:13). In addition, according to Mark 16:17, Jesus said: "And these signs will accompany those who believe: in my name they will cast out demons; they will speak in new tongues; they will pick up serpents; and if they drink any deadly thing, it will not hurt them; they will lay their hands on the sick, and they will recover." Similarly, "And they went forth and preached everywhere, while the Lord worked with them and confirmed the message by the signs that attended it" (Mark 16:20).[33] Signs and wonders—extraordinary,

---

[31]In addition to Acts 2:43, supra, see 5:12—"Now many signs and wonders were done among the people by the hands of the apostles"; 14:3—regarding Paul and Barnabas: "So they remained for a long time [at Iconium], speaking boldly for the Lord, who bore witness to the word of his grace, granting signs and wonders to be done by their hands"; 15:12—"Barnabas and Paul . . . related what signs and wonders God had done through them among the Gentiles." Compare also Romans 15:18-19 where Paul says: "For I will not venture to speak of anything except what Christ has wrought through me to win obedience from the Gentiles, by word and deed, by the power of signs and wonders, by the power of the Holy Spirit. . . ." Paul also says: "The signs of a true apostle [literally, "truly the signs of the apostle"—*ta men sēmeia tou apostolou*] were performed among you in all patience, with signs and wonders and mighty works [or, 'powerful deeds'— *dunamesin*]" (2 Cor. 12:12). This latter statement, incidentally, while again affirming that through Paul miracles took place, does not speak of them as apostolic certifications (hence, limited to apostles). The "signs of a true apostle"—which Paul does not describe in this text—were performed with "all patience"; such "signs" (even certifications) were accompanied by "signs and wonders and mighty works."
[32]*dunameis megalas*
[33]It is true that many ancient manuscripts of the Gospel of Mark do not include chapter 16, verses 9-20. However, even if these verses are a later addition, the very fact that signs are ascribed to believers in general—"those who believe"—shows an early recognition that miracles are not limited to apostles, or apostles and deacons, such as Stephen and Philip.

58

miraculous deeds—are the practice of the whole Christian community.

It is abundantly clear that the performance of mighty works—signs, wonders, miracles—belongs to the gospel proclamation. The early Christians testify *and* perform signs and wonders. The proclamation is powerful word *and* miraculous deed, both by the Holy Spirit, that bear witness to the gospel. The deed is the confirmation of the word—the visible assurance of the message of salvation. The greatest wonder of all is that of new life, new birth wrought by the word, but this is invisible; hence, when a visible sign accompanies the word there is undeniable attestation to the actuality of what has been inwardly wrought by the message of salvation.

Thus it is a serious error indeed to relegate miracles to the past. It is pathetic to hear among those who vigorously affirm the message of salvation—the necessity of regeneration—that "signs and wonders" are not to be expected any longer. If through the proclamation of the word in the power of the Spirit the miracle of rebirth can and does occur, will not that same Spirit also work other "signs and wonders"? For, surely, other miracles—no matter how extraordinary[34]—are less significant than the miracle of new life and salvation.

Let us say further that it makes little practical difference whether one affirms that the miracles in Acts (and elsewhere) are simply legendary accretions to the record—and thus really did not happen—or that they did happen then but no longer occur in our time. Both views deny the reality of the living God who is always free and able *in any time* to perform His extraordinary works through men. The "Bible believer" who affirms that miracles were for then but not for now is actually farther removed from a living faith than the "liberal" who has not gone so far as to lock the power of God into past history. Both, however, need to hear the words of Jesus: "Is not this why you are wrong, that you know neither the scriptures nor the power of God?" (Mark 12:24).

[34]Even the raising of the physically dead (to which reference is made several times in the Scriptures) is less a "wonder" than the raising of the spiritually dead by the proclamation of the Good News. For the raising of the physically dead in Acts, see the accounts of Peter raising Tabitha (9:36-42) and Paul restoring Eutychus to life (20:9-12).

Fortunately the spiritual renewal of the twentieth century has recaptured the early church's belief in and practice of mighty works. Miracles are no longer thought of as belonging to past history or as being merely legendary additions to the biblical witness; they belong to the life of the believing community and to the proclamation of the gospel.[35] "Expect a miracle" is a commonly heard expression—and those who expect God to perform mighty works are not disappointed.

The performance of mighty works, made possible by the gift of the Holy Spirit, includes a wide range of extraordinary phenomena. We shall note two of these in particular, beginning with *healing*.

In the ministry of Jesus, as is well known, next in importance to His preaching and teaching was His ministry of healing. For example, "He went about all Galilee, teaching in their synagogues and preaching the gospel of the kingdom and healing every disease and every infirmity among the people" (Matt. 4:23). Another text reads: "The power [*dunamis*] of the Lord was with him to heal" (Luke 5:17); and thereupon he healed a bedridden paralytic. This *dunamis* of God is precisely what Jesus promised His disciples would be theirs through the gift of the Holy Spirit. And so it was—and is.

As we look again at the record in Acts, it is relevant that the first specified mighty work is that of healing. Following the gift of the Holy Spirit at Pentecost and the formation of the Christian community (Acts 2) is the narrative about the healing of the lame beggar at the gate of the temple (Acts 3:1-8). Peter speaks to the man: "I have no silver or gold, but I give you what I have; in the name of Jesus Christ of Nazareth, walk" (v. 6). Thus it is the combination of the power of the Spirit ("what I have") and

---

[35]E.g., see *Nine O'Clock in the Morning*, by Dennis Bennett, chapter 6, "More to the Package." Shortly after Father Bennett's baptism in the Spirit, he found miracles of many kinds beginning to happen. At the fellowship meeting, he said: "Sometimes nearly everyone in the room had some kind of a report to give: not what God did years ago, or even last year, but what He did last week, yesterday, today!" (p. 47). One further, and beautiful, statement by Dorothy Ranaghan, in *As the Spirit Leads Us*, might be added: "The victorious life of Christ becomes known in the now. Healing, discernment, miracles, prophecy—all these signs, manifestations or demonstrations of the Spirit cry out to men as they did in the New Testament times: 'Jesus is alive! Jesus works wonders! Jesus is the Lord!' " (p. 14).

the name of Jesus Christ that leads to the miraculous healing.

What follows is quite significant. Peter addresses the assembled crowd, amazed at the healing of one they had seen many times begging at the gate, and tells them that "the faith which is through Jesus has given the man this perfect health in the presence of you all" (Acts 3:16). These words lead to the proclamation of the gospel to the crowd—"Repent therefore, and turn again, that your sins may be blotted out, that times of refreshing may come from the presence of the Lord . . ." (3:19). Thereafter, taken into custody by the Temple authorities who inquired, "By what power or by what name did you do this?", Peter "filled with the Holy Spirit" replied, ". . . be it known to you all, and to all the people of Israel, that by the name of Jesus Christ of Nazareth, whom you crucified, whom God raised from the dead, by him this man is standing before you well" (4:7-10). Peter concludes with the message of salvation: "And there is salvation in no one else, for there is no other name under heaven given among men by which we must be saved" (4:12).

What is particularly important in this narrative of miraculous healing is the way in which it becomes the occasion for proclamation of the gospel. Indeed, as a result "many of those who heard the word believed; and the number of the men came to about five thousand" (4:4). Thus, it is similar to the Day of Pentecost when miraculous speaking in tongues became the occasion for drawing a crowd together, and consequent preaching of the gospel led to the salvation of some three thousand (Acts 2:41). "Signs and wonders" thus are shown not only to be confirmations of the word (as we have seen); but also they are occasions for the word. They set forth visibly, tangibly, undeniably that an inexplicable power is present and at work, making way for the message of salvation.

It is apparent that the performance of such a mighty work as healing is vitally connected with the preaching of the gospel. It is not merely the matter of healing being an additional thing—as if the commission were to preach *and* heal. The Good News, to be sure, does include healing; hence, a missionary outreach that does not have concern for men's bodies is inadequate. However, the relationship between preaching and healing is more intimate than that. Healing, as well as other "signs and wonders," is

61

not just supplemental, it is instrumental. It can become the avenue for the proclamation of salvation in Jesus Christ.[36]

What all of this suggests is that when the church, the believing community, is seen to be the arena of God's supernatural activity, people are bound to take notice. Wherever the gospel is proclaimed in the context of "signs and wonders"—whether they precede, accompany, or follow—it is obvious that something extraordinary is going on. At Pentecost with the speaking in tongues "all were amazed and perplexed, saying to one another, 'What does this mean?'" (Acts 2:12); at the healing of the lame man "they were filled with wonder and amazement" (Acts 3:10). Such amazement, perplexity, wonderment, betokening a shocking sense of supernatural presence, prepares the way for the powerful ministry of the word.

It is significant to note again the prayer of the community of disciples following the prohibition of the council about testifying to Jesus: "And now, Lord, look upon their threats, and grant to thy servants to speak thy word with all boldness, while thou stretchest out thy hand to heal, and signs and wonders are performed through the name of thy holy servant Jesus" (Acts 4:29-30). The prayer of the disciples is for the speaking of the word to be accompanied or followed by healing, signs and wonders. Such visible demonstration of the supernatural activity of God will confirm the message, and make many come to a living faith. So whether preceding, accompanying or following, the occurrence of miracles underscores the reality of the proclaimed word as the power of God unto salvation.

The power of God to heal continues to be manifest in the early Christian community. The sick of Jerusalem are brought in great numbers to the body of the disciples, many hoping for at least the shadow of Peter to fall upon them; and then people

---

[36]A vivid illustration of this is cited in the book by J. Herbert Kane, *Understanding Christian Missions* (Grand Rapids: Baker, 1974), about the preaching of French evangelist Jacques Girard in the Ivory Coast soccer stadium: "Morning and evening for *six* weeks thirty to thirty-five thousand people crowded into the stadium. During the first part of the crusade the evangelist emphasized the power of Christ to heal. Hundreds were healed, including some high government officials and their relatives. . . . During the second part of the crusade Mr. Girard emphasized the power of Christ to save. Having already witnessed the healing of the body, the people responded in droves" (p. 424).

begin to come from surrounding towns and villages and "bringing the sick and those afflicted with unclean spirits, and they were all healed" (Acts 5:14-16). Likewise in the ministry of Philip at Samaria "the multitudes with one accord gave heed to what was said by Philip, when they heard him and saw the signs which he did. For unclean spirits came out of many who were possessed, crying with a loud voice; and many who were paralyzed or lame were healed" (8:6-7). Peter, later, in the town of Lydda, speaks to a man named Aeneas, bedridden and paralyzed: "'Aeneas, Jesus Christ heals you; rise and make your bed.' And immediately he rose. And all the residents of Lydda and Sharon saw him, and they turned to the Lord" (9:34-35). In the case of Paul who spent two years in Ephesus proclaiming the word, the Scripture adds: "And God did extraordinary miracles[37] by the hands of Paul, so that handkerchiefs were carried away from his body to the sick, and diseases left them and the evil spirits came out of them" (Acts 19:11-12). Paul ministers later at Malta to Publius's father who "lay sick with fever and dysentery"; Paul "visited him and prayed, and putting his hands on him healed him." Thereafter "the rest of the people on the island who had diseases also came and were cured" (28:8-9). Such incidents demonstrate over and over that the power of the Spirit makes for abundant healing.

A number of matters in these instances of healing may be reflected upon. First, there is again the close connection between the proclamation of the word and healing. In one case (Samaria), it is hearing the gospel in conjunction with seeing healings occur that leads to the multitude giving heed to what is said; in another case (Lydda), seeing the healing is itself the direct cause of people coming to faith. Second, in another situation (Jerusalem), healing refers to the cure of the sick and deliverance from "unclean spirits," thus both physical ailments and spiritual bondage. Third, there is evidently no limitation to the kinds of sicknesses healed—as if perhaps healing occurred to the psychosomatic but not the organic. The sick, whatever their infirmities, were healed. This calls to mind the earlier words about Jesus, that He healed "every disease and every infirmity" (Matt. 4:23).

---

[37]"Extraordinary miracles" in the Greek—*dunameis ou tas tuchousas*—"powers not the ordinary." "*Dunameis*"—"powers"—is often best translated as "miracles."

The same is true for His Spirit-filled followers who minister in His name. Fourth, in two of the cases (Jerusalem and Malta) all were healed; in another (Samaria) many were healed—many who were paralyzed and lame.

On this last point let us comment further about the totality of healing in two situations above, and its partiality in another. One of the most significant and exciting aspects of the gift of the Spirit is the fact that it makes healing possible for all. "They were all healed"—the sick, the afflicted, the tormented—is a beautiful testimony to what the Holy Spirit can do through one like Peter who is an open channel and instrument. It remains a testimony to this day that the power of God to heal is still present wherever His Spirit abounds. Even as salvation—the forgiveness of sins—is available to all, so is healing of all manner of physical, mental and emotional ailments. There only needs to be, as in the New Testament time, persons filled with God's Spirit who in proclaiming the gospel of new life in Christ also minister healing in Jesus' name. Believing that God wills both salvation and health for all men, the Christian witness of our day needs boldly to engage in this total ministry.

However, as we have observed, not all are healed in every situation: "many" but not everyone. Why this was the case in Samaria is not specified; however, it may have been due to the lack of receptivity on the part of those who were not healed. The people "with one accord gave heed to what was said by Philip" and of these, many are healed. "Giving heed" or "paying attention,"[38] however, does not necessarily lead to that openness, reception, faith wherein a healing may occur. Healing, while for everyone, may not be received by all.

We may reflect for a moment on the ministry of Jesus and observe that in most situations He healed all who were present. It is frequently recorded that Jesus healed everyone; for example, "He cast out the spirits with a word, and healed all who were sick" (Matt. 8:16); "Many followed him, and he healed them all" (Matt. 12:15). Scriptures like these may be multiplied.[39]

---

[38]The Greek word is *prosechō*, to turn one's mind to, notice, give heed to, pay attention, follow.
[39]E.g., Matthew 14:14; Luke 4:40, 6:19 (". . . power came forth from him and healed them all").

However, there are other occasions when the biblical record speaks not of all but of many: "And he healed many who were sick with various diseases, and cast out many demons . . ." (Mark 1:34); and again there is reference not to many but to a few: "He laid his hands upon a few sick people and healed them" (Mark 6:5). In the latter event, occurring at Nazareth, it is clear that healing was restricted by the lack of receptivity, the unbelief, of His own townsfolk: "They took offense at him. . . . And he could do no mighty work there, except that he laid his hands upon a few sick people and healed them. And he marveled because of their unbelief" (Mark 6:3, 5-6). On still another occasion, out of a large crowd at the sheep gate pool where "lay a multitude of invalids, blind, lame, paralyzed" (John 5:3), He healed only one, a man who had been ill for some twenty-eight years. Here the cause for the healing of only one does not seem to be due to an atmosphere of unbelief (although there is little suggestion that the sick multitude were expecting very much), but to Jesus' own decision to help the one upon whom He took special pity.

So we may repeat our earlier statement, based on the record in Acts and now also shown in the Gospels, that healing while for everyone may not be received by all. Such factors as a lack of receptivity, unbelief on the human side, or the sovereign decision to heal only one or a few on the divine side, may be operative. Thus it is quite erroneous and misleading to claim that all will be healed in every situation.

However, to conclude this discussion of healing affirmatively, it is highly important to recognize that the gift of God's Spirit does make possible the healing of every kind of disease. Thus, wherever people become channels of the divine power, extraordinary healings may be expected to occur.

In the spiritual renewal of our time, healing stands out as one of the most significant features. The power of God to heal, resident within the gift of the Holy Spirit, is being manifested on every hand. It is understood that the Good News includes healing for the body as well as salvation for the soul. For example, evangelists in the renewal do not hesitate to proclaim and act upon this "full gospel."[40] Since Jesus performed many

---

[40]Kathryn Kuhlman and Oral Roberts have been recognized leaders. See, e.g., Kuhlman's

healings and promised that His disciples would do even "greater works" than He, and since He has sent the Spirit to carry forward His ministry, then works of healing are to be expected. If they do not occur, therefore, it may be a negative sign, namely, that the gift of the Holy Spirit has not been received, or possibly that the gift has come, but people are failing to move out in faith and expectancy. But that healings of every kind[41] are occurring in the renewal of today is one of the clearest evidences of the presence and power of the Lord in the Holy Spirit.

In the preceding paragraphs several references have been made to casting out demons or evil spirits. We earlier called attention to one case (at Jerusalem) where healing refers to both the cure of the sick and deliverance from evil spirits; however, in the other two instances related (Samaria and Ephesus), a distinction is made between healing the sick and the expulsion of demons. This distinction is also apparent in the Scripture quoted[42] concerning Jesus' ministry where it is said He both cast out demons and healed. It may also be pointed out that in Mark 16:17 a differentiation is made: "And these signs will accompany those who believe: in my name they will cast out demons . . . they will lay their hands on the sick and they will recover." Thus we may say that among the mighty works made possible by the exalted Lord's gift of the Spirit is *deliverance*.

Let us view this matter in more detail. It might be helpful to begin in the book of Acts with one particular example of what casting out of evil spirits, or deliverance, entails. Paul and his companions going to the place of prayer in Philippi are daily followed by a slave girl who "had a spirit of divination."[43] She

---

I Believe in Miracles (Old Tappan, NJ: Spire Books, 1962) and Roberts' *The Call: An Autobiography* (Old Tappan, NJ: Spire Books, 1971). Roberts' ministry has increasingly moved in the direction of higher education. Mention should also be made of Francis MacNutt whose teaching on healing is found in the book, *Healing* (Notre Dame, IN: Ave Maria Press, 1974).

[41]The emphasis upon "inner healing" is also to be noted in the contemporary spiritual renewal. See, e.g., Agnes Sanford's *The Healing of the Spirit* (Philadelphia: Lippincott, 1966), Father Michael Scanlan's *Inner Healing* (New York: Paulist Press, 1974) and Ruth Carter Stapleton's *The Gift of Inner Healing* (Waco: Word Books, 1976).

[42]Matthew 8:16. See above.

[43]Literally, "a spirit of a python," or a "python spirit" (*pneuma puthōna*). "Python" was the name of the Pythian serpent or dragon who was said to guard the Delphic oracle. Thus "a spirit of divination" has nothing to do with the Holy Spirit, but stems from evil.

cries out for many days, "These men are servants of the Most High God, who proclaim to you the way of salvation." Paul, increasingly annoyed, finally takes action: he "turned and said to the spirit, 'I charge you in the name of Jesus Christ to come out of her.'" The result: "it came out that very hour" (Acts 16:16-18).

This account is not unlike that of various incidents recorded in the Gospels where people with such a spirit frequently cry out in recognition of Jesus, and deliverance thereafter occurs. For example, in the beginning of Jesus' ministry, a man with an "unclean spirit" cried out: "What have you to do with us, Jesus of Nazareth? Have you come to destroy us? I know who you are, the Holy One of God." Jesus thereupon "rebuked him, saying, 'Be silent, and come out of him!' And the unclean spirit convulsing him and crying with a loud voice, came out of him" (Mark 1:23-26). This incident makes a profound impression on those who observe: it is "a new teaching with authority"[44] (Mark 1:27).

It is significant that in both the accounts of Paul and Jesus, the spirit[45] in the person recognizes the truth at hand ("these men . . . proclaim to you the way of salvation"; "you are the Holy One of God"); but it is actually a foreign spirit occupying a human person, from which one needs deliverance. This foreign spirit is obviously supernatural, having instant recognition of divine presence; in that sense it is a "spirit of divination." It is also an evil spirit, making the girl a slave girl, and so binding that, in the case of the man with an "unclean spirit," it convulses him in being cast out. In both instances the spirit cannot withstand the impact of Jesus, or the name of Jesus (which Paul invokes), and immediately comes out.

It should be added that the same spirits referred to elsewhere are frequently shown to be tormenting and disruptive. They may be the deepest cause of physical or mental disability, even to the point of self-destruction.[46] Hence more is called for than

---

[44]*didachē kainē kat' exousian.*

[45]The language varies: "spirit," "unclean spirit," "evil spirit," "demon" and "spirit of an unclean demon" (Luke 4:33). A person with such a spirit is frequently described as "demon possessed" (Mark 1:32), or as a "demoniac" (Mark 5:15)—literally, "demonized" (*daimonistheis*), that is to say, "under the power of a demon."

[46]For example, there is the case of the Gadarene demoniac who could not be bound with chains, constantly committing acts of self-violence: "Night and day among the tombs and on the mountains he was always crying out, and bruising himself with stones" (Mark 5:5).

healing, which is a matter of mending what has been broken or diseased, whether of body or mind. What happens in demonic possession is deeper still: it is a matter of the human spirit being taken into bondage by an alien power. Thus there is a pernicious force at work, often affecting mind and body so disruptively that the only way to healing is through deliverance. Moreover, the only way whereby deliverance from such evil may come is through the presence or name of the Holy One who has the power and authority to deliver from even the most vicious tormenting spirit.

Let me summarize a few points. First, such possession only comes to light in the presence of Jesus Christ. Whatever may— or may not—have been the outward expression, the evil power which has lurked deep within the human personality is aroused at the coming of the Holy One. Hence, when one anointed with Christ's Spirit is ministering in His name, there are times when this very ministry precipitates a crisis in one who is demon possessed. Though such a person may have long turned away from truth, and his inner spirit taken over by this alien spirit, now there is sudden, even startling recognition. For the dimension of perception has now become totally a spiritual one—spirit knowing spirit—the one possessed with evil crying out in recognition of the Spirit of holiness. This may not be a verbal recognition—"I know who you are"—but usually some kind of an outcry or startled attitude betokening recognition of a divine presence. For the inward spirit of evil knows when the Holy Spirit is at hand. At least for the moment all the veils are dropped in the presence of the holy God. Second, not only is there inward recognition but at the same time there may also be inward torment. The demonic spirit, now exposed, feels the awful impact of the Holy Spirit. No longer hidden within the human personality but standing out, it finds almost unbearable the divine presence. It seems as if the Spirit of holiness is bent on torturing the possessed person—thus eliciting the response mentioned earlier: "Have you come to destroy us?"[47] Of course, there is no intentional torment; it is simply that the Holy Spirit, like a hot flame of purity, burns into all that is evil. Third,

---

[47]Mark 1:24. See comparable words of the Gadarene demoniac to Jesus in Mark 5:7: "I adjure you by God, do not torment me."

deliverance may now follow. The alien spirit that has long dominated a person is exposed; it feels the torment of holy presence and is ready for being cast out. The evil spirit is now dominated by another spirit, the Holy Spirit, and is totally subject to the word that casts it out: "Come out of him, in the name of Jesus Christ." The departing spirit may so convulse a person as to seem like the destruction of death;[48] however, it is verily the moment when a person experiences the marvel of deliverance into a fresh life.

This leads us back to the earlier point that this mighty work of deliverance continues only through those who truly minister in Jesus' name[49] by the power of His Holy Spirit. During Jesus' lifetime, when He was personally present with His disciples, He gave them power and authority over the evil spirits,[50] so that in His name they did exercise deliverance. Since Jesus has completed His earthly ministry, this same power and authority devolves upon those who receive the gift of the Holy Spirit: they too are enabled to perform the mighty work of liberating people from demonic possession.

It would be hard to overemphasize the importance of this ministry of deliverance. For there are countless numbers of

---

[48]In the event of the deliverance of the epileptic boy in Mark 9, after Jesus commands, "Come out of him and never enter him again," the text continues: "And after crying out and convulsing him terribly, it came out, and the boy was like a corpse; so that most of them said 'He is dead.'" However, "Jesus took him by the hand and lifted him up and he arose" (vv. 25-27).

[49]The name of Jesus, however, is not some magical power that may be conjured up by anyone to bring about a deliverance. The later account in Acts (19:13-16) of the "itinerant Jewish exorcists" who "undertook to pronounce the name of the Lord Jesus over those who had evil spirits" is a vivid case in point. They tried to do this by saying, "I adjure you by the Jesus whom Paul preaches." The evil spirit, unaffected, answers, "Jesus I know, and Paul I know; but who are you?" Rather than exorcism "the man in whom the evil spirit was leaped on them, mastered all of them and overpowered them, so that they fled out of that house naked and wounded." Conjuring up Jesus' name is ineffective, even dangerous, if not done by one who is truly ministering in Jesus' name.

[50]E.g., Luke 9:1-2: "And he called the twelve together and gave them power and authority [*dunamin kai exousian*] over all demons and to cure diseases, and he sent them out to preach the kingdom of God. . . ." (Note, incidentally, the threefold ministry of preaching, deliverance and healing.) But it is not just the twelve who have such authority, for later Jesus sends out an additional seventy who return "with joy, saying, 'Lord, even the demons are subject to us in your name!'" (Luke 10:1-17). It is important to recognize that such authority in Jesus' day was not limited to the circle of apostles, nor is it limited to any particular "official" persons since that time. Recall Mark 16:17—"And these signs will accompany those who believe [hence, *all* believers]: in my name they will cast out demons. . . ."

persons who desperately need such help. Their condition is not to be identified as such with sin (which needs forgiveness)[51] or disease (which calls for healing), but with possession, which cries out for deliverance. Their inner spirits—the inmost centers of their personhood—have been so laid claim to by an alien force, so "demonized" thereby, that they can scarcely hear the word concerning repentance and forgiveness. Their spirits are more than dead to the things of God; they have been *taken over* by another spirit. They may, or may not, give outward evidence of such possession. There may be an outward semblance of serenity—or contrariwise that of distortion and violence[52]—but the only hope is the exposure of the deep inward condition, and deliverance therefrom. If such a condition is not recognized and properly handled there is much confusion all around. Even the most faithful witness concerning the things of God, or on the other hand various attempts at healing (viewing such cases as emotional disorders), may leave the person still locked up in his spiritual bondage—and worse off than ever. But when a situation bears the marks of demonic possession,[53] the only possible way of relief is that of deliverance: by the power of the Holy Spirit.[54]

---

[51]Of course, the condition of every person outside Christ is sin; thus forgiveness is always needed. The point here, however, is that a person may be so inwardly dominated by evil that unless this is broken he is in no condition to hear the word of forgiveness (and reconciliation). It is by Christ that both occur: deliverance from the domination of Satan and forgiveness of sins. The commission to Paul, by the risen Christ, was to go to Jew and Gentile alike: "to open their eyes, that they may turn from darkness to light and from the power of Satan to God, that they may receive forgiveness of sins and a place among those who are sanctified by faith in me" (Acts 26:18). Turning from the power of Satan to God, therefore, may be essential background for receiving forgiveness of sins.

[52]For example, compare the slave girl's situation, which exhibited no obvious disturbance, with that of the demoniac at Gadara who was patently in a condition of continual misery.

[53]From what has been said, the most evident marks are the sensitivity of a possessed person to the presence of holiness and his feeling at the same time tormented by that presence.

[54]In the contemporary spiritual renewal mention should be made of Michael Harper's *Spiritual Warfare* (London: Hodder and Stoughton, 1970) and Don Basham's *Deliver Us From Evil* (Washington Depot, CT: Chosen Books, 1972). There has been some extremism in certain sectors of the present renewal with the holding of mass deliverance sessions for Christians and non-Christians alike, and an exaggerated viewing of almost every vice as demonic and therefore needing deliverance (for an effective counterbalance, see *The Dilemma: Deliverance or Discipline?* by W. Robert McAlister [Plainfield, NJ: Logos, 1976]). However, the importance, even urgency, of deliverance in many situations has come to be acutely recognized, and is being carried out.

A further word may be added about the matter of demonic possession and emotional disorders. Reference has just been made to the mistake of confusing the two so that what calls for deliverance is viewed as a disorder that calls for healing. Such healing attempted, whether it be spiritual (prayers, laying on of hands, etc.) or medical (therapy and various other kinds of treatments), may therefore actually miss the mark—because the situation is not understood *in depth*. If the case is one of possession, anything that falls short of deliverance is both inadequate and only a further compounding of the problem. But now it needs also to be emphasized, on the other hand, that there are serious dangers of viewing what are actually emotional disorders as demonic possession. To seek to exorcise a person whose situation calls for another kind of treatment—psychotherapy, medicine or otherwise—can be a critical mistake and leave a person worse off than before.

In all this, there is much need for spiritual discernment—that is, discernment by the Holy Spirit—so that the one seeking to minister may know how to proceed.[55] If there is not clear evidence of possession, it is better to proceed along other lines, or leave the situation to those better qualified to help.

Finally, it is evident that, as in the case of healing, deliverance from demonic spirits is also one of the attestations of the gospel of salvation. When people are delivered, this can be an extraordinary sign of the working of God's power that confirms the message of new life in Christ. Recall the words of Mark 16: "These signs will accompany those who believe: in my name they will cast out demons . . . ," and the result: "the Lord worked with them and confirmed the message by the signs that attended it" (vv. 17 and 20). Hence, casting out of demons is one

---

[55]Paul's response at Philippi to the slave girl's words, "These men are servants of the Most High God, who proclaim to you the way of salvation," is a good illustration of spiritual discernment. Outwardly such words might have seemed to be a confession of faith that would have pleased Paul; however, he recognized in them a "spirit of divination" that was not of God but from evil. Hence, rather than being deluded by her words, or even proclaiming the word of salvation, he casts out the demonic spirit. Later in the same day Paul, along with Silas, is thrown into jail, and thereafter speaks to the Philippian jailer the good news of salvation, "Believe in the Lord Jesus Christ, and you will be saved . . ." (Acts 16:31). There is no casting out of an evil spirit, for Paul discerned there was none such present. Rather does he lead the jailer directly to faith in Christ. Thus, through spiritual discernment, Paul acts differently in the two situations.

of the signs that shows forth the Good News about Christ. For when people behold the supernatural power of God delivering the demon-possessed, they are vividly assured thereby that the gospel must also be the power of God unto salvation.

What we have observed in this chapter is that the purpose of the gift of the Holy Spirit is power. This is enabling power to carry forward the ministry of Christ in word and in deed. There is the mighty witness in word leading to healing and deliverance. Verily, by the gift of the Holy Spirit to the believing community, the exalted Lord continues His work among men.

CHAPTER FIVE

RECEPTION

The Holy Spirit is given to those who believe in Jesus Christ. From all that has been said about the Holy Spirit being the Spirit of the exalted Lord and given for the primary purpose of bearing witness to Christ, it is apparent there can be no gift of the Holy Spirit except to those who believe in Him and are thereby called to be His witnesses. Through those who believe, Christ carries forward His ministry in word and deed.

Now it is important to note two matters: the *indispensability* and the *dynamics* of this faith in Jesus Christ in relation to the gift of the Holy Spirit. Let us consider these in turn.

It is important first to emphasize the matter of indispensability because of the possible misapprehension that the Holy Spirit may be received without such a faith in Jesus Christ. There have been those who, desiring no relationship to Christ, no faith in Him, would still like to receive the Holy Spirit in the sense of having some kind of inward experience of the fullness of God. For such persons faith in Christ is viewed as irrelevant, even misdirected, since what they seek is an immediacy and unity of the divine Spirit with the human spirit. Christ may point the way to such a mystical union of God and man, but He himself is viewed as not essential to such an achievement. From the truly Christian perspective, however, all immediacy with God is a "mediated immediacy"[1] wherein Christ alone can effect the unity of the infinite God and finite man.

Faith in Jesus Christ becomes all the more important with the realization that the barrier to the reception of the Spirit is not only human finitude but also human sin. Man is totally guilty, and it is only by belief in Jesus Christ that he can receive forgiveness. The wonder of the gospel, the Good News, is that there is cleansing and pardon of sins in the name of Jesus Christ.

---

[1]John Baillie in *Our Knowledge of God* (New York: Charles Scribner's Sons, 1939) has one of the most helpful statements along this line. See especially Chapter IV, Section 16, "A Mediated Immediacy."

Man may truly repent and receive forgiveness and become a new creature in Christ.

This faith in Jesus Christ is personally oriented. It is directed to Him as the one who lived, died and rose again from the dead. Through His death and resurrection He has made forgiveness and new life a glorious reality. This reality may be entered into by faith in Him, by faith in His name.

It is this faith, this kind of believing in Jesus Christ, that is indispensable to receiving the Holy Spirit.[2] It is, therefore, pointless to talk about the reception of the Holy Spirit except against this background.

That believing in Jesus Christ is indispensable to the reception of the Holy Spirit is apparent in all the relevant narratives in the book of Acts. Three illustrations may suffice.

Peter speaks at Caesarea to the centurion and his household, beginning with words in general about God, how He "shows no partiality, but in every nation any one who fears him and does what is right is acceptable to him" (Acts 10:34-35). From there on Peter proclaims Jesus Christ: His life, death and resurrection, and then focuses on the need for faith in Him to receive forgiveness: "To him all the prophets bear witness that every one who believes in him receives forgiveness of sins through his name" (10:43). Then it was that the Holy Spirit "fell on all who heard the word" (10:44), the word which set forth Christ and called for faith in Him. It was to those believing in Jesus, and receiving forgiveness through Him, that the Holy Spirit was given.

Philip at Samaria "proclaimed to them the Christ" (Acts 8:5). Doubtless in this message he gave them the Good News about Jesus' life, death and resurrection. As a result, the Samaritans came to faith, and were baptized: ". . . when they believed Philip as he preached the good news about the kingdom of God

---

[2]Michael Harper writes that "the benefits of the New Covenant include the gift of the Holy Spirit as well as the forgiveness of sins. From Pentecost onwards the Church faithfully proclaimed that Christ forgives *and* baptises in the Holy Spirit. They taught that all who repent and believe are justified by faith, and that all who are justified by faith may receive the Holy Spirit by faith" *(Walk in the Spirit* [Plainfield, NJ: Logos, 1968], p. 13). It is faith—nothing else—faith in Christ, that is essential to receiving the Holy Spirit.

and the name of Jesus Christ, they were baptized, both men and women" (8:12). Later Peter and John come from Jerusalem to communicate the Holy Spirit (8:14-17). The crucial background undoubtedly was the Samaritans' faith[3] which put them in a position to receive the Holy Spirit. Believing in Christ, the Samaritans were ready for the Holy Spirit to be given.

Before the Ephesians received the gift of the Holy Spirit Paul proclaimed Jesus Christ. He reminded them that "John baptized with the baptism of repentance, telling the people to believe in the one who was to come after him, that is Jesus" (Acts 19:4). Thereafter, "on hearing this" (19:5) the Ephesians were baptized "in the name of the Lord Jesus." Paul laid his hands on them, and they received the Holy Spirit. Unmistakably, the critical matter was the Ephesians believing in Jesus: it was the hearing of faith, as is further evidenced personally by their baptism in Jesus' name. Thus firm in their faith, the Ephesians were ready to receive the gift of the Holy Spirit.[4]

Thus it is apparent that the Holy Spirit is given only to those who believe in Jesus Christ. Believing in Him—not an idea or a doctrine, but in His reality as the living Lord—is shown to be the

[3]There is no suggestion in the narrative that there was anything lacking or defective in the Samaritans' faith. I cannot, therefore, agree with James Dunn in his book, *Baptism in the Holy Spirit*, wherein he claims it was only "intellectual assent to a statement or proposition" (p. 65), so that they believed Philip but did not truly believe in Christ. It was later, says Dunn, when they received the Holy Spirit, that they came "to genuine faith" (p. 67). This, I submit, is a quite inadequate reading of the text and context. "Believing Philip" surely means believing the Good News which Philip proclaimed; and undoubtedly Philip understood it that way, for he thereupon baptized the Samaritans. Would he have done this on the basis of a merely "intellectual assent"? Or was Philip perhaps misled? The question scarcely merits an answer. It is true that Simon the Magician also believed and was baptized by Philip (Acts 8:13) and later was called to repentance by Peter (Acts 8:20-21); but the text does not suggest that his earlier faith and baptism were not genuine (indeed, he asks Peter to "Pray for me to the Lord" [Acts 8:24].) The record in Acts further affirms the authenticity of the Samaritans' faith prior to their receiving the Holy Spirit in verse 14: "Now when the apostles at Jerusalem heard that Samaria had received the word of God. . . ." Receiving the word of God can hardly mean anything else than true and genuine faith (cf. Acts 11:1, where the same expression, "received the word of God," is used concerning the Caesareans' faith—the genuineness of which is beyond dispute). Thus, the apostles by no means (as is also sometimes suggested) came down to Samaria to make up for a defective faith. Rather did they come to believing and baptized people to minister to them the gift of the Holy Spirit.
[4]Neither the narrative about the Samaritans nor the Ephesians gives full details about the proclamation of Jesus' life, death, and resurrection. Neither states directly that through Jesus Christ there is forgiveness of sins. However, this is surely implied in the preaching of Christ by Philip and the testimony about Jesus by Paul. Luke, the author of Acts, quite often (as we have seen) does not include matters that are clearly implied and often have been detailed elsewhere.

critical and indispensable matter. It is not a belief directed to the Holy Spirit[5] but to Jesus Christ in whom is forgiveness of sins. So did the disciples at Pentecost believe, and likewise did Saul of Tarsus. The focus is Christ, who makes possible the gift of the Holy Spirit.[6]

We now turn, secondly, to the *dynamics* of that faith in Christ wherein the Holy Spirit is received. It is important to recognize at the outset that faith is a dynamic, moving reality. Though its object, Jesus Christ, is the fixed and focal point, faith may well be in process. It is not a static, once-for-all thing, but may develop or increase under the impact of Jesus Christ. Indeed, all who believe are called upon to "grow in the grace and knowledge of our Lord and Savior Jesus Christ" (2 Pet. 3:18), and thus faith may all the more be strengthened.[7]

This does not mean the first moment of faith lacks genuineness or significance. Quite the contrary, for initial faith directed to Jesus is the moment of realizing the marvel of forgiveness of sins and new life in His name. Hence, entrance upon the way of faith is far more important than anything that may happen thereafter. This cannot be overemphasized.

Now we may proceed to speak of faith in movement, faith in process. This may be a matter of a deepening of faith through further repentance and commitment wherein God's resources of grace are all the more experienced. This may also lead to a point of spiritual breakthrough into fuller Christian life and witness.

Such an understanding of the dynamics of faith is essential to

---

[5]It would be a mistake to say that faith has a second focus beyond Christ, namely, the Holy Spirit. Christian faith remains centered on Jesus Christ throughout. In Him is "every spiritual blessing" (Eph. 1:3), whether it be forgiveness of sins, the gift of the Holy Spirit or anything else. However, while Christian faith must always keep the focus on Christ it does also expect from Him the gift of the Holy Spirit. A failure to expect this is a less than Christ-centered faith.

[6]This whole matter of faith as the essential condition for receiving the Holy Spirit—and also for the quality of life that follows—is set forth well in *Catholic Pentecostals:* ". . . if there is any one thing which most strikingly characterizes Catholic pentecostals it is not tongues or singing or prayer groups; it is that *they came to seek a renewal in the Spirit in simple faith* [italics mine], and having received the answer to their prayer they begin to walk in a newness of faith. The people involved in the charismatic renewal are basically men and women of new, richer faith" (p. 144).

[7]Some of the Scriptures that depict faith as growing or increasing: Luke 17:5; 2 Cor. 10:15; Phil. 1:25; 2 Thess. 1:3.

proper consideration of the reception of the Holy Spirit. *There is a certain moment in faith—whether at the outset or somewhere along the way—when the Holy Spirit may be received.* This moment may or may not coincide with the moment of receiving forgiveness of sins. It may happen shortly thereafter or days, months, even years later. Whatever the case, faith in Jesus Christ is and remains the essential matter whenever the Holy Spirit is given.

Before going further, we may turn again to the record in the book of Acts. For herein is delineated in vivid manner the gift of the Holy Spirit in relation to faith.

Let us first reflect upon the narrative about the early disciples of Jesus. The gift of the Spirit to them on the Day of Pentecost was not at the commencement of their faith in Jesus. Some hundred and twenty of them are described as "brethren" (note the language of Acts 1:15-16)—brethren of one another through a relationship with Jesus Christ. It is they who await the promised gift of the Spirit. Of the hundred and twenty, many had been with Jesus since the beginning of His ministry, the apostles as well as others, and had passed through a variety of experiences. There was the original call to discipleship, months and years of fellowship with Jesus, then a forsaking of Him at the time of His crucifixion and death, and thereafter a turning again ("conversion")[8] to Jesus in His risen presence. At that time, according to the Fourth Gospel, the Holy Spirit was breathed into them (John 20:22), and some fifty days later, according to the account of Luke in Acts, the Holy Spirit was poured out.[9] Thus there was a period of some three or more years from the initial encounter to the day of the gift of the Spirit.

---

[8]One thinks of the words of Jesus to Peter just prior to the Crucifixion: "Simon, Simon, behold Satan demanded to have you, that he might sift you like wheat; but I have prayed for you that your faith may not fail: and when you have turned again, strengthen your brethren" (Luke 22:31-32).
[9]Whether the account in John 20:22 is to be understood as a preliminary or proleptic giving of the Spirit, with the full gift in Acts 2:4 or as a gift for another purpose (e.g. regeneration) than the gift at Pentecost (power for ministry) *or* as essentially identical with what Luke records (hence a "Johannine Pentecost") is not too important for our present consideration. Whatever position one may adopt on this matter, it is still apparent that there is a lengthy process of discipleship and faith.

How long had the first disciples been believers? This is not an easy question to answer. In one sense they had been believers for some time: they had long before given up everything to follow Jesus, had done mighty works in His name, including healing and casting out of demons, and seventy of them were told by Jesus not to rejoice in the latter "but rejoice that your names are written in heaven" (Luke 10:20). The statement of Jesus would suggest that their faith already was of eternal significance. According to the Fourth Gospel, Jesus told His disciples shortly before His death, "You are already made clean by the word which I have spoken to you" (John 15:3). This would suggest also that Jesus' presence and word had awakened such a response in the disciples that they had truly been made clean. Yet when it was a matter of Jesus' words about His coming resurrection, there seemed to be little faith, and it was only His risen presence that made their faith return. Their believing had taken on a deeper and more enduring quality—and this kind of believing began with the Resurrection.

Thus we may say that when the Pentecostal event occurred, it was to many who had long known Jesus, and, despite numerous ups and downs, their faith had continued to grow. However we may evaluate the quality of their faith, it is an obvious fact that the gift of the Spirit occurred to those on the way of faith, to those believing. Indeed, a later question of Peter to the apostles and brethren in Jerusalem concerning the recent gift of the Holy Spirit to the people at Caesarea clearly implies this: "If then God gave the same gift to them as he gave to us [believing][10]

[10]Here we do not follow the RSV which has "when we believed." The RSV reading would suggest that only when the disciples believed did they receive the gift of the Holy Spirit. However, the Greek word is *pisteusasin*, an aorist participle, which usually expresses action antecedent to the main verb, or, less frequently, simultaneous with it. If antecedent, the translation would be "having believed" or "after believing" (the New American Standard translation) or "who believed" (KJV); if simultaneous or coincident, the translation "when we believed" (RSV) would be more satisfactory. However, the participle could contain *both* ideas, and therefore the most adequate translation would be neither the RSV "when we believed" nor the KJV "who believed" but simply "believing." This would suggest that belief had been there for some time (antecedent aorist), but rather than its being simply a past fact, it was also a continuing reality (simultaneous aorist). In other words, *on the way of faith* the Holy Spirit was poured out. F.D. Bruner, in his *A Theology of the Holy Spirit*, quotes the RSV and adds, ". . . the apostles considered *Pentecost* to be . . . the date of their conversion" (p. 196). Unfortunately, Bruner does not go into the Greek text which makes for other possible, and more likely, interpretations.

in the Lord Jesus Christ, who was I that I could withstand God?" (Acts 11:17). On the way of faith, believing, they received the gift of the Holy Spirit.

It is to be added that the experience of the first disciples points in the direction of what is happening among many people in our time. The gift of the Spirit to those who for some time have been walking the way of faith is being repeated frequently today. Many who have long known Jesus and come to faith in Him are now receiving the Holy Spirit in fullness.[11] Thus in striking manner the original Christian experience is recurring.[12]

As we move on through various other narratives that contain reference to the reception of the Spirit, it is apparent that there are other parallels to the experience of receiving the Holy Spirit along the way of faith. In the first account after Pentecost of the Holy Spirit being given, namely to the Samaritans, this occurred some days after their first coming to faith in Christ. We have already noted how Philip proclaimed the gospel and many believed. However, despite their new-found faith, they had not yet received the Holy Spirit. Several days later—at least four or five days[13]—the apostles Peter and John came down from Jerusalem and "prayed for them that they might receive the Holy Spirit. . . . Then they laid their hands on them and they received the Holy Spirit" (Acts 8:15-17). So it was along the way of faith that the Samaritans experienced the outpouring of the

---

[11]It is sometimes said that it is improper to draw any parallel between the first disciples' experience of the Holy Spirit and Christian experience thereafter. For unlike later believers they could not have received the Holy Spirit until a later time because the Spirit was not given until Jesus left them. To answer: while it is true that their experience was necessarily spread over a period of time—a rather extended way of faith—this should not rule out the possibility that many after them will follow a like pattern. *Unlike* the original disciples, we may receive the Holy Spirit at the initiation of faith; *like* the first disciples there may be—and often is—an extended period of time.

[12]E.g., see the story of Russell Bixler, contemporary renewal leader, in *It Can Happen to Anybody* (Monroeville, PA: Whitaker Books, n.d.), especially Chapter IV, "The New Creation" and Chapter IX, "The Power Flows." Several years of walking the way of faith as a Church of the Brethren pastor separate the two experiences. Incidentally, Dwight L. Moody's experience of being "filled with the Holy Spirit" (supra, Chapter 4, fn. 16) occurred fifteen years after his conversion.

[13]Samaria was approximately a journey of two days from Jerusalem. So by the time the word about the Samaritans' faith had reached Jerusalem, the apostles had met and decided to send Peter and John, and Peter and John had arrived on the scene, the minimum would have been four or five days. Quite possibly it was a few days longer, perhaps a week. The exact number of days of course is not important; clearly there was an intervening time.

Holy Spirit.

The Samaritan story likewise has numerous parallels with the contemporary scene. Many, after coming to faith in Jesus Christ, have later had hands laid upon them and experienced the fullness of the Holy Spirit. And, as with the Samaritans, earnest prayer has often been the immediate background. Frequently, also, one person has been the evangelist (like Philip) to bring people to a commitment to Christ and others have been used by the Lord in ministering the Holy Spirit.[14] Thus the whole process has occurred over a period of time from initial faith to the reception of the Holy Spirit.

We turn next to the account of Saul of Tarsus in Acts 9:1-19. There is likewise a delay of several days—in this case, three— between the time Saul first encountered Jesus and the moment of his being filled with the Holy Spirit. As the narrative discloses, a voice from heaven says, "Saul, Saul, why do you persecute me?" and Saul thereupon inquires, "Who are you, Lord?" The reply is given, "I am Jesus whom you are per- secuting." After this encounter and the beginning of faith,[15] Saul fasts and prays for three days in Damascus before a man named Ananias comes to him, and "laying his hands on him, says, 'Brother Saul,[16] the Lord Jesus . . . has sent me that you may regain your sight and be filled with the Holy Spirit.'" Thus there is a period of time—though shorter than that of the Samaritans—between the inception of faith and the reception of

---

[14]An illustration of this is the case of Dr. Charles Meisgeier, university professor, whose testimony includes hearing the evangelist Billy Graham, at a Madison Square Garden meeting, whereupon "Christ became my Lord and Saviour in a real and existential way." Years later through the ministry of Rev. Dennis Bennett, Episcopal priest, Dr. Meisgeier received the fullness of the Holy Spirit. The result: "It has been a new life for us all. There is a tremendous fulfillment in being baptized in the Holy Spirit; the Christian life goes on from there and gets better and better." See *The Acts of the Holy Spirit Among the Presbyterians Today* (Los Angeles: Full Gospel Business Men's Fellowship International Publication, 1972), pp. 56-61.

[15]In a later parallel account (Acts 22:1-16) where Paul is rehearsing this event, he states that after Jesus had designated himself "I am Jesus. . .," Saul asks, "What shall I do, Lord?" This would suggest Saul has entered upon the way of faith, acknowledging Jesus as Lord. I realize it can be argued that Saul is simply saying "Lord" *(kurie)* in the sense of "Sir" or "Master," hence expressing little or no faith. However, the context, including the words from heaven, "I am Jesus," would seem to suggest more. If Christian faith begins in a personal encounter with the living Christ, Saul's experience was hardly less than that!

[16]Ananias's greeting of Saul as "brother" is another recognition that Saul is already on the way of faith before the filling with the Holy Spirit.

the Holy Spirit.

What is important to recognize for the Samaritans and Saul alike is that there are two critical moments in their experience— although there is some diversity in details[17]—and that it is the second moment in which they receive the Holy Spirit. This sequence of events is not unlike that of many today who have "believed" (Samaritans), have called Jesus "Lord" (Saul), but who do not receive the fullness of the Spirit until later. Also, various persons may perform different functions in relation to the total experience. There may be someone who is especially the channel for initial faith (as Philip, or the Lord Jesus himself), and another—or others—is the channel for the reception of the Spirit (as Peter, John and Ananias). There is much diversity in the way these moments on the way of faith occur.[18]

One further illustration of the reception of the Spirit occurring along the way of faith is that of the Ephesians in Acts 19:1-7. Paul encounters "some disciples" in Ephesus. He thereupon questions them, "Did you, [believing],[19] receive the Holy Spirit?" After the Ephesians express their ignorance concerning the Holy Spirit, Paul leads them step by step from "John's baptism," which they had experienced, into a faith in Christ accompanied by water baptism—"On hearing this [the word about Christ]

---

[17]Such as the fact that the Samaritans were baptized in water at the inception of faith and only received the Holy Spirit several days later, whereas Saul's water baptism did not occur until after his being filled with the Holy Spirit (see 9:17-18).

[18]For a variety of testimonies in the early stages of the Roman Catholic renewal (the late sixties, see *Catholic Pentecostals*, "Bearing Witness," pp. 58-106; also *Catholics and the Baptism in the Holy Spirit* (Los Angeles: FGBMFI, 1968). For Protestant testimonies see other publications of the Full Gospel Business Men's Fellowship International on Episcopalians, Baptists, Methodists, Lutherans, Presbyterians, etc.

[19]Again an instance of the aorist participle. The term here is *pisteusantes*, translated in KJV as "since you believed" (antecedent aorist), in RSV "when you believed" (coincident aorist). My preference again is simply "believing," which catches up both antecedence and coincidence as a continuing reality. What is important, however, is that, regardless of the way the aorist participle is translated, there is the obvious implication that one believing may not yet have received the Holy Spirit. Initial faith is not necessarily accompanied by the gift of the Spirit. Even if it be argued that these "disciples" were not yet believers in a fully Christian sense, since it turns out they are disciples of John, the question still points up the possibility of believing without yet receiving. However, the fact that Luke describes these Ephesians, when first encountered, as "disciples"—the term regularly used in Acts for Christian believers—could imply that the way of Christian faith had already been entered upon. (See article on πνεῦμα by E. Schweizer in *Theological Dictionary of the New Testament* where he says, "In 19:1-7, Luke is telling about Christians who have not yet experienced the outpouring of the Holy Spirit" [Vol. VI, p. 413].)

they were baptized in the name of the Lord Jesus." The final step follows: "And when Paul had laid his hands upon them, the Holy Spirit came on them; and they spoke with tongues and prophesied." Here is a sequence of events, or moments, in which persons move from a very limited faith to a specific faith affirmed in water baptism, to a laying on of hands for the gift of the Holy Spirit. The temporal span between the first two may have covered many years; the span between the second and third is quite brief. However viewed, there is a process of Christian faith involved, a series of nonidentical events, and once again the basic fact: the gift of the Holy Spirit occurring not at the moment of initial faith.[20]

In regard to what happened at Ephesus, it might be instructive also to turn to Ephesians 1:13, where it is quite possible that the apostle is rehearsing in similar words the event of their reception of the Holy Spirit. The wording is: "In him you also, who have heard the word of truth, the gospel of your salvation, and have believed[21] in him, were sealed with the promised Holy Spirit. . . ." Unmistakably the Spirit promised[22] is the same as that in Acts 2:39: ". . . the promise is to you and to your children" and the same received by the Ephesians in Acts 19:6. Further, the word "sealing," while not used as such in Acts, is contained in the idea of consecration, dedication, empowering[23] that operates all through the book. Accordingly, Acts 19 and Ephesians 1 seem to be parallel accounts, and—the point of particular relevance here—each exhibits a reception of the Spirit after faith has begun. The Ephesians in both accounts receive the promised Holy Spirit upon the way of faith.

On the contemporary scene there are numerous parallels to the Ephesian narrative in Acts 19. Many persons today have long lived in a situation of quite limited faith. Their faith may have had a little more focus on Jesus than that of the Ephesians

---

[20]Whether one identifies the initial faith with the first or second moment, the reception of the Spirit occurred thereafter (whether years later or in immediate succession). Schweizer—in looking back over the record in Acts—writes that "Days, and in exceptional cases even weeks and years may pass before endowment with the Spirit follows faith. . ." (op. cit., p. 412). Though I should prefer to say "follows initial faith," I believe Schweizer is undoubtedly correct in his basic statement.

[21]The same aorist participle pisteusantes as in Acts 19:2 above. KJV translates it "after that ye believed." It could also be translated simply as "believing." See previous fn. 19.

[22]See earlier discussion of the promise of the Spirit in Chapter 1, A. ("The Divine Promise").

[23]One of the uses of "seal" in the New Testament (see Chapter 4, supra, fn. 2 and 6).

(maybe not); there may have been a little more knowledge about the Holy Spirit (maybe not), and they may have been viewed as disciples, or Christians, in some sense—but it was all rather nebulous. Many in looking back freely recognize how limited and inadequate their earlier faith had been. Then, much like Paul with the Ephesians, someone (or perhaps more than one) came along and led them into a faith focused clearly on Jesus, perhaps also water baptism and then through additional ministry into the reception of the Holy Spirit.[24]

Now that we have noted a number of accounts in Acts that depict the gift of the Spirit as occurring along the way of faith, one stands out particularly, bearing evidence of the Holy Spirit being given at the moment of initial faith. Hereby reference is made to the account of the Gentiles at Caesarea (Acts 10 and 11:1-18). The Apostle Peter comes to the house of the God-fearing centurion Cornelius and preaches the good news of Jesus Christ, to the effect that "every one who believes in him receives forgiveness of sins through his name." And "while Peter was still saying this, the Holy Spirit fell on all who heard the word" (10:43-44). The Spirit was given coincidental with ("while") the preaching of faith in Jesus Christ. The first moment of faith in Christ was also the very moment of their receiving the Holy Spirit. Incidentally, the fact that the Holy Spirit was given is recognized later as undeniable evidence that the Caesareans had believed. For Peter, some days thereafter appearing before the apostles and brethren in Jerusalem, tells how the Holy Spirit "fell on them just as on us at the beginning." This was what convinced Peter's audience of the validity of the Gentiles' faith and salvation. At first "they were silenced. . ." but thereafter "they glorified God saying, 'Then to the Gentiles also God has granted repentance unto life' " (Acts 11:15-18).

The parallel to contemporary experience is unmistakable. Many persons attest that there was no separation whatever in time between their initial faith in Jesus Christ and their reception of the Holy Spirit. Unlike others for whom their basic Christian experience occurred over a period of time, they

---

[24]Again, see the testimonies in the books mentioned in fn. 18 supra. Many examples may be found. From the nebulous and limited to the clear and full is a transition that many are making in our time.

simply came into it all at once.[25] This does not mean there has not been growth and development since that first moment—for there has been—but the basis for all to occur later took place at the beginning.

In reflecting on what has been said, one thing may be vigorously affirmed: it is impossible to press the operation of the Holy Spirit into a mold; accordingly, it is the same with the shaping of basic Christian experience. Moreover, contemporary Christians with their testimonies to the variety of ways the Holy Spirit has been given clearly echo the witness of the church in its early formation. So it is that we find in the biblical record ample original testimony to what is again occurring in our time.[26]

---

[25]This is often the case for persons who have long been searching for reality—the "God-seekers" of the world—who upon hearing the gospel clearly for the first time and the call to a personal faith in Jesus Christ not only receive forgiveness of sins but also the empowering of the Holy Spirit. Often they have been hungering for reality in an almost desperate fashion. I think of many of the recent so-called "Jesus people," many of whom had been involved with drugs (representing an illusory search for reality). These young people had a total experience of turning to Christ and receiving the fullness of the Holy Spirit. As an example of this see Pat King, *The Jesus People are Coming* (Plainfield, NJ: Logos, 1971), the testimony of Michael Mates, "Now I'm Free," pp. 73-92. It was estimated that, at the peak of the "Jesus movement," over 90 percent of the persons involved were charismatic, not usually by virtue of a later charismatic experience, but they became such in the initial breakthrough of Christian faith. At that very moment they became "turned on" witnesses for Jesus in the power of the Spirit. In addition to the "Jesus people," there have been many other persons, either in the church or out of it, who have long had a yearning to get beyond form and ritual into a vital experience of faith. However, no matter how much they tried to find reality, emptiness somehow remained. Then—the gospel one day got through to them: a personal encounter with the living Jesus. As they experienced His reality. His forgiveness, His salvation, they also received His Spirit. The emptiness was filled, and forthwith they became fervent witnesses of the Good News.

[26]One sometimes hears it said that the book of Acts presents so much confusing, even inconsistent, data about the reception of the Holy Spirit, that the record is of dubious value for our contemporary situation. The truth of the matter, however, is that the variety of ways in which this is described gives firm basis and example for what is happening in our time.

CHAPTER SIX

MEANS

We turn now to a consideration of the gift of the Holy Spirit in relation to water baptism and the laying on of hands. Our concern at this point is the connection between these outward rites and the bestowal of the Spirit. How essential—or dispensable—are they? Is one or the other more closely associated with the gift of the Spirit?

It hardly needs to be said that this has been an area of significant differences in the history of the Church. This is evidenced by the fact, first, that both water baptism and the laying on (or imposition) of hands have been viewed as channels for the gift of the Holy Spirit. Some traditions have held the position that water baptism is sufficient: it is the means whereby the Holy Spirit is given. Accordingly, there is no call for laying on of hands in this situation. Others have held that the laying on of hands is the critical matter: without such, water baptism is incomplete, and there is no gift of the Holy Spirit. How are we to adjudicate between such critical differences?

That this is no small matter would seem undeniable. If the gift of the Holy Spirit is what we have been describing—a veritable outpouring of God's presence and power—and if this gift is vitally related to an outward rite, then the identity of that rite, the question of its essentiality, and its proper execution are critical matters. If, on the other hand, there is no vital connection between the gift of the Holy Spirit and an outward rite, this ought also to be clarified so that we be not burdened by unnecessary concerns. That there needs to be serious reflection in this area is apparent; we can scarcely afford to be uncertain or confused in so important a matter.

Once again we turn primarily to the book of Acts as the basic historical narrative depicting the gift of the Holy Spirit, and now consider its relationship to water baptism and the laying on of hands. There will be some reference also to the Gospels and the Epistles; however, as has been the case in other previous considerations, Acts must be primary because it is the only New Testament record depicting the interrelationship between the gift of the Spirit, the occurrence of water baptism and the laying on of hands.

Let us begin with reflection upon the relation of water baptism to the gift of the Holy Spirit. We are concerned of course with water baptism as a Christian rite—and only incidentally with "the baptism of John" (which is transitional in Acts to Christian baptism).[1] How does the rite of Christian baptism relate to the gift of the Spirit? By way of reply we shall set forth a number of declaratory statements and seek to demonstrate these in the five basic narratives having to do with the gift of the Holy Spirit.

However, before proceeding further, we find that water baptism, wherever described in Acts, is performed in the name of Christ only. There are four passages that mention His name in relation to baptism: Acts 2:38; 8:16; 10:48; and 19:5—with the slight variation between "the name of Jesus Christ" (2:38 and 10:48) and "the name of the Lord Jesus" (8:16 and 19:5).[2] What is important is the fact of water baptism in the name of Christ only[3] (not the variation in the name) and how this will relate to a proper understanding of its connection with the gift of the Holy Spirit.

Now we move on to various declaratory statements. First, water baptism[4] may *precede* the gift of the Holy Spirit. We begin by observing that Peter, following his Pentecostal sermon, asserts: "Repent, and be baptized every one of you in the name of Jesus Christ for the forgiveness of your sins; and you shall receive the gift of the Holy Spirit" (Acts 2:38). Water baptism obviously is depicted as preceding the gift of the Spirit. It is not altogether clear, however, whether a logical or chronological priority is envisioned. Peter's words—"and you shall receive the

---

[1]This will be noted hereafter especially in connection with Acts 19.

[2]Three prepositions are used: *epi* (Acts 2:38); *eis* (8:16 and 19:5), and *en* (10:48). They could be translated "upon," "into," and "in." For all three, "in the name" is the usual English translation. This seems proper, since the Greek words do not, I believe, intend a difference.

[3]The formula in Acts therefore is obviously divergent from the triune emphasis of Matthew 28:19. We shall return to this later.

[4]As we use the term "water baptism" from now on, we shall ordinarily be referring to baptism in the name of Christ.

gift of the Holy Spirit"—could mean either that the gift of the Spirit follows logically and therefore immediately upon water baptism, or that it may happen at some future time. Shortly after Peter's sermon, the Scripture reads: "So those who received his word were baptized, and there were added that day about three thousand souls" (2:41). Nothing is directly said about their receiving the Holy Spirit; however, that such followed directly upon water baptism seems evident in light of the ensuing account (2:42-47).[5]

Let us turn next to the Samaritan account where again water baptism is definitely shown to precede the gift of the Spirit. In this instance, however, it is clear that there is an intervening period of several days. The Samaritans "were baptized, both men and women" (Acts 8:12). Later, Peter and John "came down and prayed for them that they might receive the Holy Spirit; for it had not yet fallen on any of them, but they had only been baptized in the name of the Lord Jesus" (8:15-16). So prayer was offered and the laying on of hands was administered with the result that the Samaritans received the Holy Spirit. Hence, there is an unmistakable separation in time between water baptism and the reception of the Holy Spirit.

This passage is quite important in demonstrating that the reception of the Holy Spirit is not bound to the moment of water baptism. It is sometimes argued that there was a special reason for this in the case of the Samaritans, namely, that because of the longstanding prejudice between Jews and Samaritans, it was fitting that the gift of the Holy Spirit be delayed after baptism until representatives from Jerusalem (Peter and John) could come down, and by ministering the Holy Spirit to the Samaritans, demonstrate love and unity. The argument, however, is tenuous indeed, for if delay could happen here, why not in other circumstances?[6] Or even if it be agreed that the Jewish-

---

[5]These verses, depicting a community of people devoted to the apostles' teaching, fellowship, prayer, community, sharing and climactically "praising God and having favor with all the people," strongly suggest a participation in the gift of the Holy Spirit. (See Chapter 2, supra, especially on the note of praise.)

[6]Another reason sometimes given for the Samaritans not receiving the Holy Spirit until after their water baptism is that the gift of the Spirit requires apostolic ministry; Philip as an evangelist could not minister the Holy Spirit, so the apostles Peter and John must come down to fulfill that function. This line of reasoning, however, seems invalid both from the perspective of the immediate context which does not intimate that Peter and

Samaritan situation was maximally one of prejudice, thus calling for additional encouragement from Jerusalem, why not a visit by Peter and John simply to express fellowship and love? Why also the Holy Spirit? In any event the evidence of the text is unambiguous, namely, that regardless of what might later happen, the Samaritans did not receive the Holy Spirit when they were baptized; and this leaves open the possibility that such could happen in other instances.[7]

That there may be such a delay in many instances is found in the Catholic traditional practice of baptism and later confirmation (the latter sometimes called "the sacrament of the gift of the Holy Spirit" or "the Pentecostal sacrament"), and also in the teaching and experience of large numbers in the contemporary move of the Spirit. In the latter case there is abundant testimony to a reception of the Holy Spirit that frequently takes place some time later than baptism in water; and, indeed, rather than this being an exceptional thing, it quite often occurs.[8] Thus—in light of much tradition and experience—the Samaritan happening is a continuing reality.

One other account in Acts likewise specifically shows water baptism as preceding the gift of the Holy Spirit, namely, that of Paul and the Ephesians. We have noted that the Ephesians had earlier been baptized "into John's baptism," but they had not

John come vested with some special sacerdotal authority, and also in light of what happens later in Acts 9 when Ananias, who is a layman, ministers the Holy Spirit to Saul of Tarsus. (See below, under "laying on of hands," for more details.)

[7]F.D. Bruner, in his *A Theology of the Holy Spirit*, has the peculiar statement: "The Spirit is temporarily suspended from baptism here 'only' and precisely to teach the Church at its most prejudiced juncture, and in its strategic initial missionary move beyond Jerusalem, that *suspension cannot occur*" (italics: Bruner), p. 178. I should think that the passage teaches exactly the opposite: that *suspension may occur*. Bruner's interpretation is actually not based on the text but on a prior view (shown many times in his book) of the inseparability of water baptism and the gift of the Spirit.

[8]There is some variation here. Those in the more Protestant tradition of the movement do not hesitate to recognize a gift of the Holy Spirit after water baptism; they see it in the biblical record, and they claim to have experienced it. Those in the Catholic tradition (Roman and Anglo-) of the movement sometimes express the view that the Spirit is given in baptism or confirmation, and that the "Pentecostal experience" rather than being a reception of the Spirit is a "realization" or "actualization of that gift." See, e.g., *Catholic Pentecostals* which speaks of "an individual's or community's baptismal initiation," being "existentially renewed and actualized" (p. 147), and Leon Joseph Cardinal Suenens' *A New Pentecost?* listing of various expressions: "a release of the Spirit, a manifestation of baptism, a coming to life of the gift of the Spirit received at confirmation . . ." (p. 81).

received Christian baptism. So it is that after Paul's words the Ephesians "were baptized in the name of the Lord Jesus. And when Paul had laid his hands upon them, the Holy Spirit came on them . . ." (Acts 19:5-6). It is to be observed that, unlike the situation in Samaria, there are no several days' delay between the Ephesians' Christian baptism and their receiving the Holy Spirit. Still there is some chronological separation, however brief, between the rite of water baptism and the laying on of hands. Once again—as in the case of Peter's message to the Jerusalem multitude with baptism following, and as in the case of the Samaritans—the administration of baptism precedes the gift of the Holy Spirit.[9]

Second, water baptism may *follow* the gift of the Holy Spirit. On first hearing, this may seem a bit surprising in light of the aforementioned incidents, and especially in view of Peter's words at Pentecost which show an order of repentance, baptism in the name of Christ, and the reception of the Holy Spirit. However, it is apparent that the previous instances are by no means definitive, nor are Peter's words a prescription of the way it always happens. This we shall observe by turning to two other accounts.

The first of these is the narrative of Peter's ministry at Caesarea. As we have seen earlier, while Peter was still delivering his message, the Holy Spirit suddenly fell upon the centurion and those gathered together with him (Acts 10:44). Obviously there had been no water baptism of any kind. However, it is not disregarded, for shortly thereafter Peter declares: "Can any one forbid water for baptizing these people who have received the Holy Spirit just as we have?" And acting on his own declaration, Peter "commanded them to be baptized in the name of Jesus

---

[9]Reference might also be made to the account in Acts 8:28-39 of Philip and the Ethiopian eunuch. The eunuch comes to faith, is baptized by Philip, and ". . . when they came up out of the water, the Spirit of the Lord caught up Philip . . ." (8:39). According to some early manuscripts the text reads: "And when they came up out of the water, the Holy Spirit fell upon the eunuch and an angel of the Lord caught up Philip. . . ." The point of this reading is undoubtedly to emphasize that, as with the Samaritans, the eunuch's baptism was followed by the gift of the Holy Spirit. (See F.F. Bruce's statement to this effect in his commentary, *The Acts of the Apostles* [Grand Rapids: Eerdmans, 1951], p. 195.) Thus, in addition to the accounts in Acts that specify the gift of the Spirit to follow water baptism, such may be implied in Acts 8:39.

Christ" (10:47-48). Thus water baptism in this case unmistakably follows upon receiving the gift of the Holy Spirit.

The other incident concerns Ananias's ministry to Saul of Tarsus. Ananias lays hands on Saul that he might be filled with the Holy Spirit (Acts 9:17). The next verse reads: "And immediately something like scales fell from his eyes and he regained his sight. Then he rose and was baptized. . . ." Hence it is subsequent to Saul's receiving the Holy Spirit that he is baptized in water by Ananias.

What has been described about water baptism following the gift of the Holy Spirit is not at all unusual in our time. Many persons who have come to a living faith in Christ and the reception of the Holy Spirit have thereafter been baptized in water.[10] Often this stems from an intense desire to "go all the way with Christ," to participate corporally in His death and resurrection, to be wholly united to Him. Moreover, such baptism is seldom viewed as optional. Christ instituted it,[11] Peter commanded it (see above)—it belongs to Christian initiation and discipleship. So when one adds command to desire, if such persons have not before been baptized in water, it is quite likely to follow![12]

We may properly raise a question about the 120 who were filled with the Holy Spirit at Pentecost. What about their water baptism? This is not an easy question to answer. Though doubtless many[13] (like the later Ephesians) had participated in John's baptism, it is obvious they had not been baptized in Jesus' name

[10]Donald L. Gelpi, S.J. in his *Pentecostalism: A Theological Viewpoint* (New York: Paulist Press, 1971) suggests the case of a "Robert Z" who "a week before his sacramental baptism, while attending a prayer meeting . . . receives Spirit-baptism and immediately begins praying in tongues," p. 178. Probably Father Gelpi had witnessed this, since he refers to such as "concretely possible." However, the problem for Catholic theology is simply this: how does one relate such an experience to the traditional view that the Holy Spirit is received in baptism or confirmation? (In this case it does not help to speak of Spirit-baptism as the actualization of the gift of the Spirit received in the sacraments when there has been no sacramental participation!)
[11]According to Matt. 28:19.
[12]There are instances in the contemporary spiritual renewal of persons who received baptism as infants being baptized as adults. In some instances such adult baptism is sought because of a growing conviction of the invalidity of infant baptism; in other cases, adult baptism is viewed as not denying the validity of infant baptism, but as its fulfillment through personal, believing participation. Generally speaking, however, people in the renewal who have had prior baptism do not follow this pattern. I am referring, therefore, in the text above to those who have had no prior experience of baptism now becoming participants.
[13]Possibly all—but the Scriptures give no certain information.

before the event of Pentecost. Hence, the 120 would seem to fall into the same category as Saul of Tarsus and the Caesareans who without Christian baptism received the Holy Spirit. However, unlike in the narratives of Saul and the Caesareans, the Scriptures do not specify that after the 120 had been filled with the Spirit they were baptized in Jesus' name. Quite possibly they were so baptized, along with the 3000 later that day (Peter may have commanded it as he did later with the Caesareans), but there is no clear-cut statement to that effect. It may have been, on the other hand, because of their unique position as original disciples, who existentially were participants in Christ's death and resurrection (living through Good Friday and Easter) and recipients of His life-bestowing forgiveness, that they needed no further tangible rite. For in a certain sense, even more intensely than others after them, they had been baptized into Jesus' reality. In any event, whatever may be the right answer to the question of whether or not the original 120 later received water baptism in Jesus' name, they were similar to Saul of Tarsus and the Caesareans in that they received the Holy Spirit prior to any possible Christian water baptism.

Third—and following upon what has just been said—water baptism is *neither a precondition nor a channel* for the gift of the Holy Spirit.

It is surely clear by now that water baptism is not a precondition. The very fact, for example, that Saul of Tarsus and the Caesareans received the Holy Spirit before they were water baptized rules out the idea of any precondition. Hence Peter's words, "Repent, and be baptized . . . and you shall receive the gift of the Holy Spirit," cannot be viewed as a rule that water baptism must occur before the reception of the Spirit. His words, while pointing to what may be the usual pattern, do not establish water baptism as a precondition. Furthermore, if Peter's words were the rule, the rule had just been broken in his case! For as one of the 120 he had received the Holy Spirit with no prior water baptism in Jesus' name.

Many people in the spiritual renewal of our day bear testimony to receiving the gift of the Holy Spirit without a prior Christian baptism. Especially is this the case for those who, like the Caesareans, received the Holy Spirit at the very inception of faith. Everything happened so fast and powerfully that there was no opportunity for any ritual action!

The one precondition (as we have earlier noted) for receiving the Holy Spirit is faith: not faith and something else.[14] Baptism, for all its importance, cannot function as a precondition or prerequisite for the reception of the Holy Spirit.[15]

Now we need to add that neither is water baptism to be understood as a channel for the gift of the Holy Spirit. In none of the narratives in Acts is there representation of the Holy Spirit as being given through water baptism. Though there may be a close approximation of water baptism to the gift of the Spirit, there is no suggestion that such baptism is the medium or channel. Even less is there any picture of water baptism as conferring the gift of the Spirit. The Holy Spirit comes from the exalted Lord who himself confers the gift, and surely does not relegate such to a rite conducted by man.

Indeed, we should add, there is obviously no essential connection between water baptism and the gift of the Holy Spirit. It might be supposed that, though water baptism is not a precondition for the gift of the Holy Spirit, whenever such baptism occurs it is the outward form for the occurrence of the inward spiritual reality. From this perspective it is not so much that water baptism conveys or confers the gift of the Spirit as that the two are related as the outward to the inward; accordingly, water baptism and the gift of the Spirit, or Spirit baptism, make one united whole. According to this view, wherever there is water baptism there is also Spirit baptism: the visible action and the spiritual grace are essentially one.[16] However, to answer, we must emphasize strongly: there is *no essential connection* between water baptism and Spirit baptism,[17] no relation of one

---

[14]Not even the laying on of hands (to which we shall come shortly).

[15]Faith alone prepares the way. So Schweizer writes (in specific response to the Caesarean account as interpreted by Peter in Acts 15:8f): "Faith, not baptism, purifies for the reception of the Spirit . . ." (Article on πνεῦμα in *Theological Dictionary of the New Testament*, Vol. VI, p. 414.)

[16]In the words of F.D. Bruner: "Baptism and the reception of the Spirit are so synonymous as to be identical. Christian baptism is spiritual baptism" (*op. cit.*, p. 190). This view, fortunately, is not held by James Dunn who says, "Spirit-baptism and water-baptism remain antithetical . . ." (*op. cit.*, p. 227).

[17]E. Schweizer in his analysis of the Spirit in Acts writes that "the Spirit is not tied to

to the other as outward to inward. The reason: they are dealing with two closely related but nonetheless different spiritual realities. Water baptism is for another purpose than the reception of the Holy Spirit, and unless such is clearly seen there will be continuing confusion. We now turn to this matter.

Fourth, water baptism is connected with the *forgiveness of sins*. Here we arrive at the important point that water baptism is related primarily to the forgiveness of sins. To use the language of Peter at Pentecost: it is "for" the forgiveness of sins. "Repent and be baptized . . . in the name of Jesus Christ for the forgiveness of your sins. . . ." The climactic spiritual reality Peter attests to is the gift of the Spirit, but there is also the reality of forgiveness of sins which is first mentioned, and it is with this spiritual reality that water baptism is directly connected.

What then is the connection? We turn again to the statement of Peter in Acts 2:38 that baptism in Jesus' name is "for the forgiveness of your sins." The word *eis*, "for," could suggest "for the purpose of," "in order to obtain," thus requirement for forgiveness to be received. However, *eis* may also be translated "concerning," "with respect to," "with reference to," "with regard to,"[18] and thus designates baptism as having to do with forgiveness but not necessarily for the purpose of obtaining it. Either translation is possible, although the latter would seem more likely in that there is no suggestion elsewhere in Acts that water baptism of itself obtains forgiveness. The point then of Acts 2:38 is not to specify water baptism as a requirement for forgiveness of sins; for forgiveness of sins comes by faith not by baptism, but when baptism does occur it is specifically related to that forgiveness.

What then is the nature of the relationship? The answer would seem to be, first, that while water baptism does not of itself

---

baptism. Once He comes on men before baptism (10:44), once without it (2:1-4), once on a disciple who knew only John's baptism (18:25) . . ." (*op. cit.*, p. 414).

[18]For example, note the earlier use of *eis* in the same chapter, verse 25, where Peter prefaces a quotation from a Davidic psalm thus: "For David says concerning him [the Christ]. . . ." The word translated "concerning" (RSV and KJV) is *eis*. *eis* here clearly means "regarding," "in reference to," etc. For other similar use of *eis* cf. Rom 4:20 (*eis* translated as "concerning" RSV, "with respect to" NAS); Eph. 5:32 (*eis* translated as "concerning" KJV, "with reference to" NAS); and 1 Thess. 5:18 (*eis* translated as "concerning" in KJV).

obtain forgiveness—hence, is not required for that purpose—it does serve as a *means*. Forgiveness comes from faith in the exalted Lord; thus it is He who grants forgiveness; it can be obtained no other way. Nonetheless, the channel or means for this forgiveness to be received is water baptism. This doubtless was the case for the 3000 who responded affirmatively to Peter's message: "Repent, and be baptized, every one of you for the forgiveness of your sins. . . ." Being baptized, each one of them, was a visible, tangible expression of faith and repentance, an outward cleansing, through which forgiveness was mediated. Thus water baptism was the means of receiving the grace of forgiveness and new life.

It would be a mistake, however, to view this as baptismal regeneration in the sense that the water itself, or the act of baptism, brings about forgiveness and new birth. On a later occasion Peter says: "God exalted him at his right hand as Leader and Savior, to give repentance to Israel and forgiveness of sins" (Acts 5:31). Here though Peter again (as in Acts 2:38) refers to repentance and forgiveness, there is no mention of water baptism but only of the exalted Lord who gives both repentance and forgiveness, and therefore new birth. Hence, when—as in Acts 2:38—water baptism is specified, it is obvious that such a rite does not, and cannot, bring about forgiveness and regeneration. But—and this is important—whenever water baptism is administered in the context of genuine faith and repentance, that baptism does serve as the medium for forgiveness to be received.

A second answer to the matter of the relationship of water baptism to forgiveness is that it serves as a *sign* and *seal*. On the one hand, water baptism is a vivid portrayal of the cleansing that forgiveness brings about, and signifies becoming a new creation. It is a public demonstration of the totality of the divine forgiveness[19] and the complete cleansing and renewal that Christ accomplishes. Such baptism, since it is in Christ's name, testifies that in and with Him there is death and burial of the

---

[19]Water baptism as immersion—the whole body covered—best symbolizes this. However, the pouring of water over the person may likewise represent this totality. Sprinkling (in accordance with Ezek. 36:25, "I will sprinkle clean water upon you, and you shall be clean from all your uncleannesses . . .") is a third possibility.

self and resurrection into newness of life.[20] Forgiveness is the remission of sins—and remission is nothing less than a release from all that is past and the beginning of the wholly new. Water baptism thus is peculiarly the sign of the forgiveness of sins.

On the other hand, water baptism functions as a seal of faith and forgiveness. It is a tangible impression and certification of the reality of the remission of sins. In the waters of baptism there is "brought home" to a person the wonder of God's total cleansing: the spiritual reality of complete forgiveness being mediated and confirmed in the totality of the baptismal experience. In the combination of the divine gift and the corporal action there is a sealing of the two: what is received in faith is confirmed in the waters of baptism. One who is so baptized in faith is a marked person—cleansed, forgiven, made new in Jesus Christ.[21]

Now we return to our original point, namely, that water baptism is directly connected with the forgiveness of sins. The specific nature of that relationship (which we have just been discussing) is less important for our concerns than the fact of the connection. The reason for emphasizing this point is that frequently this connection is not seen and water baptism is mistakenly viewed as having directly to do with the gift of the Holy Spirit. It is quite important to keep this matter clear, or there will be continuing confusion in this vital area.

Before leaving the discussion of water baptism it is important to add that though such baptism is not directly connected with the gift of the Holy Spirit this does not mean that there is no relationship. On the contrary, where there is faith and forgiveness mediated through water baptism, the Holy Spirit is indubitably at work. It is the Holy Spirit who empowers the

---

[20]E.g., see Rom. 6:4—"We were buried . . . with him by baptism into death, so that as Christ was raised from the dead . . . we too might walk in newness of life." Cf. Col. 2:12 and Gal. 3:27. Water baptism by immersion most vividly demonstrates burial and resurrection.

[21]This matter of baptism as sign and seal relates to what Paul says, in Rom. 4:11, concerning how Abraham "received circumcision as a sign or seal (*sēmeion elaben peritomēs sphragida*) of the righteousness which he had by faith while he was still uncircumcised." Water baptism is clearly the New Testament parallel, and thus no more than circumcision brings about righteousness or forgiveness, but is a sign and seal of it.

word of witness, convicts of sin, thus bringing about repentance. Here then by the Holy Spirit is the origin of faith that leads to the forgiveness of sins and baptism in the name of Christ. All of this is apparent, for example, in Acts 2:22-38 where the outpoured Spirit is the agent in each of these matters. Thus the Holy Spirit is very much involved in the whole process of salvation. Since this process may include water baptism, it is the Holy Spirit who gives spiritual significance to the act of baptism (otherwise it is nothing but an empty rite). It is clear then that water baptism is closely connected with the activity of the Holy Spirit.

However—and here is the critical matter—this just-described activity of the Holy Spirit is by no means the gift of the Holy Spirit. The gift ordinarily follows upon forgiveness and baptism, even as a promise attached thereto: "Repent, and be baptized every one of you in the name of Jesus Christ for the forgiveness of your sins; and you shall receive the gift of the Holy Spirit. For the promise is to you and to your children and to all that are far off, every one whom the Lord our God calls to him" (Acts 2:38-39). The gift does not have to do with forgiveness, but with what is promised to those who repent and are baptized for forgiveness.[22] It is a promise to all whom God calls to himself—such calling implemented through the working of the Holy Spirit—that they will receive the gift of the Holy Spirit.

Another matter to discuss briefly concerns the formula for water baptism as set forth in Matthew 28:19 being different from that set forth in the book of Acts. We earlier have observed that water baptism is invariably depicted in Acts as being in the name of Jesus only, but we did not actually deal with the fact that in Matthew the formula is a triune one:[23] "Go therefore and make disciples of all nations, baptizing them in the name of the Father and of the Son and of the Holy Spirit. . . ."

Though there is no simple solution to the difference in formula, a few comments relevant to our concerns may be made: first,

---

[22]As earlier noted, water baptism is not so integral a part of forgiveness that it may not occur later. Particularly recall the account of the Caesareans in Acts 10:43-48. However, ordinarily the sequence is that of Acts 2:38-39.

[23]Mention was made of this formula in footnote 3 above, but there was no elaboration of its significance.

the longer Matthean statement suggests that water baptism is entrance into[24] a new relationship to God as Father, Son and Holy Spirit. Second, the shorter Lukan formula (in Acts) specifies that at the heart of this relationship is the forgiveness of sins which comes in the name of Jesus Christ (the Son). Third, since in Jesus is "the fulness of the Godhead,"[25] baptism in His name only (as in Acts) is actually in relation to the fullness of the divine reality: it is also, by implication, in the name of the Father and Holy Spirit. Thus there is no essential difference between the Matthean and Lukan formulas: the former highlights the fullness of the relationship into which one enters at baptism, the latter specifies the purpose of that baptism.

It might also be suggested that the words about baptism in Matthew which include reference to the Holy Spirit—"in the name . . . of the Holy Spirit"—emphasize that Christian initiation is also entrance into the sphere of the Holy Spirit's reality and activity. At the heart of such initiation is the forgiveness of sins (to which baptism in the name of Jesus, or the Son, points), but at the same time it is the beginning of a new relationship to the Holy Spirit (to which baptism in the name of the Holy Spirit points).[26] By this is meant not only that the Holy Spirit is active in bringing about forgiveness—as we have noted—but that henceforward life is to be lived in the sphere of the Spirit.[27] Though this is not identical with the gift of the Holy Spirit, it may be preparation for it, and even a kind of invocation for that gift to be received.

---

[24]The Greek word for "in" ("baptizing them in . . .") is *eis* which though it may simply mean "in" (see footnote 2) may also be translated "into." As we have earlier noted, *eis* may also signify "with reference to," hence "in relation to."

[25]For in him the whole fulness of deity [*to plērōma tēs theoētos*—"the fulness of the Godhead" KJV] dwells bodily" (Col. 2:9).

[26]The same thing is true about the Father—a new relationship to him: by adoption one becomes a son of God and is able to address God as "Father" (cf. Rom. 8:15; Gal. 4:5-6).

[27]In my book, *The Pentecostal Reality* (Plainfield, NJ: Logos, 1972), chapter 6, "The Holy Trinity," I wrote: "The purpose of that part of the Great Commission, 'Go therefore . . . baptizing' is not to make learners out of people in regard to God, but to introduce them into life lived in the reality of God as Father, Son, and Holy Spirit" (p. 102). On the matter of the Holy Spirit, later words are: "This means life claimed by God through Jesus Christ in a total kind of way, the Spirit of the living God probing the depths of the conscious and the unconscious, releasing . . . new powers to praise God, to witness compellingly in His name, to do mighty works that only He can do. Do we know this?" (p. 107).

We turn now to a consideration of the relationship between the laying on of hands and the gift of the Holy Spirit. In coming to this matter we will again be reflecting primarily upon the five basic passages in Acts. What part does the laying on of hands play in the reception of the Holy Spirit?[28]

It is apparent, first of all, that the Holy Spirit may be given *without* the laying on of hands. Again reviewing the Acts narratives, we observe that in two of five cases, namely, in regard to the gift of the Spirit at Jerusalem and at the centurion household in Caesarea, there is no laying on of hands.

Concerning the Jerusalem narrative two observations may be made: first, it is obvious that there could have been no laying on hands on the 120; as the first disciples they must receive the Holy Spirit before ministering to anyone else. Second, it seems likely that though the 3000 later that day are baptized, they do not receive the laying on of hands. It will be recalled that Peter said: "Repent and be baptized . . . and you shall receive the gift of the Holy Spirit" (Acts 2:38); but there is no mention of imposition of hands for this gift to be received. Indeed, it is quite probable that Peter, having just experienced the bestowal of the Spirit as a sovereign, unmediated action by the exalted Lord, expected all to receive the gift the same way the 120 had. However, whatever his expectation, it would seem that the 3000 also received without the laying on of hands.

In the Caesarean situation it all happened so fast—"While Peter was still saying this [i.e., still preaching his message], the Holy Spirit fell on all who heard the word" (Acts 10:44)—that there was no time for hands if anybody had been so minded! Incidentally, Peter this time might have expected to lay on hands because of the intervening incident when he and John had laid hands on the Samaritans for the reception of the Holy Spirit (Acts 8:14-17). However, as in Jerusalem, God sovereignly moves and pours out His Holy Spirit upon all who hear.

What we have been describing is by no means an uncommon occurrence in the contemporary spiritual renewal. The Holy

---

[28]There are other instances in Acts of the imposition of hands which are not directly concerned with the gift of the Holy Spirit: Acts 6:6—the dedication of seven "deacons"; 13:3—the commissioning of Barnabas and Saul; and 28:8—the healing of Publius' father. While such instances of the laying on of hands are not for the gift of the Spirit, they obviously represent Spirit-inspired activities.

Spirit is frequently received with no human mediation of any kind. This may happen at the end of a period of time as at Jerusalem or with the suddenness of a Caesarea, but in neither case has there been the imposition of hands. This extraordinary, unmediated event is for many a source of continuing amazement and wonder.[29]

It is apparent then—from the biblical record and contemporary experience—that the laying on of hands is not essential for the Holy Spirit to be received. Moreover, there is no suggestion in Acts that, following such a reception, hands are later placed as a kind of confirmation of what has already happened. Any idea of hands as being necessary or confirmatory is ruled out by the evidence.

Perhaps these things are most important to emphasize in relation to churchly traditions that variously seek to canalize the gift of the Holy Spirit. There are those who hold that the Holy Spirit may *only* be received through the laying on of hands;[30] thus without personal ministry the Holy Spirit may not be given. Over against such a binding of the Holy Spirit to an outward action we need to stress the sovereignty of the Holy Spirit to move as He wills.

Second, the Holy Spirit may be given *with* the laying on of hands. Returning to the Acts record, we observe that in three of the five accounts of the Holy Spirit being received, this occurred in connection with the laying on of hands. Peter and John, ministering to the Samaritans, "laid their hands on them and they received the Holy Spirit"[31] (Acts 8:17). At Damascus, Ananias, ministering to Saul, ". . . laying his hands on him he

---

[29]The earliest testimonies in *Catholic Pentecostals*, "Bearing Witness," pp. 24-37, of students who were baptized in the Holy Spirit at the "Duquesne weekend" especially depict an unmediated happening. One participant testifies: "There were three other students with me when all of a sudden I became filled with the Holy Spirit and realized that 'God is real' . . . . The professors then laid hands on some of the students, but most of us received the 'baptism in the Spirit' while kneeling before the blessed sacrament in prayer" (pp. 34-35). *The Acts of the Holy Spirit* [among Presbyterians, Baptists, Methodists, etc.] contains a large number of testimonies of the Holy Spirit being given without the laying on of hands.

[30]Or, as we have noted, through water baptism. Sometimes the view is entertained that there may be *two* gifts of the Holy Spirit: one at water baptism and the other with the imposition of hands.

[31]Literally, they "were laying [*epetithesan*—imperfect tense] their hands on them and they were receiving [*elambanon*—also imperfect] the Holy Spirit." The Greek tense suggests an action over a period of time, and possibly that the Samaritans one by one were receiving the Holy Spirit.

said, 'Brother Saul, the Lord Jesus who appeared to you on the road by which you came, has sent me that you may regain your sight and be filled with the Holy Spirit' " (9:17). And Paul, ministering to the Ephesians, when he "had laid his hands upon them, the Holy Spirit came on them . . ." (19:6). There is obviously a close connection between the laying on of hands and the gift of the Holy Spirit.

It is apparent once again that water baptism is not placed in an immediate conjunction with the gift of the Holy Spirit. Water baptism, as earlier mentioned, is related to forgiveness of sins, whereas laying on of hands is connected with the gift of the Holy Spirit. The symbolism is unmistakable: water baptism vividly portrays the cleansing of sin in forgiveness, the laying on of hands the external bestowal of the Spirit. Each of the outward acts is congruent with the spiritual reality to be received.

Looking more closely in the Acts narrative at this conjunction of the Holy Spirit and the imposition of hands, we observe that the Holy Spirit may be given *through* the laying on of hands. Thus it is not only a temporal conjunction, so that the gift of the Holy Spirit coincides with, or follows immediately upon, the laying on of hands; but also an instrumental conjunction, namely, that the imposition of hands may serve as the channel or means for the gift of the Spirit. Just following the words quoted above about the Samaritans (in Acts 8:17), the text reads: "Now when Simon saw that the Spirit was given through the laying on of the apostles' hands. . . ."[32] The word "through" (*dia*) specifies the instrumentality of hands in the reception of the gift of the Holy Spirit. The laying on of hands is thus the means of grace whereby the Holy Spirit may be received.

The laying on of hands for the gift of the Holy Spirit has continued variously in the history of the Church. The practice belongs particularly to the Western tradition of Christianity, but with diverse understanding of what is conveyed in the gift. Sometimes it is assumed that through the laying on of hands there is the completing or perfecting of what was given earlier in water baptism; or, again, it is held that water baptism needs

---

[32]The text continues with the recitation of Simon the magician's vain and sordid attempt to buy the power to confer the gift of the Spirit through his own hands. However, despite his perfidy, there is no question in the text that Simon correctly perceived it to be through the laying on of Peter and John's hands that the Holy Spirit was given.

no completion or perfection, so that what happens through the imposition of hands is rather a confirming or strengthening of the person for the Christian walk. However, there is seldom in the traditional church any expectation that through the laying on of hands an extraordinary spiritual event will take place, namely, the gift of the Spirit as the veritable outpouring of God's presence and power.

Here, again, is where the contemporary spiritual renewal is recapturing the biblical witness. Through the laying on of hands, people are receiving the gift of the Holy Spirit, not in the sense of completion or perfection of confirmation (though it may include elements of both), but in the sense of a divine visitation so overwhelming as to release extraordinary praise and channels of powerful ministry. There is the exciting expectation that when hands are laid on a person, the Holy Spirit himself will be given.[33]

Here two points need emphasis: first, as we have already observed, there is no necessity for hands to be laid on persons for them to receive the Holy Spirit. The exalted Lord may dispense with all ordinary means and sovereignly pour forth the Holy Spirit. Second, though the Holy Spirit may also be given through the laying on of hands, it would be a mistake to assume that this happens invariably, i.e. by virtue of the objective action.[34] We

---

[33]See, for example, the second set of testimonies in *Catholic Pentecostals*, "Bearing Witness," pp. 58-106, having to do with Notre Dame. Most cases of baptism in the Spirit occurred through the laying on of hands. (It might be suggested that Duquesne was more like the first unmediated biblical outpourings on Jews and Gentiles at Jerusalem and Caesarea, Notre Dame more like secondary outpourings upon Samaria and Ephesus.) Incidentally, I think Father Gelpi is on the right track in not seeking to relate Spirit-baptism to either water baptism or confirmation (as some Catholic theologians do): ". . . Spirit baptism is *not* a sacrament . . ." (*Pentecostalism: A Theological Viewpoint*, p. 182). In his view the laying on of hands for Spirit baptism is not to activate something already given in a sacrament but is a prayer for "full docility to the Spirit of Christ" (p. 183).

[34]E.g., the traditional Roman Catholic view of sacraments (baptism, confirmation) as being efficacious "*ex opere operato*"—"by the work performed." Father Kilian McDonnell, while holding that "the fullness of the Spirit is given during the celebration of initiation," speaks of "the scholastic doctrine of *ex opere operantis* [wherein] we receive in the measure of our openness." Thus, though there is an objective—in that sense invariable—gift of the Spirit in "the celebration of initiation," there is no receiving without subjective appropriation. (This quotation may be found in an article entitled, "The Distinguishing Characteristics of the Charismatic-Pentecostal Spirituality" in the magazine *One in Christ*, 1974, Vol. X, No. 2, pp. 117-18.) Despite my appreciation of Father McDonnell's attempt to relate the reception of the Spirit to sacramental rites, I think it is too limited a view. For while *ex opere operantis* is surely an important concept

have earlier commented that faith—believing—is the essential element in the reception of the Holy Spirit; thus in all the biblical incidents of the laying on of hands it is upon believers that hands are laid. For only those who believe in Jesus Christ may receive from Him the blessed gift of the Holy Spirit.

What then is the importance of the laying on of hands? If, on the one side, there is no necessity, and if, on the other, there is no guarantee, why not dispense with such? The answer would seem clear: the laying on of hands is a divinely instituted means of *enabling* persons to receive the gift of the Holy Spirit. Hands signify contact, community, sharing—a human channel for the divine gift; the laying on of hands represents, as seen earlier, the coming of the Holy Spirit upon someone.[35] Thus, though a person may receive the gift of the Holy Spirit without human mediation, the imposition of hands may greatly facilitate this reception.

Third, the laying on of hands for the gift of the Holy Spirit is *not limited* to the apostles. As we have noted, the apostles Peter and John do minister the Spirit to the Samaritans and the Apostle Paul does the same for the Ephesians. However, it is a Christian brother, Ananias, with no claim to apostolic authority,[36] who is the minister of the Holy Spirit to Saul of Tarsus. Thus, it would be a mistake to interpret the words of Acts 8:18—". . . the Spirit was given through the laying on of the apostles' [Peter and John's] hands . . ."—as the only way it could happen. Since Ananias, a lay brother, could minister the Holy Spirit to Saul, there is no inherent reason that Philip, the deacon-evangelist, could not have done the same for the Samaritans.[37]

---

in the matter of sacramental appropriation, it is inadequate in comprehending the subjective side of "baptism in the Holy Spirit." For since there is no guarantee that "the fullness of the Spirit" is given objectively by sacramental action (whether of baptism or confirmation) *ex opere operato*, there may be nothing to receive *ex opere operantis*.

[35]Father Edward O'Connor in his book, *The Pentecostal Movement in the Catholic Church* (Notre Dame: Ave Maria Press, 1971) writes: ". . . the gesture [of laying on of hands] does symbolize graphically the fact that God's grace is often mediated to a person through others, and especially through the community. God seems to bless the faith from which this prayerful gesture proceeds; again and again people find that they have been helped in a powerful and manifest way by it . . . the baptism in the Spirit is usually received thus" (p. 117).

[36]Ananias is simply described in Acts 9 as "a disciple at Damascus" (v. 10).

[37]It is interesting that when Philip later proclaims the gospel to the Ethiopian eunuch,

A few words might be added about the ministry of Ananias to Saul. Though little is said about him, a few things stand out: first, he was a man of faith and prayer, the Lord speaking to him in a vision: "The Lord said to him in a vision, 'Ananias.' And he said, 'Here I am, Lord' " (9:10). Second, he was a man of obedience, for though, because of Saul's evil reputation, he first hesitated at the command of Christ—"Rise and go" (9:11)—he nonetheless went. Third, Ananias, as later described by Paul, was "a devout man according to the law, well spoken of by all . . ." (22:12), hence a man of strong character and perhaps peculiarly prepared through his devotion to the law to minister to Saul the Pharisee. Thus, it may be suggested, a combination of factors made Ananias an effective minister of the Holy Spirit, and particularly suited to exercise the role of ministering to Saul's need.

It would seem apparent that the basic qualification for the laying on of hands is not apostolic office but other more important matters. And so it continues into our own day and generation. Countless numbers of people are receiving the gift of the Holy Spirit through the ministry of lay people. To be sure, many "official" clergy are likewise ministering the Holy Spirit with great effectiveness.[38] However, what really counts is not office (not even "apostolic succession") but attributes such as faithfulness, prayer, readiness, obedience, devoutness and boldness. The ministering of the Spirit, including the laying on of hands, is happening through such Christian people everywhere. Indeed, this ministry belongs to the whole people of God.

---

and baptizes him (Acts 8:38), the next words according to the Western text (as we earlier noted) are: "And when they came up out of the water, the Spirit of the Lord fell upon the eunuch. . . ." Though this is likely a later textual addition, it does reflect some early church understanding that Philip was by no means dependent on apostolic help for the Holy Spirit to be given.

[38]In my book, *The Era of the Spirit*, I sought to summarize the laying on of hands thus: ". . . wherever this laying on of hands occurs it is not, as such, a sacramental action. It is, rather, the simple ministry by one or more persons who themselves are channels of the Holy Spirit to others not yet so blessed. The 'ministers' may be clergy or laity; it makes no difference. . . . Obviously God is doing a mighty work today bound neither by office nor by rank" (p. 64).

CHAPTER SEVEN

CONTEXT

The matter before us next is that of the context in which the Holy Spirit is given. Already we have emphasized that the gift of the Holy Spirit comes to those who believe in Jesus Christ; thus faith is the only requirement. Hence we are not now speaking of additional requirements, but of the context or situation in which the gift is received. We have earlier seen that the gift of the Holy Spirit frequently occurs along the way of faith. Now we note the context, even atmosphere, wherein this takes place.

The primary thing that must be stressed is *God's sovereign disposition*. The divine context of God's will and intention is altogether basic. From within the pattern of God's purpose, whereby He works all things according to the counsel of His will, God gives His Holy Spirit. Thus whatever may be and must be said on the human side about the situation, context, and atmosphere is altogether secondary to God's sovereign action. In this sense, God gives when He wills, not according to the human condition but according to His overall design and purpose. Hence, there is a continuing mystery and, humanly speaking, unpredictability about the giving of the Holy Spirit.

This was surely true of the first Pentecost in Jerusalem. God had long purposed (and promised) the outpouring of His Spirit, and when the divinely planned time had arrived, the Holy Spirit was given. The opening words of Acts 2:1 suggest this: "When the day of Pentecost had come . . . ," or, better, "had been fulfilled. . . ."[1] So when the day was fulfilled, the Holy Spirit was given. This was God's timetable—not man's. It had basically to do with God's overarching plan in salvation history. It was an event of "the last days" (Acts 2:17) according to the divine promise.

---

[1] The verb is *sumplērousthai*—"to be fulfilled." According to the *Theological Dictionary of the New Testament* this means (in Acts 2:1) "fulfilled according to God's plan . . . the verb itself points to the fulfillment of God's saving will in the event which takes place" (Vol. VI, p. 308). The KJV is closer than RSV (and many other versions) in translating *sumplērousthai* as "was fully come."

Likewise, it is important to emphasize that the movements of the Holy Spirit throughout history to the present day are grounded in the sovereign purpose of God.[2] The fact that in our present century there has been a crescendo of the Spirit's outpouring, and that the movement has now become worldwide, points basically to the divine intention. God is doing it again—and with such a universality ("upon all flesh") that we may surmise that "the last days" are being fulfilled, and history is reaching its consummation. However that may be, the critical point to score is the divine sovereignty.

All of this needs first to be emphasized—the divine context—lest we too quickly come to the human situation. *Primarily* it is not a matter of our human concern but God's concern. Like the original disciples who participated in the coming of God's Spirit because it was God's time, so do we participate in our own day. We are privileged to be alive in what may be the climactic outpouring of the Spirit at the end of the age. Our concern is not unimportant, even our readiness to participate in what God is doing, but the basic matter again is God's sovereign purpose.[3]

Further, since it is a matter of the *gift* of the Holy Spirit, there is nothing man can do to earn it. By definition a gift is freely bestowed: it cannot be worked for or bought. It would be a serious mistake to think that while forgiveness is by grace, the gift of the Holy Spirit is by works. Here Paul's rhetorical questions are most apropos: "Did you receive the Spirit by works of

---

[2]I have sought to delineate some of these movements in my book, *The Pentecostal Reality*, chapter 3, "A New Era in History."

[3]In a booklet entitled *Theological and Pastoral Orientations on the Catholic Charismatic Renewal* (Notre Dame: Word of Life, 1974) prepared at Malines, Belgium, by an international team of Catholic theologians and lay leaders, there is a section entitled "The Spirit is Sovereign and Free." It includes these words: "Alongside the declaration that subjective dispositions affect what one gives and receives [the section before had dealt with such 'dispositions'] is a companion declaration that in no ultimate sense is the Spirit of God radically dependent on the subjective dispositions of communities or individuals. . . . The Spirit is sovereign and free. He blows when, where, and how he wills. . . . The Spirit has and retains the initiative at every moment of the community's life" (p. 19). Ralph Martin, one of the lay leaders at Malines, powerfully set forth God's action in his book, *Fire on the Earth* (Ann Arbor, MI: Word of Life, 1975), subtitled "What God is Doing in the World Today." He writes: ". . . God is moving now, today, to rekindle that fire and fan it to the mighty blaze he desires to see. He is acting now, across the world, to turn the hearts of people back to him, to heal the wounds of division, to baptize with the Spirit and with fire. He intends to restore the full vitality of his people and resurrect the full power of the body of Christ. He is casting down his fire anew. . ." (pp. 5-6).

the law, or by hearing with faith? . . . Does he who supplies the Spirit to you and works miracles among you do so by works of law, or by hearing with faith?" (Gal. 3:2, 5). On the matter of being bought, the words of Peter to Simon the magician—who offered money for the power to confer the Holy Spirit—are vividly relevant: "Your silver perish with you, because you thought you could obtain the gift of God with money!" (Acts 8:20). The gift of the Holy Spirit cannot be earned no matter how great the effort, nor can it be purchased no matter how large the amount.

Having said these various things about the divine sovereignty and the Holy Spirit as a gift, we are ready to move on to consider further the human context or situation. As we have earlier noted on the human side, it is through faith that the Holy Spirit is received. Hence, however true it is that God sovereignly grants His Holy Spirit, it is to those believing in Jesus Christ—those upon the way of faith.[4] Thus as we now move on to observe the context in which the Spirit is given, we continue to stand within the sphere of faith. We do not add one iota to faith—as if it were faith plus something else. Rather are we now dealing with various expressions *within* faith—constituents of faith, in a sense—so that the context is not extraneous to faith but its vital demonstration.

We may properly begin with the matter of *obedience*. The Holy Spirit is given within the context of obedience—to those who obey God's command. In this regard one verse in the book of Acts stands out: "And we are witnesses to these things, and so is the Holy Spirit whom God has given to those who obey him"[5] (5:32). This is obedience occurring within the area of faith: the obedience which suffuses the atmosphere surrounding those

---

[4]Refer back to Chapter 5 for our earlier elaboration of this matter.

[5]Literally, "the Holy Spirit whom God gave to the ones obeying him" (*to pneuma to hagion ho edōken ho theos tois peitharchousin autō*). F.D. Bruner errs in saying that "the obedience spoken of in Acts 5:32 rather than being a condition is the result of the gift of the Holy Spirit" (*op. cit.*, p. 172). There is no suggestion here of obedience as a result; it is rather that God gives to those obeying. E. Schweizer is correct in writing that "obedience must . . . precede the reception of the Spirit according to [Acts] 5:32" (article on πνεῦμα, *Theological Dictionary of the New Testament*, Vol. VI, p. 412). Also see John Rea, *The Layman's Commentary on the Holy Spirit* (Plainfield, NJ: Logos, rev. ed., 1974), pp. 74-78, entitled "Acts 5:32—Obedience and the Gift of the Holy Spirit."

who become recipients of the gift of the Holy Spirit. It is, indeed, the obedience of faith.[6] God grants His Spirit to those who in faith obey His command.

The quotation above, from Acts 5:32, is taken from Peter's words before the Jewish council. He speaks for all the apostles (as the passage shows), and accordingly refers to their obedience wherein the Holy Spirit was given. This then leads us back to the situation prior to Pentecost, and to the important matter of the nature of their obedience. The book of Acts begins with the words: "In the first book, O Theophilus, I have dealt with all that Jesus began to do and teach, until the day when he was taken up, after he had given commandment[s][7] through the Holy Spirit to the apostles whom he had chosen" (1:1-2). Thus as men of faith they are under obedience to Christ's commands as transmitted through the Holy Spirit.[8] The apostles accordingly give themselves to obedience—as men under orders. Thereafter specifically comes the commandment: ". . . he charged them not to depart from Jerusalem,[9] but to wait for the promise of the Father [the gift of the Holy Spirit]" (1:4). Then what follows, over a period of ten days, is the obedient act of waiting for the fulfillment of the promise. As men under orders—and with others joining them until the number comes to be about 120 (1:15)—they await the promised gift of the Holy Spirit.

A like obedience of faith is demonstrated in the case of Saul of Tarsus who, following his encounter with the risen Christ, is commanded by him: ". . . rise and enter the city [of Damascus], and you will be told what you are to do" (Acts 9:6). Saul obeys,

---

[6]The expression, "the obedience of faith," is used by Paul in Romans 1:5—". . . through whom [Christ] we have received grace and apostleship to bring about the obedience of faith [eis hupakoēn pisteōs] for the sake of his name among all the nations. . . ." Also see Romans 16:26 for the same expression. In Arndt and Gingrich, *A Greek-English Lexicon of the New Testament* (under *hupakoē*) the translation of *eis hupakoēn pisteōs* is suggested as "*with a view to (promoting) obedience which springs from faith.*" Obedience which springs from faith is an excellent way of describing the obedience which is the context for the gift of the Holy Spirit.

[7]The RSV has "commandment," in the singular; however, the Greek word *enteilamenos* is plural.

[8]Though the Holy Spirit himself has not yet been given, He is already present as the medium for Jesus' words. This prior presence of the Holy Spirit illustrates a point earlier made, namely, that the gift of the Holy Spirit by no means rules out the previous presence and activity of the Holy Spirit among people of faith.

[9]According to the Gospel of Luke (the "first book" referred to in Acts 1:1), the words are "to stay [*kathisate*—also "to sit"; in KJV "to tarry"] in the city" (chapter 24:49).

and after three days is visited by Ananias, who likewise acts in obedience to a vision and a command of Christ (9:10-11), and Saul thereafter is filled with the Holy Spirit. The atmosphere, the context, for the gift of the Holy Spirit is obedience on both sides: Ananias who ministers and Saul who receives.

Quite similar is the story of the Roman centurion Cornelius at Caesarea who, along with his kinsmen and friends, receives the outpoured gift of the Holy Spirit. Cornelius is commanded by the Lord in a vision: ". . . send men to Joppa, and bring one Simon who is called Peter . . ." (Acts 10:5). Peter, who likewise has a vision, is sent for by Cornelius; and Peter is told by the Spirit: "Rise and go down, and accompany them [the servants of Cornelius] without hesitation . . ." (10:20). Thereafter, in an atmosphere of the obedience of faith,[10] the Holy Spirit is received.

These three accounts illustrate acts of specific obedience that relate immediately to the gift of the Holy Spirit. This is important. Also there is the statement in Acts—as we noted—that the specific obedience to the command to wait in Jerusalem is preceded by other commandments that Jesus gave through the Holy Spirit. Hence, His disciples are called to a total obedience to whatever Jesus commanded: such is the larger context for the gift of the Holy Spirit. This is vividly set forth in the words of Jesus in the Fourth Gospel: "If you love me, you will keep my commandments. And I will pray the Father, and he will give you another Counselor [the Holy Spirit], to be with you for ever, even the Spirit of truth . . ." (John 14:15-17). The Holy Spirit— the "Counselor," the "Spirit of truth"—will be given to those who obey Jesus' commands.

All of this suggests that those who seek faithfully to walk in the way of Christ are living in an atmosphere conducive to the reception of the Holy Spirit. Such a walk in obedience, not done grudgingly or seeking a reward, is an expression of a heart right before God. There may—and will—be failures, but the essential intention and direction is that of obedience to the word of the Lord. Already in some sense walking in the way of holiness,

---

[10]At the moment of the Lord's command to the centurion, Cornelius is not yet a believer. However, he does become a believer, at which moment the Holy Spirit is poured out (10:43-44). Hence his obedience is caught up in faith. To such a one the Spirit is given.

such persons are in a position for a further implementation of the Holy Spirit (who is the Spirit of holiness). The way of obedience wherein God's word is gladly honored and heeded is context for the gift of the Holy Spirit.[11]

This means, on the other hand, that one of the barriers to the reception of the Holy Spirit may be that of disobedience. If a person is not walking in the way of faithful obedience to Christ's commandments, for example, the injunctions of the Sermon on the Mount (Matt. 5-7); if he is harboring anger, lust, bitterness in his heart; if love has grown cold and holiness is aggrieved— such a one is hardly in a position to receive God's *Holy* Spirit.[12] For obedience lies at the heart of faith—and it is by faith alone that the Holy Spirit is received.

So to conclude this section: obedience in general to the command of Christ—His word, His teaching, His direction—and specifically to "wait for the promise" are aspects of the context for receiving the Holy Spirit. There may be no waiting—as in the case of the centurion whose prior obedience[13] is caught up into the obedience of faith and the Spirit is poured out at His commencement of faith. But in every instance the Holy Spirit is

---

[11]Here I should like to make reference to a nineteenth-century book by Andrew Murray, *The Spirit of Christ* (New York: Randolph & Co., 1888), the section subtitled, "The Spirit Given to the Obedient," pp. 69-77. Murray writes: *"The obedient must and may look for the fulness of the Spirit"* (italics: Murray). He speaks of this as "the promise of the conscious, active indwelling of the Spirit," and adds: "A living obedience is indispensable to the full experience of the indwelling. . . . Let each of us even now say to our Lord that we do love Him and keep His commandments. In however much feebleness and failure it be, still let us speak it out to Him. . . ." Murray, a Dutch Reformed pastor in South Africa, is one of the predecessors of the twentieth-century spiritual renewal. On the contemporary scene John Rea puts it well in saying: ". . . Christian obedience is a product of the inner heart, not of outward duty. It springs from gratitude for grace already received (Rom. 12:1-8) not from desire to gain merit . . ." (*Layman's Commentary on the Holy Spirit*, p. 77). It is *this* obedience—which is not a work—that is context for the gift of the Spirit to be received.

[12]This does not mean that one must be without sin to receive the Holy Spirit. If such were the case, no one would be a recipient; for all continue to sin. Hence, views of certain "Holiness" churches that call for "complete sanctification" or total "heart purification" as necessary for the reception of the Holy Spirit are asking for the impossible. What is important is not the attainment of perfection, but ever seeking—regardless of many a failure—to walk in the way of obedience.

[13]It was not mentioned before that the centurion is described as a God-fearing man: "a devout man who feared God with all his household" (Acts 10:2) and a man who "does what is right" (Acts 10:35). Thus, against a broad background of devoutness of life and righteous concerns, Cornelius's obedience to the command of the Lord stands forth vividly.

110

given in the atmosphere of obedient faith.[14]

We turn next to observe the importance of *prayer* as context for the gift of the Holy Spirit. Prayer is of course an essential element in the totality of Christian living—in its many aspects of praise, thanksgiving, confession, supplication and dedication—but in a special way it is the atmosphere in which the Holy Spirit is given.

This may be seen first in Jesus' own experience and teaching. We are told that following His baptism in water by John, the Holy Spirit came upon Him. In that sense Jesus is the precursor of those whose water baptism is followed by the gift of the Holy Spirit.[15] It is quite relevant that the Gospel of Luke records the context of the Spirit's coming upon Jesus to be prayer: "Now when all the people were baptized, and when Jesus also had been baptized and was praying, the heaven was opened, and the Holy Spirit descended upon him in bodily form, as a dove . . ."[16] (3:21-22). It is to be particularly noted here that, though the coming of the Spirit followed directly upon Jesus' baptism, the

---

[14]This has been noted in three cases: the original disciples in Jerusalem, Saul of Tarsus and the Caesareans. As far as the Samaritans are concerned, the situation is less clear. However, it may be that one of the reasons for the delay of several days in the gift of the Holy Spirit to them was the need for more time after the beginning of faith for obedience to develop. The Samaritans had long been caught up in idolatrous adulation of Simon the magician—"they all gave heed to him, from the least to the greatest, saying, 'This man is that power of God which is called Great' " (Acts 8:10)—and were "amazed" by his magical practices (8:11). Hence, though the Samaritans had entered the way of faith, they may have needed more time for commitment—and obedience—to Christ to replace their deep-seated idolatry of Simon.

In the case of the Ephesians, we read nothing directly about obedience. However, the atmosphere is that of readiness to do what John the Baptist had commanded, and thereafter to follow Paul's injunctions. (See Acts 19:4-6.)

[15]See again Acts 2:38; 8:12-17; 19:5-6.

[16]That this was Jesus' own baptism in the Spirit is apparent in many ways: (1) Although the imagery of the dove differs, e.g., from the wind and fire of Pentecost, the picture is clearly of a coming from without of the Spirit; (2) Jesus is said immediately thereafter to be "full of the Holy Spirit" (Luke 4:1)—thus a parallel to the disciples being "filled with the Holy Spirit" (Acts 2:4); (3) the Holy Spirit came at the Jordan to inaugurate Jesus' ministry even as at Pentecost to initiate the disciples'; (4) the Spirit that came is the Spirit of power: Jesus is said thereafter to move "in the power [*dunamis*] of the Spirit" (Luke 4:14); likewise the disciples were promised to receive power (*dunamis*) (Acts 1:8) when the Holy Spirit should come upon them; (5) in the parallel passage in John's Gospel the descent of the Spirit upon Jesus is tied in with Jesus' baptism of others in the Holy Spirit—"I myself [John the Baptist] did not know him; but he who sent me to baptize with water said to me, 'He on whom you see the Spirit descend and remain, this is he who baptizes with the Holy Spirit' " (John 1:33).

111

statement about prayer links the two events together. Though water baptism prepared the way[17] for the gift of the Spirit, it occurred to one in an attitude of prayer.

The importance of prayer in connection with the gift of the Holy Spirit is further underscored in Luke's Gospel by the words of Jesus: "If you then, who are evil, know how to give good gifts to your children, how much more will the heavenly Father give the Holy Spirit to those who ask him!" (11:13).[18] The asking is earlier set forth in the story of a man who, having no bread to share with a visitor, goes to a friend's house at midnight, and though the friend is in bed with his children, the man continues to call out and knocks again and again. Jesus adds: ". . . though he will not get up and give him anything because he is his friend, yet because of his importunity[19] he will rise and give him whatever he needs. And I tell you, Ask, and it will be given you; seek, and you will find; knock, and it will be opened to you . . ." (11:8-9). Hence importunate, persistent, unrelenting prayer is the context for the gift of the Holy Spirit. Now it would be pushing the story too far to suggest that God only grudgingly gives His Spirit; for the climax describes how God goes far beyond earthly fathers in His giving. The point, however, is that God is pleased to give to those who earnestly desire something—else the gift may mean very little. But where there is intense desire, the

---

[17]The water baptism in Jesus' case, unlike that of others, was not "for the forgiveness of sins" (cf. Acts 2:38). According to the Gospel of Matthew, when John the Baptist is described as remonstrating against baptizing Jesus ("I need to be baptized by you, and do you come to me?") Jesus replied, "Let it be so now; for thus it is fitting for us to fulfil all righteousness" (3:14-15). Though Jesus was not a sinner needing baptism and forgiveness, baptism did represent identification with God's righteous purpose signified therein. Thus—and of relevance to our concerns—Jesus' water baptism, which fulfilled God's righteousness before the Spirit was given, illustrates for persons thereafter that faith-righteousness which precedes the gift of the Holy Spirit.

[18]In the parallel Matthean account (7:11) instead of "the Holy Spirit" the expression is "good things" (agatha). Of all "good things" the gift of the Holy Spirit cannot be excelled. So the Expositor's Greek Testament (New York: George H. Doran Co., n.d.), Vol. One: "The Holy Spirit is mentioned here [in Luke's Gospel] as the summum bonum, and the supreme object of desire for all true disciples" (Commentary on Luke 11:13). E.G.T. notes also: "In some forms of the Lord's Prayer (Marcion, Greg. Nys.) a petition for the gift of the Holy Spirit took the place of the first or second petition." Since Luke 11 begins with the Lord's Prayer, and is the background for all that follows about prayer, climaxing with prayer for the gift of the Spirit, it is at least conceivable that the whole passage (11:1-13) is an elaboration of the petition for the Holy Spirit and what is involved therein.

[19]The Greek word is anaideian, literally "shamelessness," hence a persistence or importunity that is almost indecent!

fulfillment of the prayer is all the more full of joy and thanksgiving.[20]

But now let us move on to the book of Acts where, again, the atmosphere of prayer is shown in several instances to surround the gift of the Holy Spirit. First, this is especially apparent in the account of Acts 1 leading up to Pentecost. As we have seen, Jesus charged the apostles to stay in Jerusalem and to await the promised Holy Spirit. Obeying this command, the apostles returned to the city, and joined by various women who had been with Jesus, including Mary and His brothers, they gave themselves to prayer: "All these with one accord devoted themselves to prayer"[21] (Acts 1:14). Thus it was not simply an idle waiting, but a waiting in prayer; and not just prayer now and then but that to which they devoted themselves. Later, the number of those waiting grew to about 120 persons (1:15), and on one occasion there was the selection by the company of an apostle to succeed Judas (1:16-26), but the atmosphere continued to be one of prayer. For on the Day of Pentecost it was to a group of people in an attitude of prayer that the Holy Spirit was given.[22]

It should be pointed out that the disciples had no idea as to exactly when the Holy Spirit would be poured out. They were not told by Jesus to wait for a given number of days, nor did they set aside so many days for prayer after which they would turn to something else. No, they simply gave themselves to prayer unlimited—prayer doubtless in connection with the promised gift of the Holy Spirit—and God at the proper time[23] sent forth

---

[20]Here the writer would like to testify personally how true this is. After some three days of continuing prayer specifically for the gift of the Holy Spirit, God marvelously granted the request. It seemed many times that God (like the man in bed at midnight) would never answer, but, because of the deep desire, importunate praying continued, and at last when the answer came, it was all the more a thing of wonder and praise.

[21]Or, "were continuing steadfastly in prayer" (ēsan proskarterountes tē proseuchē). This more literal Greek reading points to the fact of their continuous devotion.

[22]The account in Acts 2:1-4 of the coming of the Spirit does not directly say that the disciples were praying when this happened. However, it would seem clearly implied both from the words of Acts 1:14 (suggesting a continuing devotion to prayer) and the setting of Acts 2:1-4 where they were "all together in one place" (2:1) (suggesting a unity in prayer) and were "sitting" (suggesting an attitude of prayerful waiting) when the Holy Spirit came.

[23]We have already spoken of God's sovereign purpose—His own timetable—being fulfilled on the Day of Pentecost. However, again this is not to be understood as making irrelevant the human context of prayer. God fulfills His purpose through those who prayerfully await His action.

His Spirit.

Thus if one brings together Luke 11 and Acts 1 (both written by the same author), it is apparent that much stress is laid on the need for prayer in the reception of the Holy Spirit. Even though the promise of the gift is clearly there in both cases, there is a call for continuing, persisting prayer. Just as truly as this was the case for the disciples prior to Pentecost in Jerusalem (Acts 1), so it is for other of God's children who know their need (Luke 11). God delights to give His Spirit to those who earnestly ask Him.[24]

The importance of prayer in the reception of the Holy Spirit is, second, to be found in the account of Saul's being filled with the Holy Spirit. After his encounter with the risen Lord, Saul was led by the hand into Damascus and "for three days he was without sight, and neither ate nor drank" (Acts 9:9). That this time of fasting was also a time of praying seems evident from the fact that when Ananias was told in a vision to go and minister to Saul, the Lord said of Saul, ". . . behold he is praying . . ." (9:11). This expression bespeaks a continuing in prayer, a waiting on the Lord during which time, as the Scripture records, Saul likewise had a vision, namely, of Ananias coming and laying hands upon him. There were visions on both sides, prayer, fasting, waiting—and in that context God gave the Holy Spirit.

Third, and similarly, much prayer was the environment and background for the coming of the Holy Spirit upon the Gentiles at Caesarea. Cornelius, at the outset, is described as "a devout man who feared God with all his household, gave alms liberally to the people, and prayed constantly to God" (10:2). In that atmosphere Cornelius had a vision wherein he was told that his prayers and alms had "ascended as a memorial before God" (10:4), and he was instructed to send for Simon Peter in the town of Joppa. Peter thereafter also in prayer—he "went up on the housetop to pray" (10:9)—likewise had a vision which resulted

---

[24]The point is sometimes made that the account of the disciples waiting and praying prior to Pentecost cannot afford an example for others thereafter, since the Holy Spirit had not yet been given—in the words of John, "the Spirit had not been given, because Jesus was not yet glorified" (7:39). Hence, there could be no reception of the Spirit prior to Jesus' glorification. However—to that point—Jesus *had* been glorified (i.e., returned to the Father's presence, as Acts 1:9-11 records it) before Pentecost, and yet they waited some ten days. When this fact is realized, and such a Scripture as Luke 11:1-13—which seems clearly applicable to God's children at any time—is also considered, it is apparent that earnest prayer continues to be the context for the gift of the Holy Spirit.

in his willingness to go to a Gentile home and proclaim the gospel. Then the Holy Spirit fell upon Cornelius and his household. The whole situation, much like that at Damascus, was one of continuing prayer, vision and waiting on the Lord.

Finally, in the narratives concerning the Samaritans and Ephesians (unlike the previous instances) there is no mention of those receiving the Holy Spirit being in prayer. However, the Scripture does record that prior to the Samaritans' reception of the Holy Spirit, Peter and John prayed for them: they "came down [from Jerusalem] and prayed for them that they might receive the Holy Spirit" (Acts 8:15-17). After such intercession, the apostles laid their hands upon the Samaritans for the reception of the Spirit.[25] While it may be surmised that the Samaritans were in an attitude of prayer also, the emphasis rests on the prayers of Peter and John. In any event, it was against the background and in the context of believing prayer that the Holy Spirit was received.

Now looking back at these several accounts, it is apparent that prayer lies close to the gift of the Holy Spirit. Such prayer was shown variously to be: earnest, asking, even importunate (Luke 11), a matter of steadfastness and devotion (Acts 2), of day by day continuation (Acts 9), of intercession (Acts 8) and of constancy (Acts 10). There is no suggestion of prayer as a condition for securing the Holy Spirit, but over and over prayer is shown to be the background, the context, the atmosphere wherein God delights to grant His Holy Spirit to those who believe.[26]

In the contemporary situation this proves to be the case wherever the spiritual renewal is occurring. The testimonies vary—some had been praying for some time, some only for a short period, some were prayed for by others, some had

---

[25]In chapter 6, "Means," supra, it was pointed out that there was no automatic reception of the Holy Spirit through the laying on of hands by Peter and John. Though hands were the medium, the gift came only to those who believed in Jesus. Now we are noting a further point, namely, that it was not simply a matter of laying hands (apostolic or otherwise) upon believers. Rather, prior to hands, and still more basic (as an expression of faith in operation), was prayer.

[26]One of the questions in the *Heidelberg Catechism* (Q. 116) is: "Why is prayer necessary for Christians?" Then follows the striking answer: "Because it is the chief part of the gratitude which God requires of us, and because *God will give his grace and Holy Spirit only to those who sincerely beseech him in prayer without ceasing*, and who thank him for these gifts" (italics mine). See *The Heidelberg Catechism*, tr. by A.O. Miller and M.E. Osterhaven (United Church Press, 1962).

expressed little overt prayer—but it was in a prayerful atmosphere of waiting before God that the Holy Spirit was poured out.[27]

This leads us next to a brief consideration of *expectancy* as context for the gift of the Holy Spirit. Though the word is not used in any of the Acts accounts, there is unquestionably an atmosphere of expectancy that can be sensed. People looking for something to happen are particularly candidates for the reception of the Holy Spirit.

This was obviously true in the case of the disciples waiting before Pentecost. We have remarked on their obedience and their steadfastness in prayer; now we are noting the further important matter that they were all expecting something to happen. They had not only received a command to wait; they had also received a promise that the Spirit would be given. Thus their praying was expectant praying, looking toward the coming outpouring of the Holy Spirit.

The atmosphere of expectancy may be sensed in other accounts. Peter and John prayed for the Samaritans to receive the Holy Spirit and doubtless built up expectation before the laying on of hands occurred; Ananias as he was laying hands on Saul spoke about his being filled with the Holy Spirit and thus created anticipation; and Paul's question to the Ephesians, "Did you receive the Holy Spirit when you believed?", may well have brought about an expectation for what later was to happen.

Of significance surely in creating expectation were the words

---

[27]Prayer as background for the outpouring of the Spirit has been evidenced since the early twentieth century. The usual dating for the beginning of the Pentecostal/charismatic renewal is New Year's Day, 1901, in Topeka, Kansas. There, at Rev. Charles Parham's Bible School, a devout prayer service had been held on New Year's Eve, and all New Year's Day God's presence was felt "stilling hearts to wait upon greater things to come" (Klaude Kendrick, *The Promise Fulfilled*, p. 52). About 11:00 P.M. Miss Agnes Ozman, one of the students, was prayed for to receive the gift of the Holy Spirit and the Holy Spirit "fell" (see Chapter 2, supra, fn. 9). The second outburst occurred in Los Angeles on April 9, 1906, among a group of people, whites and blacks, who had prayed and fasted for ten days, asking for God to send His Spirit. On the tenth day, a young black man spoke in tongues, followed shortly by six others. Such early twentieth-century beginnings are repeated variously in our time. For example, it was at a prayer meeting that Dennis Bennett had his experience, and in prayer that the gift of the Spirit came. A friend prayed over him, and then Bennett "prayed out loud for about twenty minutes" before he began "to speak in a new language" (*Nine O'Clock in the Morning*, p. 20). Examples can be multiplied.

of Peter to the multitude in Jerusalem: ". . . and you shall receive the gift of the Holy Spirit. For the promise is to you . . ." (Acts 2:38-39). Earlier the crowd had participated in the extraordinary event of everyone hearing in his own language what the disciples were saying, and were told thereafter by Peter that this had happened through the outpouring of the Holy Spirit. Now he tells them that (following repentance and baptism in the name of Christ) they will also receive the same gift. Against the background of their own participation in an amazing event, and now Peter's promise of their likewise receiving the gift, their expectation must have been very great.[28] Thus the atmosphere wherein the gift was received was laden with intense expectation.

Now to carry the role of expectancy forward, even to the present day, it will be recalled that Peter said the promise of the gift of the Spirit was not only to his immediate audience, but also ". . . to your children and to all that are far off, every one whom the Lord our God calls to him" (2:39). "Far off"[29] suggests distance in both space and time, thus people of all places and ages, and particularly Gentiles, since Peter had already included later Jewish generations in the expression "to your children." Hence the promise of the Spirit continues to our day, and for those who truly hear it and desire it and believe it, expectancy is once again the atmosphere.

So it has been with countless thousands of people across the world in our time who in hearing about the gift of the Holy Spirit have demonstrated a growing expectancy, even excitement, about the promise being fulfilled on their behalf. Nor have they found this expectation to be a delusion, for God has generously poured out his Spirit.[30] Contrariwise, when people

---

[28]In the words of Peter: "Repent, and be baptized every one of you in the name of Jesus Christ for the forgiveness of your sins; and you shall receive the gift of the Holy Spirit." The multitude were promised two things: forgiveness of sins and the gift of the Spirit. Thus one could speak of there being a twofold expectation. It is important to emphasize again, however, that the latter is based on the former, for without the forgiveness of sins expectation of the gift of the Spirit is in vain.

[29]*eis makran.*

[30]"The presupposition of the charismatic renewal today . . . is an expectant faith, a faith that expects God to do what he said." So writes Steve Clark, a coordinator of the Word of God community in Ann Arbor, in an article "Charismatic Renewal in the Church" (found in *As the Spirit Leads Us*, p. 22). Jim Cavnar, also active in the Ann Arbor community, in speaking about his own experience says: "I knew that the baptism

have expected little and expressed satisfaction to remain where they are, they have received little if anything. But those who wait to receive everything God has to give, those who desire great things from God, those who stand on tiptoes of expectation—it is they whom God delights to bless. Expect a miracle, and miracles begin to happen!

Finally, the context for the gift of the Holy Spirit is that of *yielding*. It is in an atmosphere of surrender to the lordship of Jesus Christ that the Holy Spirit is given. When persons are ready to give up everything for the sake of Christ and the gospel, and lay themselves completely at His disposal, God vouchsafes the abundance of His Spirit. Another way of putting this is to speak of emptiness before the Lord to which comes the answer of His divine fullness. When self is broken of all prideful claim, and there is looking only to Jesus, a new power is released—the power, the anointing, of God's Holy Spirit.

In the New Testament accounts concerning the original disciples of Jesus, Pentecost stands forth as the climax of a movement toward the all-sufficiency of Jesus Christ. Peter himself is a vivid illustration of one who, earlier in response to the word of Jesus that the twelve would deny Him, had boastfully replied: "Even though they all fall away, I will not" (Mark 14:29). It is a quite different Peter who after Pentecost is shown no longer to look to himself but wholly to Christ, for example, saying to a cripple: ". . . in the name of Jesus Christ walk" (Acts 3:6), and then to spectators astounded at what had happened: "Men of Israel, why do you wonder at this, or why do you stare at us, as though by our own power or piety we had made him walk?" (3:12). Something had happened to Peter between the time of his self-affirmation—and ensuing denial of Jesus—and the time of his total Christ-affirmation. A transformation had occurred. It was prepared for by post-resurrection encounters wherein Jesus ministers new faith, new life and a new commission,[31] but actually occurred only after a period of

in the Spirit was received in faith by asking the Father for the outpouring of the Spirit promised by his Son. I felt that the most important thing was to ask in faith, with confidence in God and full of expectation . . ." (*Catholic Pentecostals*, p. 63). This note of expectant faith is found throughout the contemporary renewal.

[31]In the Gospel of John the resurrected Jesus appears to the disciples in a closed room

waiting that lasted to Pentecost. This was the final time of preparation—and of transition from self-dependency to complete dependence on Christ. The ten days in the Upper Room were surely days of yielding more and more of self until the final barrier was breached, the self was emptied of all vain striving, and the Holy Spirit rushed in to fill the vacuum with the presence and power of God. Thereafter, for Peter and the other disciples, it was to be life lived in the fullness of the Holy Spirit.

Essentially the same thing must have happened with Saul of Tarsus over a three-day period. Though Saul had been set on a new course by the risen Jesus—180 degrees opposite from his former direction—and now believed in the one he formerly persecuted, doubtless there was much yet needed by way of yielding and surrender to his new Lord before he would be able to receive the commission from Ananias to preach Christ. Saul of Tarsus had been extremely self-reliant, proud and defiant,[32] and though he had now received new life and direction, it would take these days of blindness, prayer and fasting for the full surrender to occur, so that all his strength henceforward would be from the Spirit of Christ, the Holy Spirit. The words of Paul to the Romans at a later time are quite apropos: ". . . yield yourselves to God as men who have been brought from death to life" (Rom. 6:13). A new life, after death, and then a yielding of the total self to God!

Yielding makes for total availability—one thereby becoming an instrument wholly devoted to the Master's service. It is not only to know Jesus as Savior but also as Lord; it is to be "sold out" to Him. Yielding is not sanctification but servanthood[33] wherein

---

saying, "'Peace be with you. As the Father has sent me, even so I send you.' And when he had said this, he breathed on them, and said to them, 'Receive the Holy Spirit'" (20:21-22). Further evidence of this ministration of new life and new commission is found later in the Gospel of John where Jesus feeds several of the disciples bread and fish and then three times commissions Peter to feed His sheep and lambs (21:15-17). Likewise in the Gospel of Luke there is the ministry of faith and life through His unmistakable resurrection presence (Luke 24:36-43) and the declaration of a new commission (24:46-48). Such is prior to Pentecost, as Luke specifies in the book of Acts, and thus points to a further period of instruction, waiting, and yielding to the Lord.

[32]A Roman citizen, tribe of Benjamin, graduate of Tarsus, Pharisee of the Pharisees, master of legal righteousness, fierce against the church (see e.g., Phil. 3:4-7): this was the Saul encountered by Jesus on the road to Damascus.

[33]According to Paul, in Romans 6, the "fruit" of such yielding is "unto holiness," but the yielding itself is that whereby one becomes a servant, or slave, of God. "But now being

the whole of life is placed at the disposal of Christ. Thereby the Spirit of the Lord possesses a person in totality—body, mind, spirit—and all of life becomes a "living sacrifice"[34] to God.

Such yielding means no longer one's own will but the will of God—"not my will, but thine be done." It is to have "the mind of Christ," which means to humble oneself and become obedient unto death.[35] It means to surrender the tongue, which is "an unrighteous world among our members, staining the whole body . . . set on fire by hell. . . . With it we bless the Lord and Father, and with it we curse men,"[36] so that it may become attuned only to the praise of God.

Yielding may also signify not only submission to God but also submission to other persons. In four of the Acts accounts relating to the gift of the Holy Spirit it is apparent that persons receiving this gift did so through the ministry of others. It was through the ministry of Peter and John that the Samaritans received, through the ministry of Ananias that Saul of Tarsus was filled with the Spirit, through the ministry of Peter that the Caesareans were blessed, through the ministry of Paul that the Ephesians received the gift. In three of these instances the Holy Spirit was given through the imposition of hands of a fellow Christian. The very willingness to have hands laid on one's head signified an act of submission, a readiness to receive from other brethren what God had to give. This submitting to the ministry of others, it should be added, is frequently the best antidote to a kind of religious pride that desires to deal only with God directly (as in private prayer). However, the Lord often makes use of human—and sometimes quite humble—vessels for His blessing.

---

made free from sin, and become servants [or 'slaves'] of God, ye have your fruit unto holiness, and the end everlasting life" (v. 22—KJV).

[34]The language of Romans 12:1, where again Paul calls for a life of total commitment. All of life is to be poured out on the altar of complete self-giving.

[35]See Philippians 2:5-8.

[36]See James 3:6-10. The importance of surrender of the tongue—the "unrighteous world among our members"—can scarcely be exaggerated. It desperately needs control and direction by the Holy Spirit. As we have earlier noted, when the disciples at Pentecost— and many others later—were filled with the Holy Spirit they "began to speak in other tongues as the Spirit gave them utterance." In their total yielding, which included the tongue, the Spirit gave them this new utterance which was to the praise and magnifying of God. So it continues to be in the contemporary movement of the Holy Spirit where speaking in tongues, among other things, is a sign of complete yielding to God. The tongue no longer "set on fire by hell" is aflame with the glory of God!

It is not always easy for a prominent Saul to submit to an unknown Ananias, but such may be the Lord's way of working.

One of the things that has been learned in the contemporary movement of the Holy Spirit is the importance of this ministry of fellow Christians. Though in many cases God sovereignly pours out His Spirit without human mediation, most often people receive God's gift through the laying on of hands. And the hands may be those of a cleric or layman (as in the book of Acts), whomever God chooses. This calls for submission, and a kind of yielding that may not hitherto have been experienced.[37]

It would be difficult to overemphasize this whole matter of yielding. It is at the heart of receiving the gift of God's Holy Spirit. For it is only when a person lays himself totally at the disposal of God, holding back nothing, that the Spirit moves in to take full possession. There are no shortcuts, no simplistic formulas, no outward manifestations that can bring this about. The Spirit is given only to those who let everything go, who are empty before the Lord, who thereby may be filled with His fullness. This yielding may mean the willingness to give up earthly reputation, security and ambition—that God may be glorified. It is absolute and irrevocable surrender.[38]

Yielding is an act of faith. It is not something beyond faith but is faith in its profoundest expression. Whether such yielding occurs at the inception of faith, or somewhere along the way of faith, it represents that total surrender wherein the Spirit of the living God comes to have complete sway.

---

[37]In the writer's own case it was not easy to be prayed for by an ordained minister from another denomination. It seemed a bit humiliating to one also ordained (and a theologian at that!), but God blessed this act of submission, and the gift of the Spirit was received.
[38]John Rea writes about yielding thus: "The individual seeking to be baptized and filled with the Spirit must be willing to yield control of every part of his being to the Holy Spirit . . . you should yield yourself completely unto Jesus, as one who is alive from the dead, and also every member and faculty of your body as an instrument of righteousness. . . . Yield your will so that your motives are pure. . . . Yield your members, especially your tongue as the organ of expression of the Holy Spirit through you . . ." (*Layman's Commentary on the Holy Spirit*, p. 65). Donald Gelpi speaks of praying for "full docility to the Spirit of Christ." He adds: ". . . [this] is in effect to express one's willingness to do whatever God may be calling one to do, no matter what the personal sacrifice or suffering that call might entail. The person who cannot pray such a prayer and mean it is not yet ready for 'Spirit-baptism' " (*Pentecostalism: A Theological Viewpoint*, p. 183). Yielding, "full docility"—indeed total surrender—is essential for the reception of the fullness of God's Spirit. What Rea and Gelpi speak about is illustrated countless times in the contemporary renewal.

CHAPTER EIGHT

EFFECTS

We come finally to a consideration of the effects or results of the gift of the Holy Spirit. Our concern is not so much with long-range effects, though they are certainly not excluded, as with the immediate results of the Spirit being given. A number of these may be noted.

First of all, there is an extraordinary sense of *the reality of God.* As has been observed, the gift of the Holy Spirit is the gift of God's own presence. It is not something the Holy Spirit grants—such as life, power, wisdom—but it is the Spirit himself who is given. Since the Holy Spirit is God in His essential being, the reception of this gift means the reception of God himself. This then signifies the stupendous fact of the coming of God, the Holy Spirit, in fullness to lay claim to His creature, and to pervade the totality of human existence. In this action, God without ceasing to be wholly transcendent is also wholly immanent as He possesses the heights and depths of creaturely life. This extraordinary event of the divine self-giving is at the same time a divine self-disclosure, a revelation of the divine reality. The reality of God, His divine presence, is made known to man with compelling force.

Further, the God who comes through the gift of the Holy Spirit is the triune God. Hence, though it is the Spirit who is given—and thus not the same personally as Father or Son—nonetheless His very presence also makes real other persons of the Godhead. He constantly points to, glorifies, makes real the Son, the exalted Jesus Christ, and through the Holy Spirit the exalted Lord constantly makes himself known to His believing people. Jesus Christ, though now at the "right hand" of the Father and not bodily present, becomes spiritually present among those who believe in Him. Likewise, the Holy Spirit makes real God as Father, for it is through the Spirit's indwelling and moving presence that the fatherhood of God takes on more intimate and personal meaning. By the Spirit we say "Abba! Father!" not as address to a distant deity but as the cry of the heart to one near at hand.[1] To summarize: the reality of God as Father, Son and Holy Spirit is vividly disclosed through the gift of the Holy Spirit.

As we turn again to the book of Acts, it is apparent that the reality of God is the paramount fact in everything that occurs. When the Spirit is given at Pentecost, the company immediately begins to declare the marvelous works of God and thus to exult in His wonderful presence. It matters not that thousands are gathered around them, for so full are they of God's Spirit that they go right on praising Him. The reality of God's presence has gripped them as a community, as individuals, and in such fashion that in all that follows they sense God moving in their midst.

For example, in the case of Peter's ministry it is clear that the reality of God's presence pervades everything. In his message to the large Jewish audience in Jerusalem (Acts 2:14-39) he speaks of God with authority, of Jesus Christ with the assurance of personal knowledge, of the Holy Spirit with the certainty of profound experience. He later pronounces healing in the name of Jesus Christ as in the name of one who is powerfully and personally present (Acts 3:6), and "filled with the Holy Spirit" he does not hesitate to proclaim salvation even to the rulers, elders and high priests (Acts 4:8-12). So real is the presence of God in the community of believers that Peter declares that to lie about a certain matter is to lie against God—"You have not lied to men but to God" (Acts 5:4). Further, the witness of Peter and the others about Jesus is known by them to be a co-witness with the Holy Spirit—". . . we are witnesses to these things, and so is the Holy Spirit whom God has given. . ." (Acts 5:32). Also, the Holy Spirit, prior to Peter's going to Caesarea, speaks directly and personally to him—". . . the Spirit said to him, 'Behold, three men are looking for you. Rise and go down, and accompany them without hesitation; for I have sent them'" (Acts 10:19-20).

Likewise, from the outset of Paul's ministry there is a compelling sense of God's reality. The personal self-disclosure of the risen and exalted Lord to Saul of Tarsus—"I am Jesus . . ."

---

[1]See below for fuller discussion.

(Acts 9:5) and the ensuing experience of being "filled with the Holy Spirit" (9:17) made of Saul a man whose life and activity thereafter were dominated by the reality of God's living presence. "Immediately he proclaimed Jesus, saying, 'He is the Son of God' " (9:20); and this proclamation, like all else Paul thenceforward did, stemmed from the indubitable certainty of God's pervading presence and action. One telling illustration of the presence of God in Paul's missionary activity is that wherein the apostle (with Timothy) is led by the Holy Spirit to cross over from Asia Minor into Europe. First, he was "forbidden by the Holy Spirit to speak the word in Asia," and, second, when he purposed to go in another direction, "the Spirit of Jesus did not allow them" (Acts 16:6-7). Herein is unmistakable testimony to the reality of the divine presence and direction in whatever Paul did. Throughout Paul's ministry there is a continuing sense of the activity of the Holy Spirit.[2]

The book of Acts is the record of a church intensely aware of the presence of God. When the prophets and teachers of the church at Antioch meet together, the Holy Spirit is markedly present—"While they were worshiping the Lord and fasting, the Holy Spirit said, 'Set apart for me Barnabas and Saul for the work to which I have called them' " (Acts 13:2). When the apostles and elders of the church in Jerusalem convene to make a decision about the matter of Gentile circumcision, they send a letter which includes the words: ". . . it has seemed good to the Holy Spirit and to us to lay upon you no greater burden. . ." (Acts 15:28). Throughout, it is a church—whether in Jerusalem, Antioch, or elsewhere—moving and acting in the reality of God's spiritual presence.

The book of Acts, accordingly, is far more than the acts of men—or "Acts of the Apostles."[3] For though men are everywhere

---

[2] E.g. Acts 19:21: ". . . Paul resolved in the Spirit to pass through Macedonia and Achaia and go to Jerusalem. . . ." Acts 20:22-23: ". . . I am going to Jerusalem bound in the Spirit . . . the Holy Spirit testifies to me . . . that imprisonment and afflictions await me."

[3] "Acts of the Apostles" is a title frequently given to the book. The title is doubly misleading: first, the book of Acts while mostly containing narrations about apostolic activity also relates the acts of "deacons" such as Stephen (Acts 6 and 7) and Philip (Acts 8), of churches such as at Antioch and Jerusalem (see above), of teachers such as Apollos, Priscilla and Aquila (Acts 18:24-28) and of a prophet such as Agabus (Acts 11:28 and 21:10-11); second, the focus of the title is off center, for the main feature is not the acts of

involved, it is basically the acts of God, of Jesus Christ, of the Holy Spirit that stand forth. God is present in a compelling manner, the sense of His presence and action is markedly known and experienced. All that happens finds its source and direction from Him. That God is real is the basic fact in the life of the early Christian community.

Now what has been said about the experienced reality of God in the early church is again being confirmed in the contemporary movement of the Holy Spirit. A spiritual breakthrough is occurring wherein people are being made profoundly aware of the divine presence. Through the outpoured gift of the Holy Spirit, God in His divine reality is manifesting himself. That God is *real* is being affirmed by countless thousands, not as simply an affirmation of distant faith, but of vivid, undeniable experience.

Living in a day of the "absence" of God—the "eclipse" of God, even the "death" of God[4]—this spiritual breakthrough is a tremendous fact.[5] For the unreality of God has become the actual situation for vast numbers of people. This is the case not only for the secular world but quite often for people inside the church. It is a matter of the Real Absence rather than the Real Presence. Often even when the gospel is preached, the Bible fully accepted as the Word of God, the sacraments regularly shared in, there is little spiritual vitality. This may be the case also for churches that lay much stress on evangelistic and missionary activity; there is little excitement about the presence of the living God in the midst of His people. But now through the outpouring of God's Spirit, all is changing for many persons: there is spiritual rejuvenation, renewal—an overwhelming sense of the divine presence.[6] For God is possessing His people in

the apostles or any other believers but the acts of the Holy Spirit, or the acts of the exalted Lord through the Holy Spirit, the continuation of "all that Jesus began to do and teach" (Acts 1:1) in His earthly life.

[4]"Death of God" terminology used by Nietzsche, and taken up in the mid-sixties by so-called "death of God" theologians, says far more about the human than the divine condition. For all practical purposes God is dead when there is utterly no sense of His living reality.

[5]"In an era that cries, 'God is dead,' and questions whether 'Christianity' has a future, the charismatic renewal comes as a vigorous affirmation that God is indeed a living God, and that *Jesus Christ* is active in the world with sovereign power." So begins *Pentecost in the Modern World* (Notre Dame: Ave Maria Press, 1972) by Edward D. O'Connor, C.S.C.

[6]In his autobiography, *Nine O'Clock in the Morning*, Dennis Bennett describes the sense

126

a profound manner, pervading the heights and depths of creaturely existence, even through the conscious to the subconscious life, and becoming the recognized primary actor in all that takes place.

Thus the community of believers, experiencing the divine visitation, is becoming much like the early church. As at Pentecost, people are declaring with full fervor the mighty works of God, they are witnessing to the gospel with tremendous enthusiasm and boldness, and signs and wonders are occurring on every hand. They are looking to the Holy Spirit for a "Thus saith the Lord," and like Peter, Paul, and others, they are hearing a word and moving by divine direction. When God is real and powerfully present, all of life is set in a different key—and the church becomes afresh the church of the living God.

Second, another effect of the gift of the Holy Spirit is *fullness of joy*. Wherever the Holy Spirit is received there is a great upsurge of joy. Sometimes the joy is so great as to be almost uncontainable. In the language of 1 Peter 1:8 it may be "joy unspeakable and full of glory."[7]

It is apparent that on the Day of Pentecost there was great rejoicing in the Lord. As we have noted, the Spirit-filled disciples immediately began to speak forth the "mighty works of God," and they did so in such fashion that many mockingly declared them to be "filled with new wine." However, it was not fruit of the vine but fruit of the Spirit—not an artificial joy soon to fade but a genuine joy that was thereafter to penetrate their whole existence.

Indeed, this deep joy is further demonstrated in an entirely different setting where the apostles, having already been put in

---

of Presence that came to him just following his receiving the gift of the Holy Spirit: "The Presence of God that I had so clearly seen in earlier days to be the real reason for living, suddenly enveloped me again after the many, many years of dryness. Never had I experienced God's presence in such reality as now. It might have frightened me, except that I recognized that this was the same Presence of the Lord that I had sensed when I first accepted Jesus . . . only the intensity and reality of my present experience was far greater than anything I had believed possible. If those earlier experiences were like flashbulbs, this was as if someone had suddenly turned on the floodlights! The reality of God was something that I felt all the way through. . ." (p. 24). Here, verily, is *the* answer to "the death of God"!

[7]KJV. The RSV translates the text as "unutterable and exalted joy."

jail, are now beaten and charged by the Jewish high council not to speak further in the name of Jesus. "Then they left the presence of the council, rejoicing that they were counted worthy to suffer dishonor for the name" (Acts 5:41). Hence the joy that they, along with many others, had experienced on the Day of Pentecost was not only a joy related to favorable cicumstances, but also one that continued in the midst of persecution and disrepute. It was the great rejoicing about which Jesus spoke when He told His disciples: "Blessed are you when men hate you . . . and revile you . . . on account of the Son of man! Rejoice in that day and leap for joy. . ." (Luke 6:22-23). Truly this is fullness of joy!

This fullness of joy, as a promise to His disciples, was mentioned by Jesus in the Gospel of John several times on the night of His betrayal. The words are found first in 15:11: "These things I have spoken to you, that my joy may be in you, and that your joy may be full."[8] It is to be noted that the joy comes from Jesus—it is "my joy"[9]—and that the promise is twofold: the joy to be "in" His disciples and their joy to be "full." Hence, it is not only a promise of indwelling joy but also a promise of being filled with joy. Looking ahead, it could be said that the Resurrection was the coming of joy,[10] but only at Pentecost and thereafter did the disciples know the fullness of that joy.

Returning to the book of Acts we find several other accounts where joy, or rejoicing, is mentioned. First, just following the baptism of the Ethiopian eunuch by Philip, the Scripture reads: "And when they came up out of the water, the Spirit of the Lord caught up Philip; and the eunuch saw him no more, and went on his way rejoicing" (8:39). Second, at Iconium, ". . . the disciples were filled with joy and the Holy Spirit" (13:52). Third, the Philippian jailer who had come to faith in the Lord Jesus and

---

[8]Cf. also John 16:24: ". . . ask, and you will receive, that your joy may be full," and John 17:13: "these things I speak . . . that they may have my joy fulfilled in themselves."

[9]The joy of Jesus may be observed, for example, upon the return of seventy disciples from a successful missionary journey: "In that same hour he rejoiced ['rejoiced greatly' or 'exulted'—ēgalliasato] in the Holy Spirit. . ." (Luke 10:21). Here is fullness of joy in (or "by") the Holy Spirit—which the disciples also were to experience later.

[10]E.g., the women, told that Jesus was risen, ". . . departed quickly from the tomb with fear and great joy (charas megalēs). . ." (Matt. 28:8). Later Jesus appeared to the larger group who experienced "joy and . . . marveling" (charas kai thaumazontōn) (Luke 24:41 NAS).

was baptized thereafter ". . . rejoiced greatly,[11] having believed in God with his whole household" (16:34, NAS). In all of these accounts, joy is closely connected with the Holy Spirit, quite possibly as an immediate effect of the gift of the Holy Spirit.[12]

Beyond Acts we may also observe, first, how Paul writes the Thessalonians that they ". . . received the word in much affliction, with joy inspired by the Holy Spirit" (1 Thess. 1:6). That the Thessalonians had received the gift of the Holy Spirit is apparent from Paul's prior words: ". . . our gospel came to you not only in word, but also in power and in the Holy Spirit and with full conviction" (v. 5). Hence, the "joy inspired by the Holy Spirit" came out of the fullness of their experience of the Holy Spirit—a joy that even amid "much affliction" broke forth. The result, Paul adds: ". . . you became an example to all the believers in Macedonia and Achaia" (v. 7). Second, Paul writes the Romans, praying: "May the God of hope fill you with all joy and peace in believing, so that by the power of the Holy Spirit you may abound in hope" (Rom. 15:13). "All joy" comes out of God's "filling," out of "the power of the Holy Spirit."

The fullness of joy expressed by these various Scriptures is being exemplified across the world in the contemporary outpouring of the Holy Spirit. Many who have received the gift of the Spirit attest that one of the immediate effects is an intensity of joy. Often the experience is that of an inner movement of the Holy Spirit wherein the whole being is flooded with joy.[13] There

---

[11]The Greek term is *ĕgalliasato*, the same as in Luke 10:21 (supra).

[12]We may recall (see chapter 6, fn. 9) that the Acts 8:39 passage in a number of early manuscripts reads: "And when they came up out of the water, the Holy Spirit fell upon the eunuch and an angel of the Lord caught up Philip. . . ." The point of this reading, as we before observed, is undoubtedly to emphasize that the eunuch's believing and baptism were followed by the gift of the Spirit. Accordingly, the rejoicing of the eunuch springs out of his experience of the Holy Spirit. In regard to the Acts 16:34 passage, nothing is said directly about the Holy Spirit. However, since once again the rejoicing— or great rejoicing—is closely connected with faith and baptism, the implication of the text is quite likely that of the reception of the gift of the Holy Spirit.

[13]Earlier we quoted the words of Larry Tomczak about his baptism in the Holy Spirit: "I felt the rapturous and exultant joy of the Lord surging through me. . . . Then, just at the right moment words began to flow from my heart" (supra, chap. 3, fn. 4). Then Tomczak adds: "At the same time, like a mountain stream—pure, sparkling, cool, crystal clear—living joy began to flow upward and outward through my entire being." His concluding words: "Jesus Christ touched me that night, and, oh, the joy that filled my soul. . . . I opened the door and seemed to float through it. Looking up at the cool, crisp, early morning sky, I grinned foolishly, drunk for joy" *(Clap Your Hands,* pp. 112-13). Also see the moving life story by Sister Mary Bernard, *I Leap for Joy* (Plainfield, NJ: Logos, 1974).

is about this joy something quite different, or other, than ordinary joy or happiness: it is the joy of the Lord. In one popular chorus, based on 1 Peter 1:8, the wording goes: "It is joy unspeakable and full of glory, and the half has never yet been told!"

Further, this is a joy which thereafter may have its ups and downs, but regardless of what occurs in the life of faith it continues as a wellspring ever bubbling up and overflowing. Jesus also said about the joy which He promised His disciples that ". . . no one will take your joy from you. . ." (John 16:22). So it is: since this joy is fulfilled through the gift of the Holy Spirit, and this joy is the Lord's own joy, nothing can take it away. It is joy everlasting. Surely the words of Isaiah are appropriate: "And the ransomed of the Lord shall return, and come to Zion with singing; everlasting joy shall be upon their heads. . ." (Isa. 51:11).

Third, still another effect of the gift of the Holy Spirit is that of providing *an assurance of God's act of salvation.* The Holy Spirit bears witness to what has been done, confirms the status of sonship and God's abiding presence and affords an earnest or pledge of what is yet to come.

It is significant that on two occasions (Acts 11 and 15) after the gift of the Holy Spirit to the Caesareans, or the Gentiles, Peter appears before the Jerusalem council of apostles and brethren to argue the Gentile cause. On each occasion Peter refers to the gift of the Holy Spirit which the Gentiles had likewise received as a kind of confirmation or witness. In the first instance the question basically was whether the Gentiles really were included in God's purpose of salvation, and Peter's argument was simply that "the Holy Spirit fell on them just as on us at the beginning" (11:15). Further, "if then God gave the same gift to them as he gave to us [believing][14] in the Lord Jesus Christ, who was I that I could withstand God?" (11:17). This silenced the audience; then ". . . they glorified God, saying, 'Then to the Gentiles also God has granted repentance unto life'" (11:18). The fact that God had given the Holy Spirit to the

---

[14]The RSV reading "when we believed" as earlier noted (Chapter 5, fn. 10) is misleading. "Having believed" or "believing" is preferable.

Gentiles was certification to the apostles and brethren that the Gentiles had indeed been granted salvation. On the second occasion, Peter stands again before the council to argue against the obligation of Gentiles to be circumcised in order to be saved. In the context of this argument Peter speaks of how it was God's choice that ". . . by my mouth the Gentiles should hear the word of the gospel and believe" (15:7). Then Peter immediately adds: "And God who knows the heart bore witness to them, giving them the Holy Spirit just as he did to us; and he made no distinction between us and them, but cleansed their hearts by faith"[15] (15:8-9). Here the gift of the Holy Spirit is described as a witness to the Gentiles themselves that they had indeed been granted cleansing and salvation. Thus to summarize the two accounts: the gift of the Holy Spirit was viewed as both a testimony to others, an external witness, and an internal testimony that "repentance unto life," cleansing, salvation, had unmistakably occurred.

On the matter of the testimony to others, or external witness, one of the interesting features of the contemporary outpouring of God's Spirit is the way in which it has caused many people in churches or denominations that have been long separated from and even antagonistic to one another to change their attitude. For example, many Protestants who received the gift of the Spirit in the early to mid 1960s were ill prepared to accept the movement of the Spirit among Roman Catholics that began in 1967[16] for the reason that they (the Protestants) were not at all sure any Catholics had experienced salvation. Then it began to happen among Catholics—exactly as among Protestants—and all the Protestants could do, like the apostles and brethren, was to glorify God and say, "Then to the Roman Catholics also God has granted repentance unto life!"

One other Scripture passage related to external witness is Hebrews 2:3-4: "How shall we escape if we neglect such a great salvation? It was declared at first by the Lord, and it was

---

[15]Such cleansing of the heart therefore obviated the necessity of circumcision. Or, to put it a bit differently, what really counted was not circumcision of the flesh but circumcision of the heart. And God himself had performed the operation!

[16]For Roman Catholic beginnings see *The Pentecostal Movement in the Catholic Church* by Edward D. O'Connor. Also see *Catholic Pentecostals*, which contains much of the story.

attested to us by those who heard him, while God also bore witness by signs and wonders and various miracles and by gifts of the Holy Spirit distributed according to his own will." Here again God himself bears witness to the "great salvation" through the operation and activity of the Holy Spirit. Salvation which belongs to the inward and invisible realm is attested by the outward and visible—signs, wonders, miracles, various gifts of the Holy Spirit. This passage in Hebrews is somewhat different from Acts 11 and 15: the gift (or gifts) of the Holy Spirit is not spoken of as testimony to other Christians that God has granted salvation, but it is rather a testimony to those who have not experienced salvation that behind such divine works stand a living God who brings salvation.

Again, to return to the contemporary scene, it is striking that in many places the proclamation of the gospel of salvation is being given visible certification through "signs and wonders and various miracles and gifts of the Holy Spirit." The word is preached, God "bears witness," for example, through miracles of healing taking place, and the message of salvation comes through with powerful effectiveness.[17] Indeed, in a day when people are bombarded by countless words and voices (in television, radio, printed page, etc.) and made innumerable offers, it is increasingly hard to hear the word about salvation and believe without some demonstration of power and reality. Is it really so? Is the message of an internal transformation valid? Does it actually happen? But when that message about invisible things is certified by visible demonstrations of the power of God, then credibility is vastly increased. The gospel truly must be, as is claimed, the power of God also unto salvation.

Now let us look further into the matter of the gift of the Spirit as internal witness. Paul writes to the Romans: ". . . you have received the Spirit[18] of sonship. When we cry 'Abba! Father!' it is the Spirit himself bearing witness with our spirit that we are

[17]For example, the Kathryn Kuhlman meetings in Pittsburgh, Los Angeles, and elsewhere during the 1960s and seventies were notable examples of how the teaching of the gospel was certified by the witness of healing. The climax of the meeting was not the various manifestations that occurred but the call to salvation. When that call went forth, amid the almost overwhelming signs of God's powerful presence, great numbers of people would come forward to receive salvation. See Kathryn Kuhlman, *God Can Do It Again* (Englewood Cliffs, NJ: Prentice-Hall 1971), especially "Miracles Do Happen," pp. 7-26.
[18]RSV has "spirit." Upper case "S" seems preferable (as in KJV).

the children of God" (Rom. 8:15-16). A beautiful effect of having "received the Spirit of sonship"—that is, the Spirit given to those who are sons by "adoption"[19]—is the internal witness that we are now the children of God. The assurance of being the children of God occurs in the cry of "Father! Father!"[20] which breaks out with great force and meaning.[21] It is the result of the Holy Spirit's bearing witness with our spirit.

Here, it should be added, is something not unlike "speaking in (other) tongues." As we have earlier noted,[22] the immediate response to the gift of the Holy Spirit is praise, and this praise frequently takes the transcendent form of "tongues" as the Holy Spirit enables. "They . . . began to speak in other tongues, as the Spirit gave them utterance" (Acts 2:4) is quite similar to "When we cry 'Abba! Father!' it is the Spirit himself bearing witness. . ." (Rom. 8:15-16). Speaking with tongues and crying, "Abba! Father!" both signalize a tremendous outbreak from deep within; both represent cries of persons in a profound relationship with God; both are cries that come from the activity of the Holy Spirit who has been given; both are addressed not to men but to God.[23]

---

[19]The Greek word translated in the RSV as "sonship" is *huiothesias*, literally "adoption" (as in KJV). Believers are "sons of God by adoption" (unlike Jesus Christ who is eternally the Son of God), and thereby can address God as "Father."

[20]The biblical expression is *"abba! ho patēr!"* "Abba" is an Aramaic word that expresses an intimate family relationship of child to father. In English the closest similarity might be "daddy" or "dad." However, since there are some connotations of this common family term that seem not altogether fitting in relationship to God, it is probably best to translate simply as "Father! Father!" while bearing in mind the intimacy of this new relationship.

[21]The word for "cry," *krazomen*, means "to cry out loudly." *Krazomen* "denotes the loud irrepressible cry with which the consciousness of sonship breaks from the Christian heart. . ." *(Expositor's Greek Testament, Commentary on Romans, in loco).*

[22]See Chapter 3, supra.

[23]This has been noticed, supra, in Chapter 3. Also the words of Paul about the operation of tongues in the Christian life are relevant: ". . . one who speaks in a tongue speaks not to men but to God. . ." (1 Cor. 14:2). It might be added that in the life of prayer speaking in tongues is a kind of prayer language closely related to the language of "Abba! Father!" Both *"another* tongue" and the *"mother* tongue" are beautiful expressions of power and intimacy.

The author's first experience of speaking in tongues came at the very moment when in the midst of God's visitation he was striving to say "Ab-ba." Hardly had the second syllable "ba" been pronounced than he began speaking a new language! Truly the Father was being praised by the Holy Spirit in language transcending even "Abba! Father!" Thereafter it has become a pattern of prayer to move from the transcendent language of the Spirit to the common language wherein, again by the Spirit, God is known and experienced as "Abba! Father!"

In this matter of internal witness we should also note the words of Paul in Galatians 4:6: "To prove that you are sons, God has sent into our hearts the Spirit of his Son, crying 'Abba! Father!' "[24] This again is not an external witness, or proof, but a profoundly internal one, for the Spirit cries from within the heart. In this very cry[25] of "Abba! Father!"—which is the cry through the Holy Spirit—we know we are the sons of God. For though it is a cry from within our hearts we are aware it does not originate from us: it is from the Holy Spirit.

One other quotation from Paul, earlier given, is now particularly relevant: ". . . our gospel came to you [the Thessalonians] not only in word, but also in power and in the Holy Spirit and with full conviction" (1 Thess. 1:5). This "full conviction," or "full assurance,"[26] is obviously connected, in Paul's statement, with the Holy Spirit; hence, it can be said to be an effect of the operation of the Holy Spirit. The Thessalonians not only heard the word of the gospel and believed but also received through the Holy Spirit the full assurance of their salvation.

Returning to our contemporary situation, it is highly significant that many people are experiencing afresh the inner witness, or confirmation, of sonship and salvation. What Paul speaks of in Romans 8:15-16, Galatians 4:6, and 1 Thessalonians 1:5 is becoming a profound fact. When the Holy Spirit is received, there is unmistakable inward assurance. Testimonies are frequently to be heard, such as, "I believed before, but now faith has taken on a deep inner certitude," or "I never really had much assurance about matters connected with salvation, but now I know I belong to Christ." It is a movement not *from* faith *to* sight but *in* faith *to* an assurance that was lacking before. It is a "I know whom I have believed. . ." (2 Tim. 1:12).

It is important to recognize that not all believers have this assurance—but it is possible and highly desirable. In the case of the Thessalonians Paul could write, as we have seen, about how

---

[24]New English Bible. "To prove that," the NEB translation for *hoti* is, I believe, preferable to "because" (in RSV and many other translations). Paul is speaking demonstratively—"to demonstrate that," as "proof of that"—rather than causally. (See also *Cambridge Greek Testament* [Cambridge University Press, 1914], *Commentary on Galatians, in loco:* " 'hoti' is demonstrative 'But as proof that,' rather than strictly causal.")

[25]The Greek word is *krazon*. See supra, fn. 21.

[26]The Greek term is *plērophoria pollē*, literally "much full assurance."

they had "full assurance" through the Holy Spirit from the day they heard the gospel preached. However, he also writes the Colossians of his desire that they may ". . . have all the riches of [the full assurance of understanding][27] and the knowledge of God's mystery" (Col. 2:2). Hence the "full assurance" which the Thessalonians had from the beginning Paul yearns for the Colossians to experience. We might also observe how the letter to the Hebrews expresses a similar desire for them to realize a "full assurance of hope": "And we desire each one of you to show the same earnestness in realizing the full assurance[28] of hope until the end" (Heb. 6:11). Later in the same letter there is the encouraging statement: ". . . let us draw near with a true heart in full assurance[28] of faith. . ." (Heb. 10:22). It is interesting to observe that, based on the three passages just quoted, there is the possibility of a full assurance of understanding, of hope, and of faith.[29] But, to repeat, the important thing is to recognize that not all believers have such full assurance, that its realization is from and by the Holy Spirit, and that it is much to be desired. For in such a realization there is the inner certainty of being a child of God and an heir of all that is to come.[30]

We have quoted Paul a number of times on the matter of certainty and assurance. It is now in order to mention a few like

---

[27]RSV reads: "assured understanding" instead of "full assurance of understanding." However the Greek expression is *plērophorias tēs suneseōs*. The word *plērophoria* is the same that Paul uses in writing to the Thessalonians (see fn., supra).

[28]The Greek word for "full assurance" in both Hebrews 6 and 10 is likewise *plērophoria*.

[29]According to the *Westminster Confession of Faith* there is the possibility of "an infallible assurance of faith" which is "founded upon the divine truth of the promises of salvation, the inward evidence of those graces unto which these promises are made, the testimony of the Spirit of adoption witnessing with our spirits that we are the children of God . . . [however] this infallible assurance does not so belong to the essence of faith, but that a true believer may wait long and conflict with many difficulties before he be partaker of it. . ." (Chapter XVIII, "Of the Assurance of Grace and Salvation," Sections 2 and 3). See Philip Schaff, *The Creeds of Christendom* (New York: Harper and Brothers, 1877), Vol. III, "The Westminster Confession of Faith, 1647," p. 638.

[30]Another obvious benefit of "full assurance" is the strength it gives to Christian witness. If "I know whom I have believed," if there is the continuing inner witness of the Holy Spirit to my being God's child, if this full assurance relates to understanding, hope and faith, then my witness to the gospel stems from a great inner fortitude and certainty. There is nothing quite so convincing as the witness that stems out of complete certainty—and yet not one's own certainty but that which the Holy Spirit constantly renews! (By such "infallible assurance," according to the *Westminster Confession of Faith*, a person's heart is "enlarged in peace and joy in the Holy Ghost, in love and thankfulness to God, and in strength and cheerfulness in the duties of obedience" Chapter XVIII, Section 3.)

references in the First Letter of John. The basic purpose of this letter is stated near the conclusion: "I write this to you who believe in the name of the Son of God, that you may know that you have eternal life" (1 John 5:13).[31] John is similarly concerned that faith becomes knowledge, assurance, certainty. And how does this knowledge come about? The answer: by the anointing of the Holy One. ". . . you have been anointed by the Holy One, and you all know" (1 John 2:20). The word for "anointing"[32] is the same as that used in Acts 10:38—". . . God anointed Jesus of Nazareth with the Holy Spirit and with power. . ."—and refers likewise to the gift of the Holy Spirit. This they have received, and by this anointing they know all things[33] pertaining to the spiritual life. As concrete illustration of this knowledge by the Holy Spirit, John also writes: ". . . by this we know that he abides in us, by the Spirit which he has given us" (1 John 3:24), and "By this we know that we abide in him and he in us, because he has given us of his own Spirit" (1 John 4:13). By the gift of the Holy Spirit "we know" all spiritual things: that we have eternal life, that Christ abides in us and we in Him, and whatever else pertains to matters of faith.

It should be emphasized that what is at stake here is not the reality itself but the knowledge of that reality. It is not, for example, that by the gift of the Holy Spirit Christ abides in us, but that through this gift we *know* He abides in us—and we in Him. It is not by the gift of the Spirit that we have eternal life but we *know* we have it. The Spirit who is given brings assurance and certainty into all such spiritual matters.

This leads us into other Scriptures which speak of the gift of the Holy Spirit as an "earnest" or "guarantee." Two passages in 2 Corinthians contain this: ". . . he [God] has put his seal upon us and given us his Spirit in our hearts as a guarantee"[34] (1:22), and

---

[31]This may be compared with the Gospel of John where the purpose is likewise stated near the end: ". . . these [things] are written that you may believe that Jesus is the Christ, the Son of God, and that believing you may have life in his name" (John 20:31). The Gospel intends faith and salvation; the Letter, written to those who have already experienced such, intends knowledge and assurance.

[32]*chrisma* in 1 John; *echrisen* in Acts.

[33]The "you all know" of 1 John 2:20 is *oidate pantes* which could be translated "you know all" (similarly KJV—"ye know all things").

[34]The Greek word for "guarantee" is *arrabōna*. The gift of the Spirit serves as an "earnest" (KJV)—a "first installment," a "down payment," a "pledge," thus a "guarantee."

"He who has prepared us for this very thing is God, who has given us the Spirit as a guarantee" (5:5). "This very thing" refers to the life to come (". . . a house not made with hands, eternal in the heavens"—verse 1). The earnest or pledge of that future life is the gift of the Holy Spirit. Through the Spirit within, the life to come is already in some sense present—the "first install-ment"—so that there is a gilt-edged guarantee of what is beyond. Another and similar passage about the gift of the Spirit as earnest or guarantee is that wherein Paul writes: ". . . [you] were sealed with the promised Holy Spirit, which is the guarantee of our inheritance until we acquire possession of it, to the praise of his glory" (Eph. 1:13-14).[35] By the reception of this gift the Ephesians have been sealed, and the result described is that the Spirit is the earnest of the future inheritance in heaven.[36]

Once again to return to the contemporary scene: one of the highlights of the widespread movement of the Holy Spirit is the strong eschatological sense. There is, first, the sense of the presence of the future. The gift of the Spirit brings about a knowledge that through faith in Christ one has already passed from death into life, and that while on earth there is already citizenship in heaven. This world seems less like a preparation for the next than an anticipation of what is to come. One of the common expressions is "Glory!"[37]—a word that conveys with

---

Incidentally the "seal" referred to, as was mentioned earlier (Chapter 4, fn. 2 and 6), suggests dedication or consecration—sealing in the sense of "endowment of power."
[35]We discussed a part of this statement (down to "the promised Holy Spirit") in Chapter 5.
[36]I recently came across the remarkable sermons of Thomas Goodwin, seventeenth-century Calvinist divine, on the first chapter of Ephesians: *The Works of Thomas Goodwin, D.D.*, Vol. I, *Containing an Exposition of the First Chapter of the Epistle to the Ephesians* (Edinburgh: James Nichol, M.DCCC.LXI.). In his sermon on Eph. 1: 13-14, he writes: "Serve your God day and night faithfully, walk humbly; there is a promise of the Holy Ghost to come and fill your hearts with joy unspeakable and glorious, to seal you up to the day of redemption. Sue [seek] this promise out, wait for it, rest not in believing only, rest not in assurance by graces only; there is a further assurance to be had. It was the last legacy Christ left upon earth . . . the promise of the Father" (p. 248). Though I would hesitate to identify directly "the promise of the Holy Ghost" with "sealing up to the day of salvation," I believe Goodwin is correct in recognizing that the sealing of the Spirit is connected with the gift of the Spirit, and therefore belongs to those who receive the promised Holy Spirit. Goodwin, accordingly, in this sense is an extraordinary precursor of the contemporary spiritual renewal. For more on Thomas Goodwin's view, see the book by J.A. Schep, *Spirit Baptism and Tongue Speaking* (London: The Fountain Trust, 1970), pp. 59-63.
[37]Peter speaks about being "a partaker in the glory that is to be revealed" (1 Pet. 5:1).

extraordinary effectiveness the sense of the ineffable presence of the future consummation. There is, in the second place, a strong sense of expectation about the coming of the Lord. On almost every hand there is the renewed cry of "Maranatha"— "Our Lord, come" (1 Cor. 16:22). This cry does not stem from a sense of His absence, or distance, but from a sense of His powerful presence. It is the Lord, vividly known through the Holy Spirit, hence in His spiritual reality, that His Spirit-filled people yearn to behold in His glorious body.[38] It is the intense desire in the Spirit for the fulfillment of beholding Him face to face.[39]

Fourth, another effect of the gift of the Holy Spirit is *boldness in speech and action.* We have earlier noted that the purpose of the Spirit being given is for that enabling power whereby the witness to Jesus is carried forward in both word and deed. The gift of this power brings about extraordinary boldness and courage.

It is apparent in the book of Acts that an immediate effect of the gift of the Holy Spirit is decisiveness and confidence of speech, courage in the face of all opposition, and readiness to lay down one's life for the sake of Christ. We may begin with Peter's sermon at Pentecost, just after the disciples had been "filled with the Holy Spirit," and can but be impressed with the confidence and directness of his words: "Men of Judea and all who dwell in Jerusalem, let this be known to you, and give ear to my words" (Acts 2:14). So does Peter begin—and the note of confidence[40] is apparent throughout. Nor in the climax does he mince words, proclaiming that "God has made him both Lord and Christ, this Jesus *whom you crucified"* (2:36). A like confidence and boldness is demonstrated even more on a later day when Peter and John, after the healing of a cripple, are brought before the Jewish

---

Already we may share in that coming glory.

[38]Paul speaks of "his glorious body," or "the body of his glory," in Philippians 3:21.

[39]Emil Brunner, writing about the Church, says: ". . . the more powerfully life in the Spirit of God is present in it, the more urgent is its expectation of the Coming of Jesus Christ; so that the fullness of the possession of the Spirit and the urgency of expectation are always found together, as they were in the primitive community." *The Christian Doctrine of the Church, Faith, and the Consummation: Dogmatics, Vol. III* (Philadelphia: Westminster Press, 1960), p. 400.

[40]E.g., "Brethren, I may say to you confidently. . ." (Acts 2:29). The Greek word for confidently is *parrēsia (meta parrēsias*—"with confidence"), the same word that is often translated "boldly" (see below).

council—the same that had called for Jesus' death—and are asked, "By what power or by what name did you do this?" Thereupon ". . . Peter, filled with the Holy Spirit, said to them . . . 'be it known to you all, and to all the people of Israel, that by the name of Jesus Christ of Nazareth, whom you crucified . . . this man is standing before you well' " (Acts 4:8-10). Then Peter adds that ". . . there is no other name under heaven given among men by which we must be saved" (4:12). The next verse begins: "Now when they saw the boldness of Peter and John. . . ." Here is boldness and courage indeed!

On another occasion, despite threats against them, the company of disciples pray: "And now, Lord, look upon their threats, and grant to thy servants to speak thy word with all boldness. . ." (Acts 4:29). The result: "And when they had prayed, the place in which they were gathered together was shaken; and they were all filled with the Holy Spirit and spoke the word of God with boldness" (4:31).

The close connection between being "filled with the Holy Spirit" and boldness is evident in each of the three preceding accounts. The immediate effect was a boldness—confidence, courage—of extraordinary character.

We note next the example of Stephen. Stephen, like the other men chosen to serve tables, was "full of the Spirit" (Acts 6:3).[41] He performed "great wonders and signs" and those who opposed him "could not withstand the wisdom and the Spirit with which he spoke" (6:8, 10). However, through secret instigation and false witnesses, Stephen is brought before the Jewish council. When asked by the high priest to give answer, Stephen proceeds with total courage and boldness, not hesitating at the climax of his testimony to say to the council: "You stiff-necked people, uncircumcised in heart and ears, you always resist the Holy Spirit," and "the Righteous One . . . you have now betrayed and murdered" (7:51-52). The result: members of the council are enraged, gnash their teeth against him; but he does not stop. Rather, Stephen "full of the Holy Spirit, gazed into heaven and . . . said, 'Behold I see the heavens opened and the Son of man standing at the right hand of God' " (7:56). Such was the boldness of Stephen—to speak against the evil of his

---

[41]Specifically, Stephen is called "a man full of faith and of the Holy Spirit" (Acts 6:5).

audience and to proclaim to them the glorified Lord—a boldness that held back nothing. Thereupon they stoned him to death, but he never flinched to the very end.

In this whole account of extraordinary and indomitable courage the fact of Stephen's witness is set in the context of the fullness of the Spirit. Being so laden with the presence and power of God, Stephen spoke with total fearlessness—even to his martyrdom.

We turn now to the narrative about Saul of Tarsus—Paul the Apostle—and observe again the connection between the gift of the Spirit and boldness of speech and action. Saul is "filled with the Holy Spirit" (Acts 9:17) and ". . . in the synagogues immediately he proclaimed Jesus, saying, 'He is the Son of God'" (9:20). The Jews in Damascus, amazed at first at Saul's complete turnabout from persecutor of Christians to proclaimer of Christ, are soon seeking to kill him (9:23-24). Saul manages to escape their plots and goes to Jerusalem. There Barnabas, bringing him to the apostles, speaks of Saul's conversion and how at Damascus he (Saul) had "preached boldly in the name of Jesus" (9:27). Soon thereafter Saul ". . . went in and out among them at Jerusalem preaching boldly in the name of the Lord" (9:28). So zealous is Saul that his life is soon again at stake, and to save him, the brethren in Jerusalem take him down to Caesarea and ship him off to his home city of Tarsus.

Henceforward in all of Paul's missionary travels the same boldness marks everything he did. For example, beginning his journeys with Barnabas, Paul encounters a magician at Cyprus who tries to block the Roman proconsul from hearing the gospel message. Thereupon ". . . Paul, filled with the Holy Spirit, looked intently at [the magician] and said, 'You son of the devil, you enemy of all righteousness, full of all deceit and villainy, will you not stop making crooked the straight paths of the Lord?'" (Acts 13:9-10). Then Paul boldly calls for temporary blindness to come upon the magician—and it happens. The result of Paul's bold word and action: "the proconsul believed" (13:12). Other examples of such boldness are shown upon a visit to Antioch of Pisidia where, despite much Jewish reviling and opposition, ". . . Paul and Barnabas[42] spoke out boldly saying

---

[42]Barnabas, like Paul, was a man "filled with the Holy Spirit." Recall the earlier description in Acts 11:24: ". . . he was a good man, full of the Holy Spirit and of faith." Hence, Barnabas' boldness came out of the same fullness of God's presence and power.

[that] 'Since you . . . judge yourselves unworthy of eternal life, behold we turn to the Gentiles' " (13:46). And immediately thereafter, despite persecution and expulsion, Paul and Barnabas go on to Iconium where ". . . they remained for a long time, speaking boldly for the Lord" (14:3). Other examples could be added, but these should suffice to demonstrate again the marked connection between being filled with the Holy Spirit and boldness of speech and action.

Once again, to leave the scriptural record and to turn to the contemporary scene, we find much the same thing being exemplified. People who have received the gift of the Holy Spirit often demonstrate extraordinary boldness in the Lord. Particularly is this true immediately after the experience of being filled with the Spirit when they show little hesitation in proclaiming the word about Jesus anywhere and everywhere— and despite all opposition.[43] Sometimes this bold witness dies down a bit, but wherever there is earnest prayer for its renewal at whatever the cost, there is a fresh filling with the Spirit and a new speaking the word with boldness.[44] And it is to be added that this contemporary boldness is often not only of word but also of deed, as people do not hesitate to minister healing, deliverance and other blessings in the name of the Lord.

We might do well also to mention the words of Paul to young Timothy, his child in the faith: "Hence I remind you to rekindle[45] the gift of God that is within you through the laying on of my hands; for God did not give us a spirit of timidity but a spirit of power and love and self-control" (2 Tim. 1:6-7). The gift of God, the Holy Spirit, may now and again need to be fanned to a flame, but whenever or wherever this happens, any spirit of timidity will again become the Spirit of boldness—the "spirit of power

---

[43]The author recalls, as one instance among many, the picture of a university professor recently filled with the Holy Spirit shortly thereafter witnessing boldly about Jesus on his own university campus to student and faculty alike—indeed, all who would hear. Ridicule, opposition—and finally expulsion from his professorship—resulted. But, like Paul, he continued to carry on. Another example: students at the author's school are often found on the streets, in the parks, on the beaches, boldly and publicly testifying of the Lord. Opposition—when it occurs—only seems to make them all the more eager to witness!

[44]As in the case of the disciples in Acts 4:29-31 who prayed for boldness and again (as at Pentecost) were "filled with the Holy Spirit and spoke the word of God with boldness."

[45]The Greek word is *anazōpurein*—to "kindle up," to "fan to a flame." The gift is always there but it may be like embers that can be fanned to a flame.

and love and self-control." Boldness in the gospel proclamation comes from the gift of God; so should it wane, by the rekindling of the gift, there will again be courageous witness.[46]

The boldness brought about by the Holy Spirit is a boldness unto death. It is a boldness, a courage, that lacking all shame and hesitation can say with the Apostle Paul: ". . . it is my eager expectation and hope that I shall not be at all ashamed, but that with full courage[47] now as always Christ will be honored in my body, whether by life or by death" (Phil. 1:20). It is a boldness that does not exclude martyrdom.

Finally, and climactically, one of the great effects of the gift of the Holy Spirit is the *deepening of fellowship*. When the Spirit is given, both individual and group are so profoundly united as to create a fellowship of great love, sharing, community. It is the "koinonia" [48] of the Holy Spirit.

On reviewing the account of what happened in the early church, there is an unmistakable stress on community. Before the Day of Pentecost, as we have noted, the disciples were "with one accord" (Acts 1:14) in prayer and when the day arrived they were "all together in one place" (2:1). The sense of unity is obviously intensified with the outpouring of the Holy Spirit as "they were all filled with the Holy Spirit" (2:4). Thereafter when Peter delivers his sermon it is not simply as an individual spokesman, but "standing with the eleven" (2:14) he addresses the crowd. A new and transcending koinonia has been brought about by the Holy Spirit.

Next, when some three thousand persons hear the word, are

---

[46]Paul proceeds to say to Timothy: "Do not be ashamed then of testifying to our Lord . . . but share in suffering for the gospel in the power of God" (2 Tim. 1:8). These words suggest that Timothy, like many others who have received the gift of the Holy Spirit, may have moments when boldness fails and shame about testifying sets in, *but* the gift is there only needing to be stirred up, fanned to a flame, and a fresh boldness and courage will again be manifest. It is important, accordingly, to emphasize that the fact of receiving the Holy Spirit is essential to a genuine boldness of witness, but there is nothing automatic about such witness. There can be a quenching of the Spirit (cf. 1 Thess. 5:19—"Do not quench the Spirit"). But where there is a stirring up of the Spirit with an earnest desire to be courageous in the gospel, boldness for the Lord is sure to become again manifest.
[47]The Greek for "full courage" is *pasē parrēsia*—literally "all boldness" (as in KJV).
[48]The Greek word *koinōnia* denotes "participation," "fellowship," "sharing." Because of the richness of meaning in the Greek word, a single translation often seems inadequate. Thus many today are simply making use of the Greek term.

baptized and receive the gift of the Holy Spirit,[49] the text immediately reads: "And they were continually devoting themselves to the apostles' teaching and to fellowship, to the breaking of bread and to prayer" (Acts 2:42, NAS). Here is a tremendous sense of togetherness—in study, breaking bread, prayer—that the Holy Spirit had brought about. One of the key terms is "fellowship," or "koinonia"; and the fact that they devote themselves to koinonia signifies their profound new commitment to one another.

This commitment to one another is shown concretely in what follows: ". . . all those who had believed were together, and had all things in common; and they began selling their property and possessions and were sharing them with all, as anyone might have[50] need" (2:44-45, NAS). This beautiful spirit of sharing and fellowship is shown also in the next statement: "And day by day continuing with one mind in the temple, and breaking bread from house to house, they were taking their meals together. . ." (2:46, NAS). They sold property and possessions wherever there was need; they opened their homes to one another: thus were all things in common.[51]

The number of disciples now increases to about five thousand (Acts 4:4). But the spirit of unity only deepens. Two examples follow: first, after Peter and John report back to the company the threats of the Jewish council, the disciples ". . . lifted up their voice to God with one accord. . ." (Acts 4:24, KJV). With one voice[52] and with complete unanimity—one accord[53]—they pray to God for boldness to continue to witness while the Lord heals and performs signs and wonders. Second, just following

---

[49]For discussion of their receiving the Spirit, see Chapter 6.

[50]Imperfect tense for all three verbs (selling, sharing, have); thus they "were selling" and "were sharing" as anyone "was having" need. According to the *Expositor's Greek Testament*, "the [imperfect] tense may express an action which is done often and continuously without being done universally or extending to a complete accomplishment" (commentary on Acts 2:45). Thus it would be a mistake to assume necessarily that all sold their property and shared. Rather the point is that selling and sharing were constantly going on in relation to any who had need.

[51]It would be a mistake to see in this a so-called Christian communism. No one is forced to give up anything; indeed, there is voluntary sharing as the Spirit leads and as there is need. There is no collective ownership of goods but a recognition through the Spirit that what each had was for the good of all.

[52]The word in Greek is *phōnēn* in the singular (hence, not "voices" as in RSV, NAS).

[53]The Greek word is *homothumadon*. "With one accord" is a better translation than "together" (as in RSV).

this prayer, wherein they are "filled with the Holy Spirit" (Acts 4:31), their unity is powerfully described: "Now the company [or 'multitude']⁵⁴ of those who believed were of one heart and soul, and no one [was saying]⁵⁵ that any of the things which he possessed was his own, but they had everything in common" (Acts 4:32). Again the commonality of possessions is expressed, but this time against the background of an intense unity in spirit: one heart and soul. It would be hard to imagine a more graphic or more extraordinary statement of unity than this—in that many thousands of people are involved.

A beautiful expression follows: ". . . great grace was upon them all" (4:33). And this great grace is demonstrated further: "For there was not a needy person among them, for all who were owners of lands or houses would sell them and bring the proceeds of the sales, and lay them at the apostles' feet; and they would be distributed to each, as any had need" (4:34-35, NAS). While the language does not imply that people sold everything they had (only lands and houses are mentioned), it does suggest a readiness to commit their most valuable possessions.⁵⁶ Nor is this a profligate selling of properties—as if there were some special virtue in getting rid of earthly things⁵⁷—but a selling for the purpose of bringing the proceeds to the apostles⁵⁸ that every need might be met.

---

⁵⁴As in KJV. The Greek word is *plēthous*.

⁵⁵The literal Greek rendering for *elegen*, imperfect tense. See fn. 50, supra.

⁵⁶Barnabas—later described as "full of the Holy Spirit" (Acts 11:24)—is also mentioned as one who sold a piece of property, a field, and brought the money to the apostles (Acts 4:36-37).

⁵⁷There is no suggestion that ownership of goods is wrong, and thus does not belong in the Spirit-filled community. There is no particular virtue ascribed here to selling what one has and perhaps entering upon a life of poverty (as is the case frequently in monastic communities). The whole point is that under the impact of the fullness of the Spirit (5:31), there was such "great grace" upon them that they gladly shared everything and gave of anything that might help those in need.

⁵⁸Another evidence that there was no required selling of property and bringing the proceeds to the apostles is found in the account of Ananias and his wife Sapphira that follows. They sold a piece of property, kept back some of the proceeds, but pretended to be giving the whole amount (Acts 5:1-11). Peter speaks severely first to Ananias, "Ananias, why has Satan filled your heart to lie to the Holy Spirit. . .?" (5:3). Then Peter makes clear that the sin was neither in owning the property nor in selling and disposing as Ananias might choose—"while it remained unsold, did it not remain your own?" (5:4). The sin—a huge one directed against the Holy Spirit who pervaded the community—was in the pretense of giving all. (Incidentally, this first recorded sin in the koinonia of the Holy Spirit brought sudden physical death to both Ananias and Sapphira [Acts 5:5, 10] even as the first sin in Eden brought spiritual death

144

It is evident then that the Spirit-filled community of over five thousand was truly a koinonia of the Holy Spirit. It was a community united in prayer, in witness, and in fellowship. When any potential source of disruption might come in—such as the dishonesty of Ananias and Sapphira (Acts 5:1-10) and the murmuring of certain Hellenists[59] (Acts 6:1-6)—the matter was promptly dealt with, and the koinonia maintained. The result: "And the word of God increased; and the number of the disciples multiplied greatly in Jerusalem, and a great many of the priests were obedient to the faith" (Acts 6:7).

Now let us seek to summarize a few things. While the disciples were all Jews at this stage, they were from across the Mediterranean and Middle Eastern world,[60] they were Greek-speaking and Hebrew-speaking, they were men and women, they were laymen and priests, they were apostles and brethren in general: an immense variety of backgrounds and former loyalties, but now all were in one accord. They studied together, prayed together, broke bread together. They went to the temple unitedly, and also from house to house. Their commitment to one another was so intense that they no longer were claiming possessions as their own, but were selling and sharing wherever there was need. They were of one heart and one soul—and great grace was manifest in all they did. In every way it was the koinonia of the Holy Spirit.

It might be added that their community life was one of constant praise to God and of great favor among the people. The earliest account mentions their "praising God and having favor with all the people" (Acts 2:47). Their joy in the Lord and liberality of Spirit were very attractive—so much so that "the Lord added to their number day by day those who were being saved" (2:47 also). But along with this there was growth of

---

to Adam and Eve.)

[59]On the matter of Ananias and Sapphira see preceding footnote. The "Hellenists" were non-Palestinian, Greek-speaking Jews who had become Christians. A murmuring arose because of some neglect of their widows in the daily serving of food. It was promptly taken care of by the appointment of seven men (including Stephen and Philip) to be in charge of this duty.

[60]It is to be recalled that the thousands to whom Peter preached on the day of Pentecost were "from every nation under heaven" (Acts 2:5). Thereafter many nations and languages are mentioned, all the way from Mesopotamia to Libya, from Asia (Minor) to Rome (Acts 2:9-11).

opposition among the religious leaders and ever increasing threats and persecution. Finally, with the killing of Stephen a "great persecution"[61] began, and all the disciples, except for the apostles, were scattered throughout Judea and Samaria. This by no means signified any less praise of God, joy in the Lord, or favor with the people in general, but it did mean that no longer could they attend the Temple together and share as a total body in one place. Still, wherever they went, and whatever the opposition, they continued to be one in Christ—the koinonia of the Holy Spirit.

Now it would be too much to say, or suggest, that there was invariable harmony or unity thereafter. For with the distance from Jerusalem, no longer the daily presence of the apostles, and most of all the dimming of intensity of the Spirit's presence, some disharmony and disunity were sure to come about. Factions and party spirit would appear in churches here and there. However, insofar as this happened, they were no longer really "spiritual people,"[62] no longer flowing in the Spirit of Christ, no longer what the Lord intended. Still, if they could remember who they were and be renewed in Spirit, once more they would be truly the koinonia of the Holy Spirit.

Along this line Paul writes to the Ephesians that they should be "eager to maintain the unity of the Spirit in the bond of peace" (Eph. 4:3), and he concludes his Second Letter to the Corinthians with the prayer: "The grace of the Lord Jesus Christ and the love of God and the fellowship [koinonia] of the Holy Spirit be with you all" (13:14). This unity which has come from the Spirit, this koinonia which the Spirit has brought about—such is to be zealously maintained and earnestly prayed for. These words of Paul are in line also with the great concern of Jesus expressed in the last prayer for his disciples "that they may all be one . . . I in them and thou in me, that they may become perfectly one. . ." (John 17:21, 23). It is in the unity of the Spirit that such oneness is a reality.

---

[61]See Acts 8:1.

[62]For example, Paul later writes to the Christian disciples in Corinth, that he was not really able to speak to them as "spiritual people" *(pneumatikois)*, but as "fleshly" *(sarkinois)* because there was "jealousy and strife" among them (1 Cor. 3:1, 3). It had become "party spirit"—"I belong to Paul," or "Peter," or "Apollos"—no longer the unity of the Spirit with which they had first begun (1 Cor. 1:10-13).

Now it is time to return to the contemporary situation. What we have seen in our own day in the movement of the Holy Spirit is the renewal of fellowship in depth. People have found themselves drawn together in a profound unity of worship, community, study and witness: the koinonia of the Holy Spirit. Such fellowship goes so much deeper than anything they had ever known, that they continually marvel at what God has done.

Through the gift of the Holy Spirit there has been a personal renewal of unmistakable quality, but at the same time it has been a community renewal of extraordinary character. People have been brought by the Spirit into such a mutual relationship that they know they belong to one another. It is not as if there were no sense of community before, but this has a richer quality. Now with a fresh enthusiasm and joy in the Lord they have an intense desire to be together, to enjoy one another's company, to hear what God has to say through a brother or sister, to minister to one another, to share whenever there is need. So full of the Lord's presence is the gathering of the community that nothing else is comparable to it; and the time spent with one another seems as no time at all. Frequency of gathering together, extended hours of meeting, going from house to house for prayer and fellowship: all are a part of the present renewal.

Further, people caught up in the renewal of the Spirit come from a multiplicity of backgrounds. Nations around the world, denominations from across Christendom, people of many races, ages, and cultures—all are represented in the present renewal. While some fellowships are more limited nationally, denominationally, age-wise and so on, the genius of the movement is clearly the way it essentially transcends all ordinary groupings. It is not unusual to find Protestants of many kinds, Roman Catholics,[63] possibly Eastern Orthodox, and people formerly

---

[63]"The oneness in the Spirit which the Lord has created among Catholics and Protestants through the baptism in the Spirit is a precious miracle of grace in our day. I do not believe we have begun to grasp the significance of this breakthrough in the unfolding of God's plan for his people. The sharing of a faith common to us all, the growth in mutual trust and understanding in areas of cultural and doctrinal differences, the growing ability to pray and worship together genuinely while maintaining our integrity—all this is creating a new, strong, bold, witness to the reality and saving power of the Gospel of Jesus Christ." So writes Kevin Ranaghan in *As the Spirit Leads Us*, in an article entitled "Catholics and Pentecostals Meet in the Spirit," p. 144.

with no church background, all together in the same koinonia of the Holy Spirit. This, however, is not a unity based on a lowest common denominator of religious belief, but on the fact that all have been brought by the Spirit into a profound and transforming relationship with one another.

As a result of this, prayer and praise fellowships, renewal communities, and transdenominational Christian centers have developed in many parts of the world. Some are communities of shared goods and properties, of a daily common life together. Some fellowships exist within the more traditional church structures and seek to exercise a renewing influence, others exist alongside (para-congregational), or function totally separate therefrom. But wherever such communities are found, it is essentially the same spirit of praise, fellowship, witness and concern.[64]

The reaction, it might be added, from those observing is often either one of attraction or opposition. Some find themselves strongly moved by the sight of people praising the Lord, meeting together many hours in lively prayer and expectation, showing great concern for one another. They have yearned for such a deeper fellowship, and want to become a part. Many have grown weary with traditional forms and seemingly lifeless patterns of religious activity, and here they sense life, power, vitality. Thus do persons in the renewal find favor (cf. Acts 2:47) with people around, and many are added to their number. But others manifest opposition to the movement. Sometimes this comes from the world at large that has little use for anything deeply religious and spiritual, but most often it comes from within an established church order. The renewal, in this case, is viewed with suspicion, even as a threat to some, and attitudes vary from cautious tolerance to strong opposition. These differing reactions—from attraction to repulsion—suggest that something is occurring in the fellowship of the Spirit of unusual significance for the whole church.

It seems quite possible that this renewal in the Spirit is the most profound ecumenical development of the twentieth century.

---

[64]For a good study of Christian community see Stephen B. Clark, *Building Christian Communities: Strategy for Renewing the Church* (Notre Dame: Ave Maria Press, 1972). Clark is a coordinator of the Word of God community in Ann Arbor, Michigan.

This century, now moving to a climax, has witnessed many attempts to bring churches together, to get beyond the scandal of division, and to recover that oneness which the church at least verbally affirms. And there have been varying degrees of success: formations of councils, mergers of some churches and surely many prayers for unity. Indeed, there is a growing sense that division is intolerable, that it is a huge obstacle to faith, and that Jesus' prayer that "they may all be one . . . so that the world may believe" (John 17:21) must somehow find an answer. Such is the growing ecumenical concern: and its solution, we affirm again, is to be found only in and through the renewal of the Holy Spirit.[65] As people, as churches, as individuals are profoundly renewed by the Holy Spirit the whole situation is transformed from a search after unity to its realization.

Surely hazards mark the way. For example, people renewed in the Spirit may allow a party spirit to set in, thus draw back into denominational enclaves or groups that no longer fellowship with others, or begin to emphasize certain minor doctrinal points to such a degree that the unity of the Spirit is increasingly broken. Sometimes spiritually renewed groups set themselves apart from other groups, and follow a particular leader or teaching, no longer recognizing the unity the Spirit has brought about. Indeed, there are hazards—and situations that need repentance and correction. However, the overarching fact is that through the renewal of the Spirit there is a new and profound gift of unity that alone can bring into fulfillment the genuine oneness of the body of Christ. When this is realized afresh, and is acted upon accordingly, the prayer of the Lord

---

[65]Dr. John A. Mackay, former president of Princeton Theological Seminary, puts it forcefully: "What is known as the charismatic movement—a movement marked by spiritual enthusiasm and special gifts and which crosses all boundaries of culture, race, age, and church tradition—is profoundly significant. . . . Because 'no heart is pure that is not passionate and no virtue is safe that is not enthusiastic,' the charismatic movement of today is the chief hope of the ecumenical tomorrow" (*World Vision Magazine*, April, 1970, article entitled "Oneness in the Body—Focus for the Future"). James W. Jones, Episcopal clergyman, analyzes it thus: "Structural ecumenism which does not grow out of a genuine ecumenical life will produce only empty wineskins, just as patterns of renewal that do not grow out of a renewed life will themselves have no vitality. The charismatic movement is *the* ecumenical movement, not because it is creating structural alignments (it isn't), but because it is bringing into being a new sense of the common life of the people of God" (*Filled with New Wine: The Charismatic Renewal of the Church* [New York: Harper and Row, 1974], p. 135).

may find its ultimate fulfillment.

It would seem appropriate to conclude with the words of Paul that "God's love has been poured into our hearts through the Holy Spirit which has been given to us" (Rom. 5:5). For truly when through the gift of the Holy Spirit the love of God is shed abroad in the hearts of all, then there is a profound creation of fellowship, sharing and unity with one another. Through such God-given love we become the koinonia of the Holy Spirit.

EPILOGUE

This book has been written with excitement and hope. If it is true that many people today are freshly experiencing the gift of the Holy Spirit, there is much to be excited about. For in this gift there is fullness of God's presence and power—and entrance into a whole new dimension of praise, witness and action. Also there is much to be hoped for: that people everywhere will become alert to the possibility of this gift, respond to God's offer of its availability and thereby receive it from the exalted Lord.

Perhaps these pages will have come as a surprise to some readers. For it is a fact that despite the high significance of the gift of the Holy Spirit, many persons have little knowledge or understanding of it. Such a question as Paul's, "Did you receive the Holy Spirit when you believed?" (Acts 19:2), may seem totally irrelevant and meaningless to many. They may never really have thought about the matter, and perhaps they have not so much as heard about it.

Others in reading may have felt disturbed. First, there may be some who have long thought of the gift of the Holy Spirit in terms of a kind of divine immanence experienced in a mystical moment. With or without the mediation of Jesus Christ it is assumed that the spirit of a person may enter into union with the divine Spirit. Accordingly, there is already a given—hence gift-like—unity of the divine and human spirit which only needs to be realized through meditation and stripping away artificial barriers. Thus to read all this about the work of Jesus Christ in redemption and forgiveness of sins as necessary to the reception of the Spirit may seem strange and unwarranted. Second, there may be other readers who have long viewed this gift as so inseparably attached to the sacramental life of the church that all persons who receive the proper sacramental action (baptism, confirmation) invariably become recipients of this gift. Accordingly, there is no point in getting excited about or looking forward to the gift. For if one has been properly baptized (or

151

confirmed, as the case may be), the gift presumably has been received. Third, there may be still other readers who view the gift of the Holy Spirit as identical with the gift of salvation; thus there is no gift to be considered beyond the new life in Christ. Indeed, some might say, does not the very idea of an additional gift detract from the all-sufficiency of Christ?

Unfortunately, these various views—which may be called, in turn, the mystical, the sacramental, and the evangelical—often stand in the way of a genuine apprehension and reception of the gift of the Holy Spirit. Perhaps sufficient answer to the first two views has been given in prior pages, but a word might be added about the last. Christianity, to be sure, is at heart the Good News about salvation—a new life in Christ. This gospel is to be proclaimed to the ends of the earth: that God has graciously gone all the way to bring man back to himself, and through the blood of His Son there is redemption, even the forgiveness of sins. Nothing should ever be said to detract one iota from the wonder of the gospel, for without God's work in salvation there would be no hope for anyone in all creation. And it comes as a gift—the gift of eternal life (e.g., Rom. 6:23—"the free gift of God is eternal life in Christ Jesus our Lord"). But the all-important point is that the gift of eternal life is *not* the gift of the Holy Spirit, though the latter presupposes the former and both are mediated through Jesus Christ. Thus Christ continues to be all-sufficient. One never goes past Him: for in Him is every spiritual blessing. The crucial question is: have we caught up with Him? If we have experienced through Him the life-changing wonder of forgiveness of sins and eternal life, have we also received the empowering miracle of the gift of the Holy Spirit?

Perhaps the greatest mistake in this area is to presuppose the gift of the Holy Spirit. The mystic may presuppose the gift of the Spirit in his meditation, the sacramentalist may presuppose the same gift in the occurrence of baptism and/or confirmation, the evangelical may likewise presuppose the gift of the Spirit in the experience of forgiveness and salvation. Each, in different manner, by the very presupposition,[1] bars his own way to the

---

[1] Karl Barth in his *Evangelical Theology: An Introduction* (New York: Holt, Rinehart and Winston, 1963), Chapter 5, on "The Spirit," writes of how "a foolish church presupposes his presence and action in its own existence, in its offices and sacraments,

reception of the gift. However, if the presupposition can be removed, there may be a new readiness for and openness to the gift of the Holy Spirit.

In this connection one purpose of the book has been to set forth biblically and theologically the whole area of the gift of the Holy Spirit. By doing this it is hoped that certain commonly held views may have been brought under question and a fresh look taken. By the very description of such matters as the background, dimensions, purpose and effects of the gift it is likewise hoped that many may have been challenged to raise the question: "Have I really—whatever my former attitude and experience—received this gift?"

Earlier it was said that perhaps these pages will have come as a surprise, even a disturbance, to some readers. It is also hoped that for others this book may have come as a source of some pleasure in that the attempt has been made to clarify much about the gift of the Holy Spirit. For it is undoubtedly the case that many persons who are either participants in the contemporary spiritual renewal, or strongly attracted thereto, are looking for a more thorough biblical and theological grounding. If these pages have been helpful in that direction, I am grateful.

It should be added that throughout the writing I have been fully aware of working in a seldom charted theological area. For the church at large has never given adequate consideration to the gift of the Spirit—"baptism in the Spirit," "the fullness of the Spirit," and other related matters—accordingly, there has been little from the past to go on.[2] Hence, though this has been largely a biblical study in the area, I trust that it has helped set

---

ordinations, consecrations and absolutions . . . a presupposed Spirit is certainly not the Holy Spirit" (p. 58). Thereafter Barth adds: "Only where the Spirit is sighed, cried, and prayed for does he become present and newly active." So it is with the gift of the Holy Spirit.
[2]Professor Hendrikus Berkhof in his book, *The Doctrine of the Holy Spirit* (Richmond, VA: John Knox Press, 1964) speaks in one place of a work of the Holy Spirit "beyond justification and sanctification," namely, being "filled with the Holy Spirit," to which "official theology" has paid little attention (p. 85). He thereupon devotes a few pages (pp. 85-92) to the subject, prefacing his remarks by saying, "I am aware of the fact that I set foot on an unexplored field and that my thoughts here . . . must be considered as preliminary and needing correction by others" (p. 85). This present book, as well as my two earlier ones, *The Era of the Spirit* and *The Pentecostal Reality*, are attempts to open up this "unexplored field."

the stage for further theological reflection.

Surely what has been dealt with in these pages is no small matter. It is verily, for those who receive forgiveness of sins and become new creatures, the gift of God's presence and power. Thereby the Spirit of God comes to fill the heights and depths of human existence, bringing forth transcendent expressions of praise, performance of mighty works, and many new aspects of Christian living. It is the outpouring of God's Spirit upon a redeemed people—a people who having been set right with God now become the arena of His reflected glory.

How much this is to be desired: for the church in our time not only to be "the ark of salvation" but also the tabernacle of the divine fullness! Thus the church may become the earthly counterpart to the praise of God in the heavenly sanctuary, the continuation of her Lord's ministry in mighty word and deed, and such a moving force against all evil that the citadels of darkness cannot withstand the mighty impact. Indeed, through the Holy Spirit the church may truly become that place of beauty and wonder that presages the final coming of Christ in glory.

And the church described consists of people—people who have become open to the mighty wave of God's Spirit in our time, and, whatever their frailties and shortcomings, are moving in the power and demonstration of the Holy Spirit. For all such persons, what God is doing is a matter of continuing joy and amazement.

Finally, as we close, it is good to be reminded once more that the gift of the Holy Spirit is a continuing promise. This extraordinary gift from the exalted Lord is not something that belongs to past history. For we have the sure word of Scripture that "the promise is to you and your children and to all that are far off, *every one* whom the Lord our God calls to him."

May it be that none of us shall fail to receive what God has so generously promised.

BIBLIOGRAPHY

Books Referred to in This Volume

Allen, Roland. *The Ministry of the Spirit*. Grand Rapids, Michigan: Eerdmans, 1960.

Arndt & Gingrich. *A Greek-English Lexicon of the New Testament and Other Early Christian Literature*. University of Chicago Press, 1957.

Baillie, John. *Our Knowledge of God*. New York: Charles Scribner's Sons, 1939.

Barth, Karl. *Evangelical Theology: An Introduction*. New York: Holt, Rinehart, and Winston, 1963.

Basham, Don. *Face Up With a Miracle*. Northridge, California: Voice Christian Publications, 1967.

Basham, Don. *Deliver Us From Evil*. Washington Depot, Connecticut: Chosen Books, 1972.

Bennett, Dennis. *Nine O'Clock in the Morning*. Plainfield, New Jersey: Logos, 1970.

Bernard, Sister Mary. *I Leap for Joy*. Plainfield, New Jersey: Logos, 1974.

Berkhof, Hendrikus. *The Doctrine of the Holy Spirit*. Richmond, Virginia: John Knox Press, 1964.

Bixler, Russell. *It Can Happen to Anybody*. Monroeville, Pennsylvania: Whitaker Books, n.d.

Bredesen, Harald. *Yes, Lord*. Plainfield, New Jersey: Logos, 1972.

Brown, James H. *Presbyterians and the Baptism of the Holy Spirit*, "Signs, Wonders, and Miracles." Los Angeles: Full Gospel Business Men's Fellowship International, 1963.

Bruce, F.F. *The New International Commentary on the New Testament: Commentary on the Book of Acts*. Grand Rapids, Michigan: Eerdmans, 1954.

Bruner, F.D. *A Theology of the Holy Spirit*. Grand Rapids, Michigan: Eerdmans, 1970.

Brunner, Emil. *The Christian Doctrine of the Church, Faith, and the Consummation: Dogmatics, Vol. III*. Philadelphia, Westminster Press, 1960.

Brunner, Peter. *Worship in the Name of Jesus*. St. Louis: Concordia, 1968.

Cambridge Greek Testament. Cambridge University Press, 1914.

Christenson, Larry. *Speaking in Tongues*. Minneapolis: Dimension Books, 1968.

Clark, Stephen B. *Building Christian Community: Strategy for Renewing the Church*. Notre Dame: Ave Maria Press, 1972.

Delling, Gerhard. *Worship in the New Testament*. Philadelphia: Westminster Press, 1972.

Dewar, Lindsay. *The Holy Spirit and Modern Thought*. New York: Harper and Brothers, 1959.

Dunn, James. *Baptism in the Holy Spirit*. Naperville, Illinois: Allenson, 1970.

Ensley, Eddie. *Sounds of Wonder*. New York: Paulist Press, 1977.

Ervin, Howard M. *These Are Not Drunken As Ye Suppose*. Plainfield, New Jersey: Logos, 1968.

Expositor's Greek Testament. New York: George H. Doran Company, n.d.

Finney, Charles G. *Charles G. Finney: An Autobiography*. Old Tappan, New Jersey: Revell, 1876.

Frost, Robert C. *Set My Spirit Free*. Plainfield, New Jersey: Logos, 1973.

Gelpi, Donald L. *Pentecostalism: A Theological Viewpoint*. New York: Paulist Press, 1971.

Goodwin, Thomas. *The Works of Thomas Goodwin, D.D.*, Vol. I, *Containing an Exposition of the First Chapter of the Epistle to the Ephesians*. Edinburgh: James Nichols, M.DCCC.LXI.

Green, Michael. *I Believe in the Holy Spirit*. Grand Rapids, Michigan: Eerdmans, 1975.

Harris, Ralph. *Spoken by the Spirit: Documented Accounts of "Other Tongues" from Arabic to Zulu*. Springfield, Missouri: Gospel Publishing House, 1973.

Harper, Michael. *Power for the Body of Christ*. London: Fountain Trust, 1964.

Harper, Michael. *Spiritual Warfare*. London: Hodder & Stoughton, 1970.

Harper, Michael. *Walk in the Spirit*. Plainfield, New Jersey: Logos, 1968.

Heidelberg Catechism, translated by A.O. Miller and M.E. Osterhaven. United Church Press, 1962.

Hull, J.H.E. *The Holy Spirit in the Acts of the Apostles*. Cleveland & New York: World Publishing Company, 1968.

Jackson and Lake, editors. *The Acts of the Apostles*. London: Macmillan & Co., Ltd., 1920.

Jones, James W. *Filled With New Wine: The Charismatic Renewal of the Church*. New York: Harper & Row, 1974.

Kane, J. Herbert. *Understanding Christian Missions*. Grand Rapids, Michigan: Baker, 1974.

Katz, Arthur. *Ben Israel: Odyssey of a Modern Jew*. Plainfield, New Jersey: Logos, 1970.

Kendrick, Klaude. *The Promise Fulfilled*. Springfield, Missouri: Gospel Publishing House, 1961.

King, Pat. *The Jesus People Are Coming!* Plainfield, New Jersey: Logos, 1971.

Kuhlman, Kathryn. *God Can Do It Again*. Englewood Cliffs, New Jersey: Prentice Hall, 1971.

Kuhlman, Kathryn. *I Believe in Miracles*. Old Tappan, New Jersey: Spire Books, 1962.

Lewis, C.S. *Transposition and Other Addresses*. London: Geoffrey Bles, 1949.

Mackay, John A. *World Vision Magazine*, "Oneness in the Body—Focus for the Future," April 1970.

MacNutt, Francis. *Healing*. Notre Dame, Indiana: Ave Maria Press, 1974.

Martin, Ralph. *Fire on the Earth*. Ann Arbor, Michigan: Word of Life, 1975.

McAlister, W. Robert. *The Dilemma: Deliverance or Discipline?* Plainfield, New Jersey: Logos, 1976.

McDonnell, Kilian. *One in Christ,* "The Distinguishing Characteristics of the Charismatic-Pentecostal Spirituality," 1974, Vol. X, No. 2.

Meisgeier, Charles. *The Acts of the Holy Spirit Among the Presbyterians Today.* Los Angeles: Full Gospel Business Men's Fellowship International, 1972.

Meyer, H.A.W. *Critical and Exegetical Handbook to the Acts of the Apostles.* New York: Funk & Wagnalls, 1883.

Moffatt Commentary: The Acts of the Apostles. New York: Harper and Brothers, 1931.

Moody, W.R. *The Life of D.L. Moody.* New York: Fleming H. Revell, 1900.

Munck, Simon. *The Anchor Bible: The Acts of the Apostles.* Garden City, New York: Doubleday & Company, 1967.

Murray, Andrew. *The Spirit of Christ.* New York: Randolph & Company, 1888.

O'Connor, Edward. *The Pentecostal Movement in the Catholic Church.* Notre Dame: Ave Maria Press, 1971.

Prange, Erwin. *The Gift Is Already Yours.* Plainfield, New Jersey: Logos, 1973.

Ranaghan, Kevin & Dorothy. *As the Spirit Leads Us.* New York: Paulist Press, 1971.

Ranaghan, Kevin & Dorothy. *Catholic Pentecostals.* New York: Paulist Press, 1969.

Rea, John. *The Layman's Commentary on the Holy Spirit.* Plainfield, New Jersey: Logos, rev. ed., 1974.

Richardson, Alan. *An Introduction to the Theology of the New Testament.* New York: Harper and Brothers, 1958.

Roberts, Oral. *The Call: An Autobiography.* Old Tappan, New Jersey: Spire Books, 1971.

Robertson, A.T. *Word Pictures in the New Testament.* New York: Harper and Brothers, 1932.

Samarin, William. *Tongues of Men and Angels.* New York: Macmillan, 1972.

Sanford, Agnes. *The Healing of the Spirit.* Philadelphia: Lippincott, 1966.

Scanlon, Michael. *Inner Healing.* New York: Paulist Press, 1974.

Schep, J.A. *Spirit Baptism and Tongue Speaking.* London: Fountain Trust, 1970.

Schaff, Philip. *History of the Christian Church.* New York: Charles Scribner's Sons, 1910.

Sherrill, John. *They Speak With Other Tongues: The Story of a Reporter on the Trail of a Miracle.* New York: McGraw Hill, 1964.

Stapleton, Ruth Carter. *The Gift of Inner Healing.* Waco: Word Books, 1976.

Stott, John R.W. *The Baptism and Fullness of the Holy Spirit.* Downer's Grove: Inter-Varsity Press, 1964.

Suenens, Leon Joseph. *A New Pentecost?* New York: Seabury Press, 1974.

Thayer. *Greek-English Lexicon of the New Testament.* New York & London: Harper and Brothers, 1899.

Theological and Pastoral Orientations on the Catholic Charismatic Renewal.
Notre Dame: Word of Life, 1974.

Theological Dictionary of the New Testament, Vols. VI & VII. Grand Rapids:
Eerdmans, 1971.

Tomczak, Larry. *Clap Your Hands!* Plainfield, New Jersey: Logos, 1973.

Tugwell, Simon. *Did You Receive the Holy Spirit?* London: Darton, Longman &
Todd, 1972.

Westminster Confession of Faith.

Williams, J. Rodman. *Era of the Spirit.* Plainfield, New Jersey: Logos, 1971.

Williams, J. Rodman. *The Pentecostal Reality.* Plainfield, New Jersey: Logos,
1972.

DATE DUE

5/31/04 -C		
6/17/05		
6-7-07		